Icelandic Sagas

Twayne's World Authors Series

Scandinavian Literature

Leif Sjöberg, Editor
State University of New York at Stony Brook

TWAS 717

Skarðsbók, AM 350 fol. The Jónsbók law codex from Skard. The historiated initial *S* represents terms of passage confirmed with a handshake (above) and a ship being prepared for sailing (below). *Used with the kind permission of the Stofnun Árna Magnússonar in Reykjavik, Iceland.*

Icelandic Sagas

By Paul Schach

University of Nebraska-Lincoln

Twayne Publishers · Boston

Icelandic Sagas

Paul Schach

Copyright © 1984 by G.K. Hall & Company
All Rights Reserved
Published by Twayne Publishers
A Division of G. K. Hall & Company
70 Lincoln Street
Boston, Massachusetts 02111

Printed on permanent/durable acid-free
paper and bound in the United States of
America.

Library of Congress Cataloging in
Publication Data

Schach, Paul.
Icelandic sagas.

(Twayne's world authors series; TWAS 717)
Bibliography: p. 198
Includes index.
1. Sagas—History and criticism.
I. Sjöberg, Leif.   II. Title.   II. Series.
PT7181.S29   1984   839'.6'09   83-12679
ISBN 0-8057-6564-6

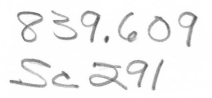
To Ruth, Joan, Kathy, and Paula

Contents

About the Author

Preface

Acknowledgments

Chronology

CHAPTER ONE
From the Discovery of Iceland to the
Fall of the Commonwealth   1

CHAPTER TWO
The Beginning of Historical Writing   23

CHAPTER THREE
The First Biographies   48

CHAPTER FOUR
Early Stories about Icelanders   71

CHAPTER FIVE
Major Sagas about Icelanders   97

CHAPTER SIX
Shorter Sagas about Icelanders   131

CHAPTER SEVEN
Late Sagas about Icelanders   155

CHAPTER EIGHT
Summary and Conclusions   172

Notes and References   179

Selected Bibliography   198

Index   208

About the Author

Paul Schach is Charles J. Mach Professor of Germanic Languages at the University of Nebraska--Lincoln, where he has taught since 1951. As a member of the Graduate College faculty, he teaches courses on Old Norse, Middle High German, and medieval German literature. Professor Schach received the A.B. degree magna cum laude from Albright College in 1938, and the M.A. in 1941 and the Ph.D. in 1949 from the University of Pennsylvania. His postdoctoral research was done in Iceland and Germany. Professor Schach has also taught at Albright College, North Central College, and as a guest professor at the University of Colorado (five summers), and the University of Pennsylvania (three summers). He has also been a guest lecturer at several European universities.

Professor Schach is a member of the American Association of Teachers of German, the American Scandinavian Foundation, the Medieval Academy of America, the Midwest Modern Language Association of America, the Society for the Advancement of Scandinavian Study, and the Viking Society for Northern Research (England). His previous publications include translations of Eyrbyggja Saga (1959, repr. 1970) and Tristrams Saga (1973), numerous articles in English and German on the Icelandic sagas and on German settlement dialects in America, and the anthology Languages in Conflict: Linguistic Acculturation on the Great Plains (1980). His honors include the Ordre de Tristan (Liège, 1966) for his research on the Tristan legend in Scandinavia, an Award for Outstanding Research and Creative Activity (University of Nebraska, 1979), and a National Council Citation (Albright College, 1980).

Professor Schach served as associate managing editor (1970-73) and as managing editor (1977-81) of Scandinavian Studies.

Preface

The Icelandic sagas have been aptly characterized as "the most extraordinary literary creation of medieval Europe" (1). Sagas are prose narratives ranging from about ten to almost four hundred pages in length. Shorter prose tales are known as þættir (sg. þáttr "strand, section"), so called because most of them have been preserved as inserts in longer texts (2). Konungasögur, "Sagas of Kings," are synoptic histories or biographies of Norwegian kings. Byskupasögur, "Sagas of Bishops," are chronicles or biographies of Icelandic bishops. Íslendingasögur, "Sagas of Icelanders," widely known as "Family Sagas," are biographies of Icelandic heroes or chronicles of Icelandic families or countrysides.

This genre has been designated as "the sole original contribution of Scandinavia to world literature" (3). The originality of the sagas of Icelanders consists in the fact that they are idealized, imaginary re-creations of the past in which the authors have portrayed their forebears with psychological realism. The cultural reference is largely heathen, but the cultural milieu is Christian. Stated differently, the Íslendingasögur depict pre-Christian Iceland as seen through the eyes of Christians.

Discussion of the riddarasögur, "Sagas of Knights," and the fornaldarsögur, "Sagas of Ancient Times," had to be omitted for reasons of space. The former are Norwegian translations and adaptations as well as Icelandic imitations of chivalric romances. The latter deal with legendary Germanic heroes and vikings who lived, or were believed to have lived, before Iceland was settled. Both genres influenced late Íslendingasögur. A chapter on Snorri Sturluson was made superfluous through the recent publication of Marlene Ciklamini's Snorri Sturluson in this series.

The long-standing controversy over the genesis of the Íslendingasögur need only be touched on here since it has been discussed compendiously by Peter Hallberg and exhaustively by Theodore M. Andersson (4). According to the "free-prose" doctrine, sagas are recordings of stories that acquired their style and structure during an oral stage of development. By contrast, Walter Baetke and his followers minimize the importance of oral traditions and regard the Sagas of Icelanders as free literary compositions (5). A middle ground is occupied by the "Icelandic school," who regard the Sagas of Icelanders as literary works based on oral and written sources (6). Andreas Heusler is widely considered a staunch proponent of the free-prose doctrine because of a few unfortunate exaggerated comments. His final position, however, seems to have been this: short sagas with linear plots are reflections of oral tales; long sagas with plot interlace are literary creations. My own present views will emerge from the discussion of individual sagas and will be summarized in the final chapter.

To be properly understood, the Íslendingasögur must be viewed against the background of the social and historical forces that helped to shape them and within the context of the literary development of which they form a major part. In this book, I propose neither to develop a thesis nor to set forth original interpretations of my own. Notes and references had to be held to a minimum. Some of the notes are for the purpose of documentation; most of them, however, are references to further sources of information including alternative interpretations. For this reason, I tried to limit the notes to recent, readily available studies, especially those written in English, which include critical discussions of, and references to, older scholarly literature. My indebtedness to scholars here and abroad will be obvious to specialists.

My method is eclectic. Emphasis is on individual sagas. This procedure brings with it a certain amount of repetition, especially in comments on saga style and structure. Several sagas that are not available in modern English translations are treated at greater length than would otherwise be the case. Questions of sources, manuscript transmission, and the like are touched on briefly in a few cases to give the general reader or the beginning student of Old Norse an inkling of the complexity of some of the problems connected with the study of this fascinating literature.

Names of Icelandic scholars and saga titles are given in Icelandic orthography in this study. Names of saga characters have been simplified, but diacritical marks have been retained. Thus Þuríðr and Hörðr appear as Thuríd and Hörd. Primary stress is on the first syllable. The Icelandic consonants ð (edh) and þ (thorn) correspond to English th, as in then and thin, respectively. Other consonants can generally be pronounced as in German. The r is an alveolar trill, f is voiced between vowels and in final position (like English v), l and n are unvoiced when preceded by h (which is not sounded), s is always voiceless, and double consonants are pronounced double when followed by a vowel. The acute indicates vowel length. Thus é is pronounced as in gate, í as in keen, ó as in note (in all cases without the offglide), a as in father, and y as in German kühn or English keen (with rounded lips). The ligatures æ and œ, which are always long, can be sounded respectively as in head and German Höhle (hale with lips rounded). The dipthongs ei and ey can be pronounced as in say, and au as in how. The short vowel ö (also written ǫ) should be pronounced as in British not or American nut (with lip rounding).

Most sagas are known by more than one name. Thus the greatest work in saga literature, Brennu-Njáls saga, "Saga of Njál of the Burning," is generally called Njáls saga and sometimes Njála. For obvious reasons, the various titles are used in the discussion of such sagas.

Begun during my first visit to Iceland in 1955, the original version of this introduction to saga literature was nearing completion when Den isländska sagan by Peter Hallberg appeared in print. Since the two books were remarkably similar in scope, method, and interpretation, there was no justification for publishing my study. Instead, I translated Hallberg's book into English and began the seemingly endless task of revising Icelandic Sagas.

After forty years of reading and translating sagas, I find that my views of this literary genre have changed substantially. These changes are reflected in the present volume, which is fundamentally different from the original book in scope and approach, and frequently quite different in the interpretation of individual sagas. The most important additions are discussions of the earlier historical writings and of the first biographies of Norwegian kings and Icelandic bishops.

Paul Schach

University of Nebraska--Lincoln

Acknowledgments

The Sisyphean task of revising this book has been lightened by grants from the American Philosophical Society, the Research Council of the University of Nebraska, and the Woods Foundation. It is a pleasant duty to express my sincere gratitude for this generous support. It is a most pleasant duty to express my sincere gratitude also to Professor Jónas Kristjánsson, Director of the Stofnun Árna Magnússonar, for providing the frontispiece; to the Cornell University Press for permission to use a quotation from Einar Ólafur Sveinsson, The Age of the Sturlungs. Icelandic Civilization in the Thirteenth Century, trans. Jóhann S. Hannesson, Islandica, vol. 36 (1953); and to the University of Manitoba Press for permission to use four quotations from Jón Jóhannesson, A History of the Old Iceland Commonwealth. Íslendinga saga, trans. Haraldur Bessason, University of Manitoba Icelandic Studies, vol. 2 (1974).

Chronology

ca. 800-870   Irish hermits in southeastern Iceland.

ca. 825   Faeroes colonized by Norsemen.

870-930   Iceland settled by Norsemen.

930   General Assembly founded.

ca. 985   Greenland colonized.

995-1000   Ólaf Tryggvason king of Norway.

999   Christianity accepted by General Assembly.

1004-1030   Skapti Thóroddsson lawspeaker of Iceland.

1005   Appelate court (Fifth Court) established by Skapti Thóroddsson.

1015-1030   Ólaf Haraldsson (Saint Ólaf) king of Norway.

1056-1080   Ísleif Gizurarson bishop of Iceland.

1082-1106   Gizur Ísleifsson bishop of Iceland.

1084-1107   Markús Skeggjason lawspeaker of Iceland.

1096   Law of tithes drawn up by Bishop Gizur.

ca. 1100   Earliest homilies and saints' lives translated and adapted from Latin in Norway and Iceland.

1106-1113   Gizur Ísleifsson bishop of Skálholt.

1106-1121 (Saint) Jón Ögmundarson bishop of Hólar.

1117-1118 Icelandic secular laws revised and codified.

ca. 1120 "History of the Kings of Norway" composed in Latin by Sæmund Sigfússon the Learned.

ca. 1122-1133 Íslendingabók, "Book of Icelanders," composed by Ari Thorgilsson the Learned.

1113 Benedictine monastery founded at Thingeyrar.

ca. 1126 Laws of religious observance encoded.

ca. 1140 First Grammatical Treatise composed.

1152 Archiepiscopal see transferred from Lund to Nidarós (Trondheim).

ca. 1160-1190 Veraldarsaga, "History of the World," translated.

ca. 1170 Hryggjarstykki, "Backbone Piece," composed by Eirík Oddsson.

ca. 1180 Historia de antiquitate regum Norwagiensium, "History of the Kings of Norway from Ancient Times," composed in Norway by the monk Theodoricus.

1180-1210 Earliest Latin and vernacular biographies of Norwegian kings composed at Thingeyrar.

1190 Icelandic chieftains forbidden to take church orders by Archbishop of Nidarós.

ca. 1190 Nóregs konungatal, "Succession of the Kings of Norway," composed in honor of Jón Loptsson.

ca. 1190 Ágrip af Nóregs konunga sögum,

"Summary of Sagas about Kings of Norway," composed in Norway.

ca. 1200-1230   Earliest sagas of Icelandic bishops and Icelandic heroes composed.

ca. 1210   Gesta Danorum, "The History of the Danes," composed by Saxo Grammaticus (ca. 1150-1216).

ca. 1220   Landnámabók, "Book of the Settlements," revised by Styrmir Kárason the Learned.

ca. 1220-1235   The Prose Edda, Egils saga Skalla-Grímsson, "Saga of Egil, Son of Skalla-Grím," Óláfs saga hins helga, "Biography of Saint Ólaf," and Heimskringla, "History of Norwegian Kings," composed by Snorri Sturluson.

1226   Tristrams saga ok Isöndar, translation of Thomas of Brittany's Tristan et Iseult, made by Friar Róbert at the behest of King Hákon Hákonarson of Norway.

1238   Norwegian bishops appointed to the episcopal sees of Skálholt and Hólar.

ca. 1240-1250   Eyrbyggja saga, "Saga of the People of Eyr," and Laxdæla saga, "Saga of the People of Laxárdal," composed.

ca. 1250   Völsunga saga, "Saga of the Volsungs," a prose harmonization of heroic poems from the Poetic Edda, composed.

1262-1264   Iceland becomes tributary to Norway.

ca. 1265   Hákonar saga Hákonarsonar, "Biography of Hákon, Son of Hákon," composed by Sturla Thórdarson.

1271   Járnsíða, "Ironside," Norwegian law code brought to Iceland by Sturla Thór-

darson, replaces the Icelandic law code
Grágás, "Grey Goose."

ca. 1280-1290 Brennu-Njáls saga, "Saga of Njál of
the Burning," composed.

1281 Jónsbók, "Jón's Book," Norwegian
law code replaces Járnsíða.

ca. 1272-1280 Íslendinga saga, "History of the
Icelanders," composed; Kristni saga,
"History of Christendom," compiled; and
Landnámabók revised by Sturla Thór-
darson.

ca. 1285 Hænsa-Þóris saga, "Saga of Hen-
Thórir," composed.

ca. 1330 Landnámabók revised by Sir Hauk
Erlendsson.

ca. 1325 Grettis saga Ásmundarsonar, "Saga of
Grettir, Son of Ásmund," composed.

ca. 1500 Fljótsdæla saga compiled.

Chapter One
From the Discovery of Iceland to the Fall of the Commonwealth

Discovery and Settlement

The Icelandic historian Sturla Thórdarson (1214-84) relates three intriguing stories about the discovery of Iceland in his redaction of Landnámabók (Book of settlements). According to the first of these, a Norwegian ship set sail for the Faeroe Islands.

> But they were driven out to sea westwards and discovered a large country there. They climbed a high mountain in the Eastfjords and looked about far and wide for smoke or for some other sign that the land was inhabited, but they saw nothing. In the fall they returned to the Faeroes, and as they were sailing away from that land there came a heavy fall of snow on the mountains, and therefore they called the country Snowland. They praised the country highly. The place in the Eastfjords where they landed is now called Reydarfjall. This is what Priest Sæmund the Learned said. (1)

If this anecdote actually derives from Sæmund Sigfússon the Learned (1056-1133), Iceland's earliest historian, it may well contain a kernel of truth. Similar tales are told in the sagas about the accidental discovery of Greenland and Vínland ("Wineland"), followed by voyages of exploration and attempted or successful colonization. The Icelandic Annals record several instances of ships that drifted out to Greenland because of fog or adverse winds or both while bound for Iceland (2).

The Norsemen may have learned the location of Iceland in the Faeroes from Irish anchorites, who had worshiped God in the solitude of that remote land for decades before it was colonized by the Norsemen. It also seems likely that the Faeroes, Iceland, Greenland,

and the North American coast had all been sighted as
arctic mirages before Europeans set foot on their
shores (3). The largest separation between Scotland
and Baffin Island is the gap of 225 miles between the
Faeroes and Iceland. Davis Strait is only 200 miles
wide at its narrowest point, and this is no doubt the
reason why Thorfinn karlsefni first sailed north toward
Disco Island when he set out from Greenland in search
of Vínland (4). Having crossed the strait, he could
sail to Vínland without losing sight of land. All of
this in no way disparages the bravery and nautical
skill of the Norsemen, who sailed the northern seas
centuries before any other peoples (except the anchorites mentioned above) ventured into those perilous
waters.

The traditional date of the first permanent Norse
settlement is 874, when a Norwegian named Ingólf
Arnarson is said to have set up house in Reykjavík,
the site of the capital of Iceland. By ca. 930 the
habitable areas, the coastal plains, are believed to
have been fully settled, with a population of ca.
30,000 to 40,000 (5). Ari Thorgilsson the Learned
(1067-1148) records Ingólf's settlement at the beginning of his Íslendingabók (Book of Icelanders).

Iceland was first settled from Norway in the days of
Harald Fairhair, at the time--according to the
opinion and calculation of my teacher Teit, the
wisest man I have known, son of Bishop Ísleif; and
of my uncle Thorkel, Gellir's son, whose memory
reached far back; and of Thuríd, daughter of Snorri
godi, who was both learned in many things and trust-
worthy--when Ívar, son of Ragnar Lodbrók, had
Saint Edmund, king of the English, put to death.
And that was 870 years after the birth of Christ,
according to what is written in his [Edmund's] saga.

A Norwegian named Ingólf, it is truly reported,
left there for Iceland for the first time when
Harald Fairhair was sixteen years old and for the
second time a few years later. He settled in the
south at Reykjavík. (chap. 1)

The settlement of Iceland resulted from a massive
exodus from Scandinavia, which was in a state of recurrent warfare throughout the Viking Age (ca. 780-1070).
Most of the settlers came from southwestern Norway, the

coast of which was vulnerable to depredation by marauders. In the oldest histories of Norway, no connection is made between King Harald Fairhair and the settlement of Iceland. According to later saga literature, however, Harald endeavored to drive the vikings from his realm when he became sole ruler of the country ca. 885. The emigrants thus included farmers fleeing from the marauders as well as marauders and other opponents fleeing from the king. Basic causes of marauding and emigration were overpopulation and a desire for land and wealth (6). These emigrants probably represented a cross section of the Norwegian population with a fairly heavy sprinkling of vikings and local warlords who were unwilling to abide by the laws imposed on the country by King Harald. Many Norwegians went to Iceland by way of the western settlements (in the British Isles and nearby islands), where they often remained for years and intermarried with Celts. Although the majority of the Icelandic settlers were pagan, a rather large contingent from the western settlements were Christian. Some were Christian for the most part, but preferred to call on their good friend, the god Thór, in dangerous situations. A few were atheists, believing in "their own might and main" (mátt sinn ok megin). The culture of early Iceland was basically Norwegian (7).

The Norwegian Heritage

Social organization. The Norwegian heritage of the Icelanders included legal and judicial concepts and institutions that had their orgins in Germanic antiquity. Around the year 930, the Gulathing Law of southwestern Norway was adapted to Icelandic conditions, and the General Assembly (alþingi) was established. This body consisted of thirty-nine (later forty-eight) chieftains with the rank of goði and was presided over by a lawspeaker, who was elected by the goðar for a period of three years. The word goði is usually translated as "pagan priest," but since the godi's cult duties were secondary to his secular ones, it seems inadvisable to use this designation (8). During his term of office, the lawspeaker was required to recite in three installments Úlfljót's Law, named for the man who had brought it from Norway. This law was passed on by word of mouth until the Latin alphabet was

introduced into Iceland following the conversion (999).
Just when the civil laws were first committed to parchment is not known.

The General Assembly, which met annually for two
weeks in June at Thingvellir ("Plains of the Assembly"), had judicial and legislative power, but there
were no provisions for the enforcement of the laws.
Execution of a sentence--usually fines or banishment
from the district or the country--was left to the
successful litigant, and his efforts to secure legal
redress often led to a new round of aggression, followed by further litigation. Because of this lack of a
central authority, men of wealth and power could ride
roughshod over weaker opponents. As Hallberg expressed
it so aptly, "the role that power and violence played
in litigation presents a sharp and strange contrast to
the formalism and subtlety that were developed in legal
procedure" (9). Magnus Magnusson went so far as to
label the legal system as "at best an uneasy substitute
for revenge" (10). The situation was further complicated by the fact that honor demanded that an injury to
a kinsman be avenged, even when legal compensation had
been effected (11). And the concept "kinsman" included
fourth cousins. Although the sagas are not a true
representation of life in Iceland during the Saga Age
(ca. 870-1050), they do reflect the weaknesses of this
system. A favorite villain of saga literature, for
example, is the ójafnaðarmaðr, a cruel, avaricious
killer who repeatedly flaunts the law with impunity
until he is finally laid low.

It is clear that political power in ancient Iceland
was completely controlled by the godar. Landnámabók records the names of about 430 settlers, whose
families owned most of the land and wealth in Iceland
for several centuries. It was from such powerful
families that the godar came (12). The power and
authority of the individual godi were designated by the
term goðorð ("authority, chieftaincy"). This office
was hereditary, but could be sold, shared, or temporarily transferred. This easy transferability of power,
combined with the lack of any central authority, made
the country vulnerable to both internal disruption and
external aggression and thus contributed greatly to the
eventual collapse of the commonwealth (1262). Each
freeman had to be a member of a godord. Theoretically
he could choose his godi, since the godord was original-

ly not territorially defined. In practice, however, most farmers swore allegiance to the godi nearest to them. Local assemblies comprising three adjacent authorities were held before and after the meeting of the General Assembly.

The relationship of the godi to his liegemen (þing-menn) was roughly comparable to that of a medieval European sovereign to his vassals: the godi protected his liegemen from outside aggression, and they in turn accompanied him to the General Assembly and supported him there and on punitive expeditions. Until recently, it was believed that the liegemen had to pay a temple tax to their godi who, in return, was obligated to maintain the temple (hof) so that it did not deteriorate and to hold sacrificial feasts in it, as we read in Eyrbyggja saga (Saga of the people of Eyr) (chap. 4). Olaf Olsen has shown, however, that this passage is a learned reconstruction based on the church system of thirteenth-century Iceland and that the heathen hof was identical with the large banquet hall found on the estates of wealthy landowners. Here convivial banquets were held, at which the blood and flesh of sacrificed animals were consumed (13).

Eddic and skaldic poetry. The Norwegian heritage of the Icelanders also included a wealth of alliterative poetry, some knowledge of which is necessary for an understanding of saga literature. On the basis of content and style, this poetry is designated as either Eddic or skaldic (14). Eddic lays provided saga authors with themes and motifs for their stories; skaldic poems and stanzas preserved old traditions on which they could construct scenes, episodes, or even entire sagas.

Edda, which probably means "poetics," was originally the name of a treatise on skaldic poetry by the historian Snorri Sturluson. Today, however, it is the designation for the corpus of Eddic poetry. Eddic lays are of two kinds, mythologic and heroic. Mythological lays, which are our chief source of information about Germanic pagan mythology, relate stories about such gods as Ódin (Woden), Frey, Thór, and Loki and about the goddesses Freyja (Frey's wife and sister), Jörd, Frigg, and others. Heroic lays tell of the tragic adventures of historical and legendary warriors such as Sigurd (German Siegfried), Attila the Hun (Old Norse Atli, Middle High German Etzel), and Gunnar (German

Gunther) and of their wives and sweethearts, the most
important of whom are Brynhild (German Brünhild) and
Gudrún (who corresponds to the German heroine
Kriemhild).

Whereas mythological poetry seems to have been
unique to Scandinavia, heroic poetry was common to most
of the Germanic tribes, although little of it has
survived except in Iceland, where the church was less
intolerant of pagan survivals than elsewhere. The
major differences between Old Norse heroic lays, such
as the Atlakviða (Lay of Atli), and West Germanic
heroic lays such as the Hildebrandslied (Lay of
Hildebrand) is that the Norse poems are stanzaic, whereas the others are not. Despite the quantity and variety of Eddic poetry, however, the Norsemen never
developed a verse epic such as the Old English
Beowulf or the Middle High German heroic epics.
Instead, about 1250, they transformed a cycle of heroic
lays into Völsunga saga (Saga of the Völsungs) (a
major source for Richard Wagner's Ring des Nibelungen), which has themes and characters in common
with the Middle High German Nibelungenlied (Song of
the Nibelungs) (ca. 1205).

Skaldic poetry differs fundamentally from Eddic
poetry in several respects. Whereas Eddic lays are
anonymous, the authors of most skaldic poems are known.
Skaldic poetry deals with recent or contemporary
figures rather than with events from the distant past.
It is predominantly descriptive rather than narrative.
Its meter is more regular and its structure more complicated than those of Eddic poetry. And finally, it
employs more, and vastly more complicated, metaphorical
compounds known as kennings than any other form of
Germanic poetry. Simple kennings of the type of Old
English hronrād ("whale road") for sea occur in
Eddic lays, in Beowulf, in Shakespeare, and in every-
day speech. But the kennings of skaldic poetry can
consist of as many as seven elements, and their content
often refers to legendary or mythological events.
Thus, for example, to understand the simple kenning
Grana byrðr ("Grani's burden") we must know that
Grani was the name of the horse that carried the gold
Sigurd won by killing the dragon Fáfnir. Therefore,
Grana byrðr is a kenning or poetic periphrasis for
gold.

Although there are many skaldic measures, the one

regarded as most appropriate for the praise and entertainment of princes--and that was the purpose of much
of this poetry--was the dróttkvætt ("court meter").
The dróttkvætt stanza consists of eight lines, each
of which has six syllables with three stresses. Two
syllables in an odd-numbered line must alliterate with
the first syllable of the following even-numbered line,
so that there are four sets of alliteration in each
stanza. In each line there are two syllables that
rhyme with each other. The odd lines have imperfect
syllabic rhyme (skothending), such as behave:above,
and even lines have perfect syllabic rhyme
(aðalhending), such as atone:only. The stanza is
divided into two half-stanzas, each of which (called a
helming or helmingr) is ideally a semantic and
syntactic unit. Stanzas could be combined to form a
relatively short poem called a flokkr or a longer,
more complicated one with one or more refrains known as
a drápa, which was considered to be the most fitting
for eulogies of kings.

Because of its complexity, skaldic poetry could be
transmitted orally for generations until finally
recorded when the Latin alphabet came to the North with
the advent of Christianity. Although scholars tend to
regard references in saga literature to the recording
of skaldic stanzas on rune sticks as a thirteenth-
century anachronism, it seems reasonable to believe
that some skaldic poetry was preserved in this manner.
Both Eddic and skaldic poetry continued to be composed
in Iceland long after the practice had fallen into
disuse in Norway. Indeed, Icelanders at an early date
replaced Norwegians as court poets in Norway and the
other Scandinavian countries.

Snorri Sturluson regarded the poems of court skalds
as the most trustworthy of all preliterary historical
sources. Unfortunately, however, the content of this
complex poetry is often both vague and meager. Many
stanzas are difficult to interpret, both because of
their interlaced, esoteric language and because they
were damaged during oral and scribal transmission.
Often the stanzas are at variance with the prose text
they are cited to authenticate, and sometimes one and
the same stanza is assigned to different poets or associated with different events. Occasionally, a series
of stanzas or even entire poems are quoted with little
or no prose comment. When there is a close fit between

a stanza and the passage in which it is embedded, we
must consider the possibility that the verse was composed by the author rather than by the skald to whom it
is attributed or that an editor altered the verse to
make it agree with the prose. Nevertheless, skaldic
poetry is an important source of old traditions, and
some historians have even tried to reconstruct the
early history of the North purely on the basis of
skaldic stanzas with complete disregard for the sur-
rounding prose. And some sagas could not have been
written if the stanzas they preserve had not been available to the authors in oral or written form.

Christianity in Iceland

The conversion. Two events mark a major turning
point in Icelandic civilization. The first of these
was the reluctant but voluntary acceptance of Christianity by the godar in the year 999, which the author of
Gunnlaugs saga ormstungu (Saga of Gunnlaug Serpent-
tongue) declared to be "the best event that had ever
occurred in Iceland" (chap. 5). Although much has been
written about Germanic mythology, little is known about
religious beliefs and practices in pagan Iceland.
Belief in the heathen gods (æsir) seems to have been
on the wane already at the time of the settlement--
partly because migration removed people from their ancestral cult sites and partly because the Northmen had
come in contact with Christianity in the British Isles
and elsewhere. Place and personal names indicate that
Thór and Frey were the most popular pagan gods in
Iceland. Aside from some skaldic verses that deal with
experiences of personal religious conflict, our main
primary source of knowledge of the conversion is Ari's
Íslendingabók, and even this is one-sided since
Ari's only named informant was the grandson of one of
the two chieftains who served as King Ólaf
Tryggvason's emissaries to the General Assembly (15).

The second crucial event was a major change in the
law code made by Lawspeaker Skapti Thóroddsson, who
held office for twenty-seven years (1004-30). In
Íslendingabók, Ari writes as follows about Skapti's
legal reforms: "He established the law of the Fifth
Court, and also brought about a law forbidding a slayer
to announce a killing committed by anyone but himself;
until then there had been the same law here on that

point as in Norway. In his day many chieftains and powerful men were fined or banished for manslaughter or assaults by the exercise of his authority and the forceful discharge of his office" (chap. 8) (16). This amendment to the constitution made it impossible for a wealthy aristocrat to blame one of his henchmen for his crimes and to send him abroad in his place when a sentence of banishment was pronounced. With its emphasis on personal responsibility, this improvement in the constitution can be regarded as an application of Christian ethics to legal and social problems.

Skapti Thóroddsson must have been one of the most powerful and influential men in Iceland for several decades. It will be enlightening to compare what is known of the historical Skapti with the conflicting descriptions of the characters who bear his name in saga literature. In the sagas no mention is made of powerful men who were fined or banished by Skapti. "The omission of such accounts in the Sagas of the Icelanders, many of which are set during Skapti Thóroddsson's term of office, is one of the features that have weakened our faith in the historicity of saga literature" (17).

The national church of Iceland. There seems to have been little church organization in Iceland until the first bishop, Ísleif Gizursson, was elected in 1056. Gizur the White, one of the earliest converts to Christianity, had his son Ísleif educated in the convent of Herford in Westphalia, Germany. In due course Ísleif was elected bishop of Iceland. He first journeyed to Rome, where his election was sanctioned by the pope. From Rome he continued to Bremen, where he was consecrated by Archbishop Adalbert. According to Adam of Bremen, the archbishop entrusted Bishop Ísleif with "letters to the people of Iceland and Greenland, reverently greeting their churches and promising them he would come to them very soon." The Icelanders, Adam declared, "hold their bishop as king. All the people respect his wishes. They hold as law whatever he ordains as coming from God, or from the Scriptures" (18). Quite the opposite was true, however, for Ísleif suffered deeply from the unruliness and immorality of his countrymen.

Ísleif contributed greatly to the intellectual improvement of the priests by founding a school at Skálholt, his ancestral estate in southern Iceland.

Among Ísleif's pupils were Jón Ögmundarson, who became bishop of Hólar and founded a school there when the diocese of northern Iceland was established (1106), and Ísleif's son Teit, Ari's teacher, who founded a school at Haukadal, not far from Skálholt. Sæmund's son Eyjólf founded a school at the nearby estate of Oddi, which long remained an important center of ecclesiastical and secular learning. Bishop Ísleif was succeeded in 1082 by his son Gizur, who had also studied at Herford.

The praise that Adam of Bremen had bestowed upon Ísleif would have been more appropriate for his son Gizur. The twenty-four years of Bishop Ísleif's term of office seem to have been a time of violence and turmoil. In Hungrvaka (Appetizer), one of the more reliable of the secondary historical sources for this period, we read that "some men engaged in viking raids and warfare, and furthermore, people committed many shameful acts [endemi] that today would be regarded as monstrous outrages [ódæmi] if people did them" (chap. 2). From other sources we learn that these outrages included the eating of things unfit for human consumption and the killing of old and helpless people by throwing them over cliffs when food was in short supply (19).

The improvement in people's behavior during Gizur's tenure can probably be ascribed to the gradual civilizing influence of Christianity and of Skapti Thóroddsson's legal reforms on the one hand and to favorable weather conditions and profitable trading on the other. The latter no doubt account in large measure for Bishop Gizur's popularity. Ari states in Íslendingabók that Gizur was "better beloved by the whole people than any other man who . . . has ever been in this country" (chap. 10). The author of Kristni saga (Saga of Christianity) goes even further in his praise: "Bishop Gizur had so restored the country to peace that there were no great quarrels among chieftains during that time, and the bearing of weapons was largely abandoned. At that time most men of rank were educated [lærðir] and took holy orders even though they were chieftains, such as Hall Teitsson . . . and Sæmund the Learned . . . [and] Ari the Learned" (chap. 13).

Bishop Gizur's greatest achievement was the enactment of the tithe law in 1097, decades before similar laws were enacted elsewhere in the North. This remarkable feat was accomplished on the advice of Sæmund and with the support of Lawspeaker Markús Skeggjason, who was "the wisest lawspeaker in Iceland next to Skapti" (chap. 12). The tithe law required all landowners to assess the value of their property and to pay an annual tax on it. This money was divided into four equal shares that went to church owners, the priests, the bishop, and for support of the indigent. The fact that the churches in Iceland were the property of the land-owners helps explain why the tithe law met with less opposition there than in other Scandinavian countries. For church proprietors who owned several churches or became priests themselves, the tithes were a major source of income. For tax purposes, chieftaincies were regarded as "power and not property." It should be noted that all books owned by priests were also exempted from this tax (20). The enactment of this law put the national church, about whose poverty Bishop Ísleif had lamented, on a strong financial footing, which was further strengthened by Bishop Gizur's donation of his paternal estate of Skálholt along with other proper-ties and chattels. Probably the last reform with which Gizur was connected was the decision of the General Assembly to have the civil law revised and "recorded in a book" during the winter of 1117-18 (21). This was done on the advice and at the home of the chieftain Haflidi Másson, and a portion of the revised code is known as Haflidaskrá (Haflidi's Scroll). A few years later (ca. 1123) the code of church law was revised and adopted (22).

Bishop Jón Ögmundarson was concerned about the esthetic, intellectual, and moral improvement of the Icelandic people. Jón is said to have gone abroad as a young man in order to "observe the customs of good people and to further his education" (23). The school he founded at Hólar flourished for decades and had close connections with the first monastery in Iceland, the nearby Benedictine house founded at Thingeyrar in 1133. Both the episcopal school and the monastery were centers of writing. According to Jóns saga helga (chap. 27), the teacher Klæng Thorsteinsson and his pupils wrote "many remarkable books, which are still to be seen at Hólar and in many other places," and during the last decades of the century, four of the earliest biographies of Norwegian kings were composed at

Thingeyrar. One of these was a Latin biography of King
Ólaf Tryggvason, written by the monk Gunnlaug
Leifsson, who wrote various other works including the
biography of Jón Ögmundarson cited above (24).

Since the early literature has surprisingly little
to say about Bishop Jón, the vernacular adaptations of
Gunnlaug's biography are our main sources of information about his educational activities. Jón, who was
an accomplished singer and harpist, stressed the study
of music, literature, and Latin. He also tried to
raise the morals in his diocese by condemning dancing
and the chanting of erotic verses to women. Especially
interesting is his severe condemnation of sorcery, for
heathen practices such as this are also strongly
denounced in saga literature. In the Íslendinga
sögur, as we shall see, pagan magic caused the downfall of otherwise invulnerable heroes (25).

The Twelfth Century

Education and travel abroad. The twelfth century
was the most cosmopolitan era in early Icelandic
history. Following the example of Ísleif, Gizur,
Sæmund (the first Scandinavian to acquire his education in France), and Jón, young men went abroad to
study. The literature studied in the schools and monasteries of Iceland was the same as that studied on the
continent and in England, but much of the literature
produced in Iceland, although European in form, was in
content an amalgam of foreign and native elements (26).
The number of Icelandic pilgrims to Rome and the Holy
Land grew so great that Nikulás Bergthórsson, abbot
of the monastery Munkathverá (founded 1155), felt
constrained to write a guidebook, Leiðarvísir ok
borgaskipan (Itinerary and a list of cities), based on
a pilgrimage he had made himself about 1150-54 (27).
It is obvious that travel and study on such a scale
must have been a drain on the wealth of the families
involved. On the other hand, however, Icelanders could
profit from foreign trade as long as they owned their
own sea-going ships.

Separation of clergy and laity. During the second
half of the century, however, certain events occurred
that helped bring about another major change in Icelandic society. In 1152 the Scandinavian archiepiscopal
see was moved from Lund to Nidarós (Trondheim) in

Norway. This facilitated the exchange of books between schools and monasteries in Norway and Iceland, but it also subjected the Icelandic national church to ever increasing pressures from abroad. In Norway, Archbishop Eystein had been able to carry out the papal demand for control of church properties largely because King Magnús Erlingsson's claim to the throne was legally questionable. To bolster his position against rival pretenders to the throne, the king had himself invested with regal power by the archbishop. In return for his dubious coronation, King Magnús had to make concessions in regard to the papal demand for church autonomy. The archbishop was not long in extending this demand to Iceland with the aid of Thorlák Thórhallsson, who had arrived in Nidarós for consecration in 1177 after having been elected bishop of Skálholt in 1174.

Instead of publicly announcing the demands of the church for control of property, tithes, and clergy, Bishop Thorlák attempted to acquire authority over individual properties by refusing to consecrate newly built edifices or by threatening to excommunicate owners of churches unwilling to relinquish them. Although the bishop was successful in cowing small farmers to his will, large landholders defied him. Jón Loptsson of Oddi (d. 1197), the most powerful chieftain in the country, wished to have a newly built church consecrated. When the bishop asked Jón whether he knew about the archbishop's letter, he is said to have replied:

> I am willing to listen to the archbishop's message, but I am resolved to set it at naught, and I do not think he is wiser or better than my forebears, Sæmund the Learned and his sons. Nor shall I condemn the conduct of the bishops in this country who honored the custom of our land in suffering laymen to exercise authority over the churches that their ancestors dedicated to God at the same time as they stipulated that they and their descendants should remain in control of them. (28)

Whether or not Jón Loptsson actually spoke these words, they represent the position of the aristocrats, who took pride in both their heritage and their profitable church estates.

Even though Bishop Thorlák was ineffectual in espousing the cause of canon law and the episcopal ownership of churches, his endeavor signifies the beginning of a split between clergy and laity in Iceland. This rift was widened in 1190, when the archbishop forbade godar to take religious orders. An important victory was won in 1238, when the archbishop refused to consecrate two bishops elected by the Icelanders and instead appointed two Norwegians to the Icelandic episcopal sees. From this time on, Icelandic bishops, who heretofore had been selected by the Icelandic chieftains, were chosen by the Norwegian archbishop and the canons of Nidarós. At this time also, priests in the archdiocese of Nidarós were forbidden to marry, and "by demanding that priests remain unmarried it [the church] succeeded in drawing a more distinct line between clergy and laity" (29).

During the last decades of the twelfth and the first decades of the thirteenth century, the monks of Thingeyrar had not supported the ecclesiastical party. Nor did they support the archbishop's cause in Iceland, to judge from a short but bitter comment found in the biography of Bishop Gudmund Arason. While still a priest with no apparent political connections or aspirations, Gudmund visited Thingeyrar, where he was cordially and ceremoniously received by "Abbot Karl and Gunnlaug the monk and many others." But this was "before that envy and arrogance arose, which were revealed by his adversaries who were rebuked by him for their misdeeds. . . . Now all of this bears eloquent testimony to how such men esteemed his counsel before they were blinded by ambition" (30).

In the spring of 1253, the General Assembly resolved that canon law should take precedence over civil law when the two were in conflict. Less than fifteen years after the Icelanders had become subjects of the Norwegian king, the General Assembly accepted most of the demands of the archbishop. The national church of Iceland, owned and controlled by prominent farmers since the time of the conversion, had become a state within a state. The separation of clergy and laity was complete.

Iceland and the Norwegian Crown

Whereas the ever increasing domination of the nation-

al church of Iceland by the archiepiscopal see of
Nidarós can be documented in detail, alleged designs
of the Norwegian crown to subjugate Iceland are more
difficult to substantiate. How unreliable the Sagas of
Icelanders are in this matter is shown by the contradictory depictions of King Harald Fairhair that we find in
this literature. Ari reports only that Harald forbade
his subjects to emigrate from Norway for fear that his
realm would be depopulated, but that he and his subjects later "came to an agreement that every man who
was not exempted and who went from there to this
country should pay the king five ounces" (chap. 1).
According to one version of Landnámabók, Harald set
a limit on the size of the settlements in Iceland in
order that later settlers would not be deprived of land
(31). The compiler of the Ágrip af Nóregs konunga
sögum (Compendium of sagas about kings of Norway)
reports that Harald "improved his realm and restored it
to peace" (siðaði vel land sitt ok friðaði). In
Egils saga Skallagrímssonar (Saga of Egil, son of
Skallagrím), however, Snorri Sturluson portrayed
Harald as a cruel, treacherous tyrant. By contrast,
the author of Vatnsdæla saga (Saga of the people of
Vatnsdal) depicted him as a stern but just monarch. In
each case, the characterization of the king reveals the
author's political bias or artistic purpose or both
(32).

King Ólaf the Saint (d. 1030), who attracted several excellent Icelandic poets to his court, seems to
have been on good terms with a number of influential
Icelanders. According to the Helgisaga, the "legendary" saga of Saint Ólaf, he employed Hjalti
Skeggjason, early proponent of Christianity in Iceland,
as a special diplomatic envoy to the court of King
Ólaf of Sweden (chaps. 42-44). In the same biography,
we read that after Saint Ólaf had conquered his rival
kings in the Uppland district, "it is said that he had
that one blinded whose name was Hrærek, and he sent
him out to Iceland to Gudmund the Mighty, and he died
there" (chap. 24). Saint Ólaf must have had an
imposing personality, for one of his court poets,
Thormód Bersason, declared that his only wish was "to
live and to die in the king's presence" (chap. 58).
Even if these statements are not factual, they reveal a
perception of this monarch that is quite different from
that of Snorri Sturluson.

On at least one occasion, the Icelanders seem virtually to have been saved from extinction through the
generosity of a Norwegian monarch, Harald the Harsh (d.
1066), as can be seen from the following passage in the
synoptic history Morkinskinna (Rotten skin):

> Of all the Norwegian kings he enjoyed the greatest
> popularity among the Icelanders. As Iceland was
> experiencing a season of great privation, King
> Harald sent four ships with cargoes of grain to
> Iceland and limited the price of each skippund
> (384 pounds) to three marks in homespun cloth. He
> allowed every indigent who so desired to emigrate
> from Iceland to Norway as soon as that person could
> obtain passage and necessary provisions. As a
> result, many paupers moved out of Iceland. And soon
> the famine in Iceland was relieved and conditions
> improved although the country had come to the brink
> of exhaustion because of the hardships. (33)

Snorri reports the same event, which he concludes as
follows: "And from this the country rallied until
harvests improved. King Harald also sent out to Iceland a bell for the church which had been built for the
General Assembly at Thingvellir with timber provided by
Saint Ólaf" (34).

Snorri sometimes introduced material into his
Heimskringla (Orb of the world) for propagandistic
purposes. One of the versions of Jómsvíkinga saga
(Saga of the Jómsvikings), for example, relates that
King Harald Gormsson of Denmark once planned a punitive
expedition to Iceland because some Icelanders had
composed scurrilous verses about him in retaliation for
the Danes' illegal appropriation of cargo from a
stranded Icelandic vessel. The king, however, was
readily dissuaded from this reckless adventure. Snorri
dramatizes the anecdote to make the threat of royal
intervention seem more ominous. Before undertaking the
hazardous expedition, King Harald dispatched a warlock
in the shape of a whale to reconnoiter in Iceland. In
each quarter of the island, the warlock encountered
fearsome creatures that prevented him from going
ashore: an enormous dragon that spit venom at him, a
huge bird, an immense bull, and a mountain giant.
These figures, which represent the guardian spirits of
the country and today comprise the national coat of

arms of Iceland, are the Babylonian cherubim described by Ezekiel. Snorri probably borrowed them from a well-known homily he must have heard read yearly in church on the feast of Saint John the Evangelist (35).

Another timely addition of this sort occurs in his Ólafs saga hins helga (Saga of Saint Olaf) (chaps. 124-26). According to this account, King Ólaf the Saint in 1024 sent his greetings to the General Assembly and expressed his willingness to be the sovereign of the Icelanders if they so wished. As a token of good will, he asked the Icelanders to give him "the island or skerry outside of the Eyjafjord which they call Grímsey." His proposition was discussed at length. Finally someone asked Gudmund's brother, Einar Thværing, why he had not expressed an opinion. His reply, which is known to every Icelander, is as follows:

> The reason I have said little about this matter is that no one has asked me. But if I am to state my opinion, then it seems to me that the best thing for the people of this country is not to submit to taxation by King Ólaf or other such impositions as he has laid on the men of Norway. For this loss of freedom we would bring not only upon ourselves, but also upon our sons and all our kin who shall dwell in this land, and this serfdom would never leave the land. . . . But if the people want to keep that freedom which they have had since this land was settled, then the thing to do is to give the king no hold on us, whether through possession of land or through our paying a fixed tax such as might be counted a sign of allegiance. On the other hand it seems to me fitting that men should send the king gifts of friendship, those who so desire. . . . These would be well spent if friendship is returned for them. But of Grímsey there is this to say, that if nothing is taken thence that can serve for food, then an army can be fed there. And if a foreign army is there and goes out from there in longships, then I think many a small farmer will find himself hard pressed. (36)

The only known source for this speech is an obscure skaldic verse attributed to Einar Thværing (37). In order to understand Snorri's motives for creating these

two episodes, we shall have to review briefly certain
events in Iceland.

The Decline of the Commonwealth

Internal dissension. As we have seen, Iceland
enjoyed a brief period of peace, prosperity, and
clement weather during the episcopal tenure of Gizur
Ísleifsson. Following his death, however, matters took
a sudden turn for the worse, as the compiler of
Hungrvaka vividly describes:

> The wisest men thought that Iceland seemed to droop
> after the death of Bishop Gizur as Rome did after
> the passing of Bishop Gregory. The death of Bishop
> Gizur presaged great distress from bad seasons, both
> in shipwrecks and the loss of human life and cattle
> that accompanied them. This was followed by hostili-
> ties and lawlessness and in addition loss of life
> throughout the entire country such as had never
> occurred since the country was settled. Two years
> after the passing of Bishop Gizur, Haflidi Másson
> was wounded at the General Assembly, and the lawsuit
> was not resolved that summer. (chap. 5)

Gizur was succeeded by Thorlák Runólfsson (d. 1133),
who seems to have fared little better than Ísleif. In
Hungrvaka, we read that "many chieftains
(höfðingjar) made trouble for Bishop Thorlák
because of their disobedience, and some because of
wickedness and infractions of the law, but he managed
as best he could under the circumstances" (chap. 7).
Haflidi Másson was the leading chieftain in
northern Iceland at this time. The injury referred to
above came about following a series of confrontations
between Haflidi and another leading chieftain named
Thorgils Oddason. A sentence of banishment was passed
against Thorgils, but Haflidi was unable to execute it
since his opponent was too powerful. In 1120, as we
read in Kristni saga, Haflidi arrived at the General
Assembly with about 1440 men and Thorgils with about
840 followers (chap. 12). Hostilities, which might
well have led to civil war, were averted through the
entreaties of men of good will. As Ursula Brown expressed it, "Haflidi's obstinacy is finally broken down
by a Christian argument of humility and forgiveness,

and the two chieftains are reconciled and remain at peace for the rest of their lives" (38). The conciliatory words attributed to Ketil Thorsteinsson, soon to become bishop of Hólar, are noteworthy. In urging Haflidi to accept private arbitration, Ketil relates an unsuccessful attempt on his part to prosecute an assailant in court: "I wanted to avenge this promptly by having the man outlawed with the support of kinsmen. We prepared the case, but then some powerful men came forth to support him and thus my case was quashed. Now it may be that some powerful men will come forth to support Thorgils, even though your case is just" (chap. 29). These words were obviously meant as a commentary on the legal system, which was as unworkable in the twelfth century as it had been a century earlier. In this case, reason and good will prevailed--with the help of threats of excommunication from Bishop Thorlák.

Historians have neglected the period 1120-1220, possibly because the sources for those years are rather meager. The fact that two chieftains could muster over two thousand fighting men as early as 1120 to settle a private squabble by force of arms could bode no good for the future of the Icelandic Commonwealth. It therefore seems strange that scholars should assume that this century was an era of relative tranquility. Indeed, a recent study of the period, based on four sagas of contemporary and recent times, indicates that this assumption is not realistic (39). Although ordinary farmers remained dependent on their chieftains for protection from aggression, a class of wealthy landholders developed during this century who were able to defy their chieftains because of their superior wealth and popularity. Just as a few chieftains gradually gained control over large areas of the country, so some of the farmers gained in wealth and power--for the most part, church proprietors, who received not only a share of the tithes but also rents from their tenants and interest on money lent to the less fortunate. The strong position of such farmers at this time (ca. 1220) must have been the outcome of social and economic dislocation during the previous century. It is clear that the horrors of the Age of the Sturlungs were not the bloody disruption of an age of peace but the climax of an accelerating process of strife and struggle. By the year 1220, six families were fighting within and among themselves to gain ownership and control of the entire country.

Thus we see that social and political turmoil in Iceland during the period 1120–1220 resulted from a combination of forces. The first was the well-documented struggle over church ownership and canon law. The second was the less well-documented struggle among secular chieftains and prominent farmers for wealth and power that culminated in large-scale battles in the thirteenth century. The third was the complete breakdown of the legal system: disputes were settled by force or by arbitration, not by the courts (40). The fourth was the ever recurring struggle for survival against natural catastrophes--severe winters, storms, ice floes that blocked harbors, volcanic eruptions, epidemics among humans and livestock, famine. The fifth factor, sometimes overlooked by historians, was the gradual disappearance of seaworthy vessels that could not be replaced for lack of wood in Iceland. Since about 1170, the Icelanders were dependent on the Norwegian crown not only for passage abroad but even for such necessities of life as grain and lumber. This dependence on Norway for trade led to several clashes between Icelandic chieftains and Norwegian merchants. One of these quarrels, instigated by the chieftain Sæmund Jónsson of Oddi, was so severe and prolonged that in 1220 Earl Skúli threatened to send a punitive force to Iceland. Earl Skúli was dissuaded from his purpose by Snorri Sturluson, who later received an oceangoing ship as a gift from the earl (41). This is the last "known instance of a ship being in the sole possession of an Icelander" (42). And finally, we must not forget that the many Icelandic poets who served as royal chroniclers from the time of Harald Fairhair became retainers of the king, as did the chieftains who sought his support in the settlement of their feuds in Iceland. This fact helps to explain the ambivalence of chieftains and the conflicting attitudes of saga writers toward the crown during the thirteenth century.

The Sturlung Age. Snorri was the son of Sturla Thórdarson (1115–83), called Hvamm-Sturla after his farm in the Hvammsfjord in western Iceland. A scheming, unscrupulous upstart, Sturla had acquired wealth and power through feuds with neighboring farmers and the sly manipulation of the law. One of these feuds was arbitrated by Jón Loptsson. When Jón returned home, he took Snorri, then three years of age, with him as his foster son. For sixteen years, Snorri remained at Oddi, center of native culture and European learning. Through two well-calculated marriages and canny legal maneuvers, Snorri became the wealthiest and, for a time, the most powerful chieftain in Iceland. Snorri and his two elder brothers, Sighvat and Thórd, placed their stamp and their name upon their time, the Sturlung Age (1200-1280), an era of barbaric immorality, cruelty, and cynical perversion of the law, but a time also of remarkable literary productivity. Sturlunga saga, a compilation of contemporary biographies and chronicles, is a grim record of this age and one of the keys to an understanding of saga literature. Most of the major sagas of kings and of Icelanders were composed during this time of strife and turmoil (43).

Snorri spent the years 1218-20 in Scandinavia, mostly with Earl (later Duke) Skúli in Norway. As already noted, Snorri was able to dissuade Earl Skúli from sending a punitive force to Iceland in retaliation for the harassment of Norwegian merchants there. In return for this favor, Snorri is said to have promised to persuade the Icelanders to become subjects of the Norwegian king. Upon his return to Iceland, however, he seems to have been somewhat less than diligent in working for the royal cause. Instead, he composed a laudatory poem in honor of Earl Skúli and King Hákon called Háttatal (Enumeration of verse forms) in which he employed a wide diversity of skaldic stanzas.

Although many Icelanders were suspicious of Snorri, he was elected to the office of lawspeaker for the second time (1222-31). He was now at the peak of his power. But Snorri had made many enemies, and in 1237 he fled to Norway, where he remained on good terms with Duke Skúli but not with King Hákon. The following year, his brother Sighvat Sturluson and four of Sighvat's five sons were slain at the Battle of Örlygsstadir. When Snorri heard of the death of his kinsmen, he returned to Iceland in defiance of the king's ban on sailing. Accused by King Hákon of high treason, Snorri was murdered on 22 September 1241. Ironically—but somehow fittingly for the Sturlung Age—Snorri's death was brought about by his erstwhile son-in-law Gizur Thorvaldsson. The king confiscated Snorri's properties. In 1256 Gizur went to Norway, to return two years later with the rank and insignia--trumpet and standard--of a Norwegian earl. In 1262-64 the Icelanders became tributary to the Norwegian crown. Snorri Sturluson's prophetic warning had fulfilled itself. Ironically, it was not Grímsey but Snorri's own estates that gave the Norwegian king a foothold on Iceland.

Perhaps the most dangerous vice of the Sturlung Age was avarice--the unscrupulous, unrelenting drive of rich and mighty chieftains and farmers for more wealth and power, with the result that "internal warfare coupled with the lack of proper administration of justice" became the "main reasons for the erosion of political authority that gradually took place" (44). The most conspicuous weakness of this age was the lack of hóf, that is, moderation and self-control. It is not simply fortuitous that hóf should become the highest virtue for saga writers (45).

The Íslendinga sögur are probably more readily enjoyable to modern readers than any other form of medieval literature. To be understood, however, they must be read against the background of the enigmatic age that created them. The two passages from Heimskringla discussed above, for example, are meaningful only to those who are acquainted with the tense Icelandic-Norwegian political relations during the years 1170-1220 and with the ambitious, ruthless, often ambivalent behavior of Icelandic chieftains including Snorri Sturluson in the thirteenth century. This also holds true for many passages in the Íslendinga sögur and even for entire sagas. The more thoroughly we know the Sturlung Age, the more fully will we appreciate its literature. Equally important is a knowledge of the earlier historical literature of the North, in which we find, in rudimentary form, rhetorical and structural techniques as well as basic themes that are developed and exploited in the Íslendinga sögur (46).

Chapter Two
The Beginning of Historical Writing

Introduction

As we have seen, the twelfth century was a time of intensive literary activity in Icelandic schools and monasteries. The literature of this period is surprisingly rich and varied, but only those works that have a direct bearing on the sagas can be considered here (1).

Early in the twelfth century, an anonymous genius devised an orthography for Icelandic based on phonemic principles. The First Grammatical Treatise, as this essay of about ten printed pages is known, differs essentially from earlier and contemporary European grammars in two respects: it presents a theory of orthography and it is written in the vernacular rather than in Latin. After praising the English for effectively adapting the Latin alphabet to their language, the "first grammarian" states that he has "written an alphabet for us Icelanders also, in order that it might become easier to write and read, as is now customary in this country as well, laws and family records [áttvísi], or interpretations of sacred writings, or also the historical knowledge that Ari Thorgilsson has recorded in books with such discerning wisdom" (2).

The significance of this statement for the literary historian is obvious. The first grammarian was especially concerned lest the imperfect orthography then in use lead to misinterpretations of the laws. The importance of genealogies was so great that their recording must have begun soon after the Latin alphabet was introduced into Iceland. Such family records constituted the basis of Landnámabók and a major source of information for later saga writers. The "many books" written by Klæng Thorsteinsson and his pupils at Hólar were certainly "sacred writings"—translations and adaptations of saints' lives, homilies, and so on (3). Homilies were written as early as the end of the eleventh century in Norway and soon thereafter in Iceland. The importance of saints'

lives as models for the composition of sagas has been
demonstrated by Turville-Petre (4). Indeed, some of
the earliest biographies of Norwegian kings and Icelandic bishops were--literally--saints' lives. Most
important of all in this quotation, however, is the
mention of Ari's books, for Ari is widely cited as an
authority in sagas of Norwegian kings and Icelandic
heroes. Before discussing the nature, purpose, and
influence of Ari's writings, however, it will be necessary to say a few words about Sæmund the Learned.

The First Icelandic Chronicles

Sæmund Sigfússon the Learned. It is generally
agreed that Sæmund, who is cited widely as a historical authority, was the author of a Latin chronicle of
the Norwegian kings that is no longer extant. A quotation from his book is found as an interpolation in the
vernacular translation of Odd Snorrason's Latin
biography of King Olaf Tryggvason, where information
about the king's punishment of pagan sorcerers is
attributed to Sæmund.

From this quotation and from the poem Nóregs
konungatal (Succession of the kings of Norway), we
gain a fairly good idea of the nature and scope of
Sæmund's survey. About halfway through the poem of
eighty-seven stanzas, the anonymous author states that
he has related the lives of ten kings, descended from
Harald (Fairhair), "just as Sæmund the Learned did."
This poem was composed about 1190 in honor of Jón
Loptsson, who was a grandson of Sæmund and of King
Magnús Bareleg. The poem suggests that Sæmund's book
was a chronicle of Norwegian kings from the time of
Hálfdan the Black (ca. 820-60) to the death of Magnús
the Good (1047), containing information about the
length of each king's reign, his achievements, and
place of burial. From other sources we know that this
book also contained miscellaneous information about
events in Iceland and Norway and that it probably
began, in typically medieval fashion, with the creation of the world (5). Svend Ellehøj has shown that
Sæmund, like Ari, exerted a pervasive influence on
later historical writing (6).

Ari Thorgilsson the Learned. Ari Thorgilsson's
Íslendingabók (ca. 1122-33) is about as long as
The First Grammatical Treatise. In ten short chap-

ters, Ari gives an account of the settlement of the country, the enactment of the civil law, the establishment of the General Assembly, the correction of the calendar, the establishment of the quarter courts, the settlement of Greenland, the advent of Christianity, the activities of lawspeakers and foreign bishops, and the election and achievements of the first two native bishops. An appendix contains the genealogy of Harald Fairhair, the genealogies of five Icelandic bishops (representing the four quarters or districts of the country), and Ari's genealogy, which is traced back thirty-nine generations to Yngvi, king of the Turks.

Ari based his history on both written sources and oral information. Although Ari mentions Sæmund only once, it seems reasonable to explain certain Latinisms as coming from that source. Ari carefully identified some of his oral informants, most of whom had died long before he wrote his book.

One obvious purpose of Íslendingabók was to establish the chronology and to record the history of Iceland, with special emphasis on the advent and development of Christianity. Ari's assurance that his informants were learned and trustworthy demonstrates that he was concerned with recording historical truth. Both internal and external evidence suggest, however, that he was pursuing additional goals. Let us first consider the Prologue:

> The Book of the Icelanders I wrote first for our bishops Thorlák and Ketil and showed it both to them and to Priest Sæmund. And according as it pleased them to have it as it was, or augmented, I wrote this one covering the same ground but excluding the genealogies [áttatala] and the lives of kings [konungaævi] while adding what has since become better known to me and is more fully related in this one than in that. But whatever is wrongly stated in this history, it is our duty to prefer that which is proved to be correct. (Prologue)

If Ari had merely wanted to record history, he would have had no occasion to omit historical material. Clearly the bishops and Sæmund must have felt that the genealogies and the lives of the kings detracted from what they perceived to be the central aims of the book. Let us now look at chapter 6, which at first glance seems to be irrelevant to the history of Iceland:

> The country that is called Greenland was discovered
> and settled from Iceland. Eirík the Red was the
> name of the Breidfjord man who went out there from
> here and took possession of land at the place that
> has been called Eiríksfjord ever since. He gave a
> name to the land and called it Greenland, and said
> that people would desire to go there if it had a
> good name. At both the eastern and western settle-
> ments they found human habitations, fragments of
> skin boats, and stone implements, from which it
> could be seen that the same kind of people had
> passed that way as inhabited Vínland and whom the
> Greenlanders called Skrælings. When he began to
> settle the country, it was fourteen or fifteen years
> before Christianity came to Iceland [984 or 985]
> according to what a man who had gone out with Eirík
> the Red told Thorkel Gellisson in Greenland. (chap.
> 6)

We recall Adam of Bremen's statement that Bishop
Ísleif had returned to Iceland in 1057 bearing an
official dispatch from Archbishop Adalbert to both the
Icelanders and the Greenlanders. This implies that
Greenland was regarded as being under the jurisdiction
of the see of Skálholt. But we read in the Annals
that three bishops attended the General Assembly in
1126 (7). The third was a certain Bishop Arnald, who
had been sent to Greenland by the Norwegian king at the
request of the Greenlanders, as we know from Einars
þáttr Sokkasonar (Tale of Einar, son of Sokki) (8).
Clearly this chapter, too, was written on behalf of the
Icelandic bishops, who must have resented the Greenlanders' impropriety in appealing to a foreign secular
power in a purely religious matter.

Ari's rather dry account blossoms into dramatic
narrative in the story about the advent of Christianity. With the country on the verge of war between
pagans and Christians, the Christians "bargained with"
the pagan lawspeaker to "proclaim the law." Lawspeaker
Thorgeir first related a fictitious exemplum telling
how the peoples of Denmark and Norway had once made
peace despite the efforts of the kings to prolong
hostilities.

"And now it seems advisable to me," he said, "that
we do not let the will of those prevail who are most
strongly opposed to each other, but so compromise
between them that each side may win part of its
case, and let us all have one law and one faith. It
will prove true that if we sunder the law, we shall
also sunder the peace." And he concluded his speech
in such a way that both sides agreed that all should
keep the law that he would proclaim. (chap. 7)

Thorgeir thereupon declared that all Icelanders should
become Christians and submit to baptism.

As a feeble concession to his own party, the lawspeaker declared that the old law should remain valid
in regard to the eating of horse flesh (associated with
sacrifice to Frey) and infanticide. People might sacrifice to the pagan gods in secret but were susceptible
to the lesser outlawry (banishment from the country for
three years) if accused of this practice by witnesses.
Thorgeir, of course, was well aware of the Icelanders'
dependence on the Norwegian crown for sustenance in
times of famine. He also knew that King Ôlaf
Tryggvason, the "missionary king," was holding hostage
four sons of leading Icelandic chieftains, one from
each quarter of the country, pending acceptance of
Christianity by the General Assembly. Thus his problem
was not to arrive at a decision, but to make the only
reasonable decision acceptable to the pagans.

Ari terminated his history with the year 1120. His
contemporaries certainly saw the parallel between
Thorgeir's exemplum, Ari's story of the peaceful
acceptance of Christianity by the godar--probably true
in essence if not in detail--and the reconciliation
brought about between Haflidi Másson and Thorgils
Oddason in 1121 through the good offices and threats of
the bishops. The three passages quoted above, Ari's
praise of the Lawspeakers Skapti and Markús, and the
inclusion of the bishops' genealogies all seem to point
in the same direction: Ari wrote the second version of
Íslendingabók, in part at least, as an exhortation
to the Icelanders to obey and support the ecclesiastical and secular authorities in their endeavors to maintain peace and order in their country (9). In other
words, Ari's Íslendingabók is more than history. It
is tendentious history that is relevant for contempo-

rary times, that is, the early twelfth century. And it
clearly reveals the author's strong ancestral and
national pride--a spirit that also characterizes many
of the Sagas of Icelanders. **Landnámabók.** Landnámabók is unique in the
history of European literature. It records with remark-
able topographical accuracy the land claims of 430 settlers. Their descendants are named, as are the ancestors of some of them. About 130 of the settlers are
said to have come from Norway and some 50 from the
western settlements, mostly from the Hebrides. In all,
the Book of Settlements contains the names of over
3,000 persons and 1,400 places. The first five books
of the Old Testament, the Book of Joshua, and the Historia regum Britanniae have been suggested as possible
models for this work (10). Like most Old Icelandic
literary monuments, Landnámabók has not come down
to us in its original form. There exist two medieval
redactions and a fragment (two leaves) of a third one.
In addition, there are two compilations from the seventeenth century. Jón Jóhannesson has unraveled the
complicated textual history of Landnáma; the relationship of its various versions to each other can be
seen from the following stemma (11):

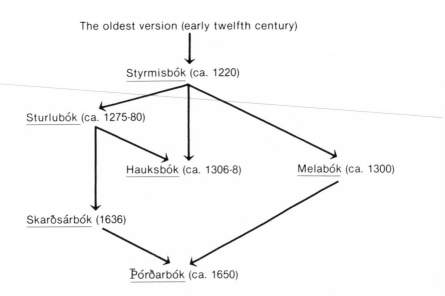

Prior Styrmir the Learned (d. 1245) revised and
expanded the original somewhat. Sturla Thórdarson
rearranged the order of the entries of this record of
the settlement, transformed it into a historical
topography of Iceland, and added many saga excerpts.
Sturla had a penchant for exaggeration and for the use
of superlatives in describing the wealth and achievements of certain illustrious Icelanders, including his
own ancestors. Sir Hauk Erlandsson (d. 1334) stated
that he compiled his redaction from Styrmisbók and
Sturlubók, preferring the fuller text when the two
differed. Sir Hauk was the kingmaker among Landnáma
redactors. Through his imaginative editing he not only
traced his own ancestry back to an Irish king, he also
made it possible for many of his countrymen to claim
descent from mythical and legendary royalty. Despite
its complicated textual history we can now use
Landnámabók with a reasonable degree of confidence
in studying the growth of saga literature, thanks to
the meticulous investigations of Jón Jóhannesson and
the exemplary edition of Jakob Benediktsson.

It seems likely that a major reason for compiling
Landnámabók was to establish an accurate record of
property ownership in connection with the collection of
tithes. The nature and purpose of this fascinating
book changed markedly, however, under the impact of
political events. In the epilogue to Dórðarbók, we
read this apologia for writing about the settlement of
Iceland:

It is the opinion of many persons that writing about
the settlement is irrelevant learning. But we think
we can better refute foreigners when they charge us
with being descended from slaves and scoundrels if
we have definite knowledge of our ancestry. And
also for those persons who wish to have knowledge
about the past or to trace genealogies it is better
to start at the beginning rather than to plunge in
at the middle. And indeed, all enlightened peoples
wish to know about the origins of their countries,
or how each one began, or about their kinsmen. (12)

This statement of the triple purpose of Landnámabók could conceivably stem from Ari's time--from the
beginning of Icelandic nationalism. But it seems to
reflect the Norwegian-Icelandic tensions of the fateful

years 1170-1220, which led to Snorri's ambivalent dealings with the Norwegian crown and eventually to his
downfall. It therefore seems reasonable to attribute
the above statement to Styrmir the Learned (13).

Eirík Oddsson. As a chronicler of Norwegian
kings, Ari Thorgilsson was followed by Eirík Oddsson,
who wrote a book called <u>Hryggjarstykki</u> (Backbone
piece, ca. 1170), which is believed to have covered the
period from 1130, when Ari's account supposedly came to
an end, until 1161, when Ingi, the son of Harald gilli,
died. Snorri Sturluson cites Odd six times in his
<u>Haraldssona saga</u> and once mentions his history. Like
Ari, Eirík based his chronicle on eyewitness accounts.

The most detailed and vivid borrowing from <u>Hrygg-
jarstykki</u> in <u>Heimskringla</u> is the description of the
death of Sigurd slembidjákn, a pretender to the Norwegian crown, who was captured after having made
depredations in Norway. Some of his captors wanted him
beheaded for his atrocities, but others demanded
vengeance for injuries suffered at his hands.

> They broke his arms and legs with the hammers of
> their axes. Then they tore off his clothing and
> stripped off his scalp and intended to flay him
> alive. But they could not do this because of the
> flow of blood. Then they took whips of walrus hide
> and flogged him until his skin was completely off,
> as though he had been flayed. And then they took a
> pole and struck his back and broke it. Then they
> dragged him to a tree and hanged him. Then they
> struck off his head and dragged his body away and
> buried it in a heap of stones. (14)

Sigurd's fortitude is stressed. Eirík states that by
the time Sigurd expired, he had sung one-third of the
psalter, and that when he spoke, his voice was no more
tremulous than usual. "It is the opinion of all,"
Eirík wrote, "both friends and enemies, that within
the memory of man, no one in all Norway had been more
capable in every way than Sigurd. But in some respects
he was pursued by ill luck" (15).

Turville-Petre comments that this passage "is more
detailed and vivid than any . . . in Ari's work now
known, and shows how the art of narration had developed
since Ari's day" (16). This, of course, is true. We
must not forget, however, that Ari's informants were

old people recalling things they had seen or heard in childhood, whereas Eirík based this account on reports of eyewitnesses of the grisly event. It is also quite likely, as Nordal has suggested, that Eirík had a strong personal interest in Sigurd (17). Snorri may also have contributed to the vividness of this scene.

Hungrvaka. As a chronicler of Icelandic bishops, Ari was succeeded by an anonymous priest who about 1200 expanded and extended the last three chapters of Íslendingabók into a synoptic history of the diocese of Skálholt from 1056 to 1176. The author named his book of thirty pages Hungrvaka (Appetizer) because its purpose was to arouse the interest of young people in the achievements of their illustrious bishops and to induce them to read books in the Norse tongue such as "laws, or sagas, or biographies (mannfræði)" (chap. 1). No doubt he had in mind such works as Eirík's Hryggjarstykki, Ágrip, Veraldar saga (History of the world), the earliest sagas of Saint Ólaf, and similar works now lost.

Except for the introductory chapter, which is written in a rambling style, the language of Hungrvaka is clear and straightforward. The main sections of the book have the same structure: the biography of each bishop is followed by a summary of events that occurred in Iceland and abroad during his tenure of office. Whether this information was culled from written sources by the author or added by a later editor cannot be determined, since this work has been preserved only in late copies.

After giving a more detailed account of the foreign bishops and of the first two native ones than Ari had done, the author of Hungrvaka characterized and extolled the achievements of Thorlák Runólfsson, Magnús Einarsson, and Klæng Thorsteinsson. Although he admired these spiritual leaders, he did not hide their defects, as can be seen in this description of bishop-elect Thorlák: "Thorlák was a man of average height and amiable, with a long face and light chestnut hair. He was not said to be a handsome man by people in general, nor was he very impressive in the opinion of most people. When he went abroad, people said that there must be a poor choice of men in Iceland, and he seemed to them to be unworthy of such an honor" (chap. 6). Klæng is described as handsome, prepossessing, and vigorous, and he was "a good writer, an excellent

scholar . . . and a great poet" (chap. 9); but when he
invited 840 priests and other men of rank to a sumptu-
ous banquet in celebration of his lavish rebuilding of
the church at Skálholt, the author comments that this
was done "more with munificence than with full pru-
dence" (chap. 10). A touch of irony is found in the
description of the grief suffered by people at the
sudden death of Bishop Ketil Thorsteinsson of Hólar
while attending a wedding at Skálholt: "But because
of the persuasions of Bishop Magnús and the excellent
drink that people had to drink there, their hearts were
lightened somewhat more quickly than they would otherwise have been" (chap. 8). The fact that the author of
Hungrvaka referred only briefly, albeit most admiring-
ly, to Bishop Thorlák the Saint suggests that he was
aware of plans to write a more detailed biography of
that church leader.

In addition to Ari's Íslendingabók, the author
of Hungrvaka seems to have known Adam of Bremen's
History. Among the foreign bishops who visited
Iceland, he mentions Jón Írski, "and some men believe
that he then went to Vindland and converted many people
to God, and was later seized and beaten, and both hands
and feet were cut off and last of all his head, and
with those tortures he went to God" (chap. 3). As
Turville-Petre has shown, this passage agrees closely
with Adam's description of the martyrdom of Johannes
Scotus (18). The author of Hungrvaka named only one
source and stated that he "composed this booklet in
order not to forget completely" what he had "heard the
learned man Gizur Hallsson say about this matter"
(chap. 1).

Gizur's name is also associated with Veraldar saga
(ca. 1160-90), a translation of a German chronicle that
derives ultimately from Bede and Isidor and Dares
Phrygius's De excidio Trojæ, with supplementary
material from the Bible, biblical commentaries, and
German historical writings (19). Fredrik Paasche
attributed Veraldar saga to Gizur on the basis of his
fame as scholar and globe-trotter (20). According to
the Haukdæla þáttr (Tale of the people of Haukadal), he had gone abroad often, had served as a marshal
of King Sigurd (the father of King Sverrir), and was
"more highly esteemed in Rome than any Icelander before
him because of his accomplishments and prowess" (chap.
4). The only known book to have been written by Gizur

is the no longer extant <u>Flos peregrinationis</u> (The supreme journey) in which he recounted his pilgrimage to Rome. Gizur's grandfather, Teit Ísleifsson, we recall, was described by Ari as "the wisest man I have known." Gizur's father, Hall Teitsson (d. 1150), is regarded by many scholars including Jón Helgason as the author of the <u>First Grammatical Treatise</u> (21). In <u>Hungrvaka</u>, we read that when Hall went to Rome as bishop-elect at the age of sixty-five, he spoke the language of each country "as if he had been born there" (chap. 8). Thus we see that for three generations the descendants of Gizur the White and their close associates were leading bearers of literary culture in Iceland.

The First Norwegian Synoptics

The <u>Historia Norvegiæ</u>. Although the Norwegians preceded the Icelanders in the translation and composition of homilies, they did not begin to record their national history until the last decades of the twelfth century. The earliest known synoptic histories of Norwegian kings are the <u>Historia Norvegiæ</u> (History of Norway, ca. 1170), composed by an anonymous Norwegian cleric at the instigation of a certain Agnellus, and the <u>Historia de antiquitate regum Norwagiensium</u> (History of Norwegian kings in ancient times), written by a monk named Theodoricus at the monastery of Nidarhólm about 1180 and dedicated to Archbishop Eystein of Nidarós (d. 1188).

According to the Prologue of the <u>Historia Norvegiæ</u>, its purpose was to present a geographical description of Norway and its "tributary islands" (including Iceland!), a survey of Norwegian kings to contemporary times, and an account of the struggle between Christianity and heathendom in Norway. Whether or not the work was ever completed is not known, since the only extant manuscript breaks off with the arrival of Saint Ólaf in Norway (1015). A major source, especially for the first part and for the treatment of Saint Ólaf, was Adam's <u>History</u>. The author's depiction of Ólaf Tryggvason, however, seems to be a deliberate refutation of Adam's characterization of this ruler as an apostate and practitioner of pagan wizardry. Matter that the <u>Historia Norvegiæ</u> has in common with other West Norse historical writing is derived by Ellehøj from Ari's konungaævi (22).

Some of the most interesting passages in this book
are those dealing with the customs, and especially the
sorcery, of the Lapps, whom the author calls Finns (as
do later saga writers), and his descriptions of the
flora and fauna of the North (chap. 4). Most remarkable are the beavers, which employ "beaver thralls,"
turned over on their backs, as sledges to transport
bark from the forest to their underwater burrows.

The importance of the Historia Norvegiæ for Norwegian history lies in the fact that in some cases it
preserves older, and perhaps more truthful, traditions
than later chronicles do; its importance for literary
history consists in the fact that it helps demonstrate
the persistent and pervasive influence of Ari's
original Íslendingabók on West Norse historical
writing.

Theodoricus monachus. Theodoricus monachus casually referred to a Catalogus regum Norwagiensium as one
of his sources. As Ellehøj has shown, the Catalogus
provided Theodoricus with the chronological framework
for his history, genealogies of rulers, data on the
achievements of kings such as church building, and
burial sites. The skeleton provided by the Catalogus
was fleshed out with material supplied by oral informants, which included ecclesiastical traditions preserved at the archiepiscopal see and tales told by
"those we call Icelanders" (Prologus). Theodoricus had
great confidence in the information supplied by Icelanders since it was based on ancient (skaldic) poems.

Although he cannot be shown to have used Sæmund's
chronicle directly, one passage in his Historia clearly derives from that source. Sturla Thórdarson's
description of the discovery of Iceland is so similar
to that of Theodoricus—and these two are so different
from all others—that there must be some relationship
between them. It is possible that Sturla knew
Theodoricus's chronicle, since it was used by Odd
Snorrason in his biography of Ólaf Tryggvason. The
similarities and dissimilarities between Sturla's and
Theodoricus's accounts are of such a nature, however,
that they could only have come from a common source
which, from Sturla's statement, must have been Sæmund.
Since Theodoricus probably did not know Sæmund's
work, he must have received this information from one
of his Icelandic informants, whom Finnur Jónsson has

identified as Thorlák Thórhallsson (23). Thorlák
had been a pupil of Sæmund's son Eyjólf, and he and
Theodoricus had much in common, for they were both
ardent proponents of Eystein's ecclesiastical policies.
The <u>Ágrip af Nóregs konunga sögum</u>. The <u>His-</u>
<u>toria</u> of Theodoricus was a major source for the
<u>Ágrip af Nóregs konunga sögum</u>, believed to have
been compiled about 1190 at Nidarós, probably by a
Norwegian cleric. The other main sources, as demonstrated by Ellehøj, included Ari's <u>konungaævi</u> and
Sæmund's chronicle, which were probably brought to
Norway by Abbot Karl Jónsson in 1185, and the <u>Catalo-</u>
<u>gus regum Norwagiensium</u> (24). In addition the author
made use of popular tales, local ecclesiastical traditions, and skaldic verses, seven of which he quoted in
whole or in part.
    Originally the <u>Ágrip</u> presumably covered the
period from Hálfdan the Black (d. 860) to the acces-
sion of King Sverrir (1177), but in its present
defective form it begins with the acceptance of Harald
Fairhair as sole ruler of Norway and breaks off shortly
after the introductory descriptions of the kings
Eystein, Sigurd, and Ingi (d. 1161). For a historical
work, the disposition of the material is deplorable:
matter of moment is treated summarily, whereas irrelevant tales are narrated in detail. In the second chapter of the extant work, for example, the author invents
a battle between Harald Fairhair and a nonexistent king
Skeidar Brand, based on a misunderstanding of the ship-
kenning <u>skeiðar-brandr</u> ("galley prow"). In the
following two chapters, he relates the charming tale of
Harald's infatuation for the Lappish witch Snjófríd,
which Snorri copied almost verbatim in his <u>Haralds</u>
<u>saga hárfagra</u> (chap. 25).
    Even if he did not succeed, the compiler obviously
tried to write in a pleasing and entertaining manner.
He was fond of antithesis and alliteration. As one
would expect, Latinisms occur frequently. In one
passage, the Latin source peeks through the translation: a son of Snjófríd <u>var . . . kallaðr</u>
<u>seiðmaðr, það er spámaðr</u> ("was . . . called a wizard,
that is, a soothsayer"), which, as Finnur Jónsson
suggested, probably renders <u>vocatus est seiðmaðr, id</u>
<u>est propheta</u> (25). The source for this passage was
probably Sæmund's chronicle (26).
    Rulers whom the author despised, such as Eirík

Bloodaxe and his sons and Sigurd Munn, the father of
Sverrir, were labeled ofstapamenn ("overbearing,
arrogant men"). Kings like Sigurd the Jerusalemfarer
and Hákon the Good, on the other hand, were characterized as listuligir ("magnificent, elegant"). Hákon
(chap. 5) was said to excel all other men at öllum
riddaraskap ok kurteisi ("in all chivalry and courtly
bearing"). It is evident from the strongly partisan
characterizations that Ágrip was not written at the
instigation of King Sverrir, as some scholars have
believed. Although not good literature, this chronicle
was an important source for later historical writing.

Orkneyinga saga

Ágrip supplied both a chronological framework and
miscellaneous information for the compiler of Orkneyinga saga (Saga of the people of Orkney, ca. 1200), a
synoptic history of the earls of Orkney and their
diverse dealings with the rulers of Norway and Scotland
from the time of Sigurd Eysteinsson (d. 890) until
1171. The original is lost; the extant version has
been expanded and continued to the time of Earl Jón
Haraldsson (d. 1231). A three-chapter introduction,
attributed by some scholars to Snorri Sturluson, provides the Orkney earls with mythical ancestors, whose
conflicts with kinsmen prefigure a major recurrent
theme of the saga. Einar Ol. Sveinsson has adduced
weighty internal and external evidence for assuming
that this history was composed under the auspices of
the Oddi dynasty (27).
Orkneyinga saga has significant points of contact
with earlier and later sagas. Aud the Deepminded, who
plays an important role in Laxdæla saga and a lesser
one in Eyrbyggja, is mentioned in chapter 5.
Rögnvald kali's adventure in Dolls Cave (chap. 61) is
a hazy analogue to Grettir's famous battle with a
monster in a cave (28). Snorri Sturluson borrowed
generously from this work for his Óláfs saga helga,
and these borrowed portions have replaced the original
ones in Orkneyinga saga. Earl Rögnvald's premonition of his death in this history seems to have been
influenced by the legendary saga about Saint Ólaf
(chap. 89). In this episode, one of the earl's men
wished to replenish the dying embers at which they were
warming themselves.

Then the earl made a slip of the tongue with these words: "When these fires are burned out, we will also have lived out our lives" [eru vér ok fullgamlir]. But he had meant to say that they would be fully warmed [fullbakaðir]. When he noticed this, he said, "I have not made a slip of the tongue before, as far as I remember. I now recall what my foster-father, King Ólaf, said at Stiklastadir when I noted his slip of the tongue: if I should ever happen to make a slip of the tongue, I should expect to have only a short time left to live. It may be that my kinsman Thorfinn is alive." (chap. 29)

Scarcely had these words been uttered when Earl Thorfinn and his men surrounded the building and set it on fire. Rögnvald made a dramatic escape by vaulting over the attackers and vanishing into the darkness, but his place of refuge was betrayed by the barking of his dog. Saint Ólaf's prophecy was fulfilled.

Rhetorically Orkneyinga saga shares several features with sagas of kings and of Icelandic heroes. Like Snorri and the creator of Laxdæla saga, the compiler of this history frequently employed the phrase sem fyrr var ritat ("as has already been written") to effect cohesion and to mark transitions in his narrative. Occasionally the scene of action is prepared in advance, as in the description of the slaying of Svein Ásleifarson in Dublin (chaps. 107-8) (29). Another noteworthy example of this foreshadowing technique is the prophecy of Edna Kjarvalsdóttir that a magic standard in the form of a raven that she made for her son, Earl Sigurd, would always bring death to the bearers but victory to the one before whom it was borne. In his first battle Sigurd was victorious, but three banner bearers were slain. Years later, however, in the battle against the Irish King Brján, "there was no one to bear the raven standard, and the earl bore it himself and fell there" (chaps. 11-12). This integral tale about Earl Sigurd sheds welcome light upon murky statements in Njáls saga (chap. 157) and in Þorsteins saga Síðu-Hallssonar (Saga of Thorstein, son of Hall of Síða, chap. 2), in both of which the episode appears in fragmented and abridged form (30).

Stylistically this compilation is uneven. As already mentioned, substantial portions are from Snorri's

pen. The characterization of Earl Magnús the Saint
and the description of his martyrdom read like translations from a hagiographic Latin _vita_ (chaps. 45, 50).
The assertion that he lived with his bride for ten
years "pure and spotless of all sins of the flesh" and
that "when he felt tempted, he sprang into cold water
and besought God's help" (chap. 45) was also made about
King Oswald of England (31). Among the most entertaining episodes is the account of Rögnvald kali's voyage
to the Holy Land, which is constructed on stanzas he
and two Icelandic skalds composed about this adventurous journey. One of these verses was composed by Earl
Rögnvald to substantiate the claim of Audun the Red to
have been the first man to board a Saracen merchant
ship in the Mediterranean Sea: "Audun the Red with
great zeal was the first to climb aboard the dark ship;
the valiant man attacked boldly. There we reddened our
weapons in the blood of men; black bodies fell upon the
deck; this was God's doing" (chap. 28). All the Saracens, the "heretics of God," were slain except the
skipper, who bade the vikings a courteous farewell when
they released him, adding that he hoped they would
never meet again.

Brutal torture and killing are realistically described. Among the memorable descriptions of barbaric
behavior is the following passage that relates the
treacherous slaying of Melbrikta Tooth, Earl of the
Scots, by Sigurd the Mighty:

> There was a fierce battle but not a long one before
> Melbrikta and his followers were killed. Sigurd had
> their heads fastened to their saddle straps as proof
> of their prowess. Then they rode homeward, boasting
> of their victory. As they were riding along, Sigurd
> wanted to spur his horse, and he struck his calf
> against the tooth projecting from Melbrikta's mouth
> and skinned it. The wound quickly grew painful and
> swollen, and that led to his death. (chap. 5)

Even more brutish is the slaying of Hálfdan Longlegs,
son of Harald Fairhair and Snjófríd, by Turf-Einar in
vengeance for the slaying of his father: "They found
Hálfdan Longlegs . . . and Einar had an eagle carved
on his back with a sword. They cut all his ribs from
the spine and drew out the lungs and sacrificed him to
Odin as a victory offering" (chap. 8).

A perusal of the text of this chronicle reveals that the compiler took pains to weld the materials from his disparate sources into a cohesive narrative, and also that a later redactor endeavored to smooth out the stylistic unevenness. The first of the major synoptic chronicles, <u>Orkneyinga saga</u> is of importance for students of Icelandic literary history as well as for students of the history of Scotland and the Orkneys.

Skjöldunga saga

Another work that Einar Ól. Sveinsson has cogently associated with the Oddaverjar is <u>Skjöldunga saga</u> (Saga of the Skjöldungs), a chronicle of the legendary rulers of Denmark from the time of Skjöld (OE Scyld), son of Óðin, to Gorm the Old, one of the earliest historical kings. The skeleton for this chronicle was provided by a genealogical table, probably compiled by Sæmund the Learned, which traced the pedigree of the Oddaverjar (and the Sturlungs) back to Óðin (32). The chieftains of Oddi were notorious for their overweening pride in their royal ancestry. When Deacon Pál, son of Sæmund Jónsson, visited Norway in 1216, for example, he was jeered by the Norwegians, who accused him of scheming to seize the throne of that country (33). It seems quite likely that one purpose for writing <u>Skjöldunga saga</u> was to glorify the Oddi family, and Bjarni Guðnason has advanced reasons for ascribing it to Bishop Pál (d. 1211), son of Jón Loptsson, whose ancestry, we recall, was traced back to King Harald Fairhair in <u>Nóregs konungatal</u>. Another purpose, Bjarni Guðnason suggests, was to relate the political history of Denmark to world history by making Óðin the father of Skjöld and having him come to the North from Asia (34). Further evidence to support this suggestion is the fact that Harald Fairhair's pedigree was extended to Adam, whom "God created first of all men" (35).

Although <u>Skjöldunga saga</u> no longer exists, we can gain a fairly good idea of its content and spirit from a Latin rendering made by Arngrímur Jónsson near the end of the sixteenth century and from borrowings from it in Snorri's <u>Edda</u> and in various other works. The skeleton provided by Sæmund's <u>ættartala</u> was fleshed out--sometimes very leanly--with material from skaldic verse, heroic and mythological poetry, and other oral

traditions. Evidence for the existence of ancient
traditions about the Danish kings is found in Beowulf
and other Old English poems (36). We must also keep in
mind the fact that for several centuries Icelandic
skalds--among them Lawspeaker Markús Skeggjason--
visited the Danish court and served in the royal
retinue. When the author's sources were sparse, he
padded out his narrative with learned speculation and
typically medieval etymologizing. During the reign of
Skjöld's son Leif, for example, conditions in Denmark
were so peaceful that his name was lengthened to
Fridleif (friðr, "peace"). Leif's son and successor
Fróði was so erudite that from his name was derived
the appelation fróðr ("learned"). His reign, too,
was marked by peace and the absence of crime, and this
time of tranquility coincided with the reign of Emperor
Augustus and especially with "the year of the birth of
the Saviour" (37). The portrayal of the bounteous
harvests from unsown grainfields is reminiscent of the
descriptions of Vínland in Adam of Bremen's History
(bk. 4, chap. 38) and in Eiríks saga rauða (chap.
5).

Skjöldunga saga is characterized by heroic spirit
permeated with Christian sentiment, as illustrated by
the following summary of a typical episode:

As an illegitimate son Áli the Brave cannot succeed
his father, Fridleif Fróðason, as king. His
brother Fróði takes possession of both the dominion
and the wealth. Áli goes marauding to gain fame
and fortune. He harries throughout Sweden and con-
quers a domain there. Suspecting that Áli will
claim a share of the inheritance, Fróði pays
Starkad the Old 120 marks of silver to kill him.
Although reluctant to do so, Starkad finally agrees
out of loyalty to his sovereign. Welcomed with
generous gifts and affection, Starkad quickly gains
Áli's confidence. He is slow to carry out his mission, however, because the young king's piercing
gaze terrifies him. One day when Áli goes to the
baths, he asks Starkad to stand guard over him.
When Áli's physical strength diminishes and the
fierce glare of his eyes mellows in the warm bath,
Starkad thrusts his sword through him. "I know that
this deed was planned by my brother Fróði," he says
with a smile. Áli dies laughing, but those present

weep. Filled with remorse, Starkad takes to harrying. He soon leaves Sweden, however, because of his
hatred for pagan sacrifice. (p. 224)

The episode is heroic except for Starkad's remorse and
his hatred for pagan sacrifice, which are Christian.
Christian sentiment is revealed also in the author's
previous praise for Fridleif's abolition of heathen
practices in his realm and his later comment that
Fródi's violent death while in the act of pagan sacrifice was a fitting punishment for fratricide.

Jómsvíkinga saga

Jómsvíkinga saga (Saga of the Jómsvikings)
begins where Skjöldunga saga ends, with King Gorm
the Old. The Jómsvikings were a band of Danish warriors whose base of operations, the Jómsborg, was
situated on the island of Wollin off the coast of
Pomerania. The climax of the story is the Battle of
Hjörungavág (ca. 980), in which Earl Hákon of Hladir
repulsed an attack by a Danish fleet. This portion of
the story is believed to be derived from a lost history
of the Earls of Hladir.
  Composed about 1200, this saga is preserved in four
thirteenth-century vernacular redactions and a Latin
rendition of a fifth one made by Arngrímur Jónsson
about 1592 (38). Despite obvious infelicities, which
vary from one version to the other, Jómsvíkinga
saga has a carefully planned and tightly structured
plot. All historical sagas contain matter intended to
entertain, but the freedom with which the author of
this work treats historical personages and events
suggests that his primary purpose was not to record
facts but to create historical fiction. Emphasis is on
action. The characters are not complex individuals but
types that complement and contrast with each other.
  The basic structural devices are foreshadowing and
the epic triad, usually employed in conjunction with
each other. At the beginning of the story, for example, King Gorm has three dreams--derived ultimately
from Pharaoh's dreams in Genesis 41:15-21--two of which
are interpreted by his wife Thyri as prophecies of
famine in Denmark. Because she succeeded in averting
the predicted disaster, Queen Thyri received the byname
"Glory of Denmark." The third dream is a prophecy of

strife in Denmark following the king's death. Similar-
ly three portents that appear to Earl Klakk-Harald are
interpreted by Queen Thyri to signify future conflict
and treachery in Denmark and the advent of Christianity
(chap. 3). One of these is a variant of the tree dream
that occurs widely in hagiographic narrative and occasionally in the sagas (39). Vagn, the most reckless of
the Jómsvikings, swears an oath to take part in the
attack on Earl Hákon, to slay Hákon's vassal Thorkel
Leira, and to sleep with Thorkel's daughter Ingeborg
(chap. 26). The threefold oath is completely fulfilled
when Vagn and Ingeborg are married in the final chapter
of the story. During the Battle of Hjörungavág, Earl
Hákon has to appeal three times for help to his
tutelary goddess Hölgabrúd. Only after he has his
youngest son sacrificed to her does she grant him
victory by raising a fierce hailstorm against the
attackers. Christianity is mentioned in the saga, but
we find little trace of Christian ethics in it. The
battle itself, which is fought in three stages, is
vividly described, as is the beheading of several of
the captured Jómsvikings. Indeed, Lee M. Hollander
declared that "it would be difficult to cite in world
literature a parallel to that unforgettable scene"
(40).

The verbose language of the older redactions of this
story was streamlined and compressed by the redactor of
the version found in Codex Holmiensis 7, quarto, into a
terse, paratactic, sometimes elliptical narrative that
conforms with the popular notion of what "oral saga
style" should be. One of his guiding principles was to
condense detailed plans for future action into a curt
statement that certain characters devised a plan. We
are kept in ignorance of the nature of the plan until
it is carried out. The purpose of this technique, of
course, was to arouse curiosity and to sustain suspense.

Færeyinga saga

The author of Færeyinga saga (Saga of the Faeroe
Islanders) (ca. 1210) goes even further. He sometimes
merely hints at the hatching of plots and even keeps us
in ignorance of how they are carried out (41). In two
successive summers, the Norwegian king's tax collectors
fail to return from the Faeroes. When King Ólaf

demands that one of his Faeroese liegemen appear before him for interrogation, it is decided that Thoralf of the island Dimun shall go. Thereupon Thránd of Gata, the chief schemer, goads his three nephews into taking a boatload of wool to Norway for sale. One dark night, Thoralf is slain and his companion hurled into the sea by unidentified assailants. Sigurd, one of Thránd's nephews, is suspected of the murder and agrees to undergo the ordeal of bearing a hot iron the following day. On the pretext that he cannot expect a just verdict from the king, he returns immediately to the Faeroes. There can be no doubt that Thránd planned the killing of the king's emissaries and of Thoralf, but this fact is not even hinted at by the author through the common device of having "the people say" or in any other way.

Thránd is a most unsavory character. He is dishonest, deceitful, avaricious, and completely unscrupulous. He comes to riches by stealing a precious gold ring at a fair in Denmark and then earning a handsome reward for_ devising a scheme for compensating the victim through donations from all the merchants present. He increases his wealth and power by having his cousins, Brestir and Beinir, killed and their sons, Sigmund and Thórir, taken to Norway in the hope that they will never return. Eventually, after a series of attacks and counterattacks, he brings about Sigmund's destruction after the latter has magnanimously (but foolishly, as Thránd himself said) spared his life. And yet the author succeeds in eliciting our grudging admiration for the scheming curmudgeon by portraying him as the embodiment of Faeroese independence as he resists--in his own devious way and not for ideological reasons--the imposition of foreign laws and a foreign religion by foreign monarchs. It was this aspect of Thránd's character that must have appealed to Snorri Sturluson, as we can see from Thránd's cameo appearances in Heimskringla (Óláfs saga helga, chaps. 135, 143). But in the end, Thránd is outwitted by Sigmund Brestisson's daughter Thóra. Through her well-laid plans, her husband Leif succeeds in killing Thránd's nephews to settle accounts once and for all. Thránd dies of grief, and Leif receives all the Faeroes in fief from King Magnús the Good, son of Saint Ólaf.

Thránd's antagonist, Sigmund Brestisson, is a paragon of heroic virtues. In the Battle of Hjörungavág,

it is his defeat of the viking Búi that wins the
victory for Earl Hákon and his son Eirík. Later he
is converted to Christianity by King Ólaf Tryggvason,
who commissions him to Christianize the Faeroes. He
accomplishes this by force after his attempt at a peaceful conversion is thwarted by Thránd. Victorious in a
series of skirmishes with his cunning kinsman, he is
finally outmaneuvered and forced to leap into the sea
to save his life. He finally reaches land but is so
exhausted that he is buffeted about by the surf for a
long time before he can muster enough strength to pull
himself up on the foreshore. Here he is murdered by a
local farmer and his sons. There is a double irony in
his death. He was killed mainly for his ring, a gift
from the pagan Earl Hákon, which Sigmund insisted on
wearing (despite King Ólaf's warnings) because of a
promise made to the giver. And his death was avenged
by his kinsman Thránd, the very one who had caused it.

This saga has many excellent qualities. There are
memorable scenes, including the powerful hero being
buffeted about by the surf and the appearance of his
ghost carrying his head in his hands, conjured up by
the wizardry of Thránd to identify his slayers. Frequently tragic scenes are prefaced by humorous ones,
with the humor usually being centered on Thránd. The
style is lucid except for the hagiographic, alliterative speech in which King Ólaf compares his youth with
that of Sigmund. Despite the fact that this saga has
been preserved only as inserts in later sagas of Ólaf
Tryggvason and Saint Ólaf, its structure is well
integrated, although most readers today will probably
regard the account of Sigmund's youth in Norway as dis-
proportionately long. We find here a rather sophisticated treatment of several saga themes, such as the woman
as inciter to vengeance (Thóra), the reluctant Christian (Thránd), and the cursed object (Sigmund's ring).

Grænlendinga saga

As a final example of early historical writing, let
us consider Grænlendinga saga (Saga of the Greenlanders, ca. 1190), the account of the accidental discovery, planned exploration, and attempted settlement of
Vínland, which is probably to be located somewhere
between the St. Lawrence and Hudson rivers (42). We
recall that the earliest reference to Vínland occurs

in Adam of Bremen's History. Adam cites as his source of information "the most learned king of the Danes," Svein Úlfsson. Fifty years later, Ari mentions Vínland so casually that a general knowledge of its existence in Iceland can be assumed. In the Icelandic Annals, we read the laconic report that in 1121 a certain "bishop of Greenland set out in search of Vínland" (43). Although the Greenlanders continued to sail to Labrador (Markland, "Woodland") for timber, they seem to have abandoned hope of colonizing Vínland and subsequently forgot its precise location.

According to Grænlendinga saga, which can confidently be accepted as a historical document in outline even though most of the details must be regarded as imaginary, Vínland was discovered about 885 by the seafaring merchant Bjarni Herjólfsson, who was driven off course while sailing from Iceland to visit his father in Greenland. About fifteen years later, Leif, son of Eirík the Red, retraced Bjarni's course from Vínland to Greenland to explore the accidentally discovered country. Subsequently, a wealthy Icelandic merchant named Thorfinn karlsefni undertook the colonization of Vínland but had to abandon his purpose because of the hostility of the natives--provoked in part at least by the barbaric behavior of the Greenlanders. Two additional voyages to Vínland and one abortive one are recorded.

During this unsuccessful undertaking, Leif's brother Thorstein died of illness in the wilderness of Greenland. Shortly afterward, his corpse sat up and made a prophecy concerning his widow Gudríd:

I am concerned to tell Gudríd her fate, so that she can better endure my death, for I have come to a place of good repose. I must tell you, Gudríd, that you will be married to an Icelander, and you will live together for a long time. Many descendants will come from you, vigorous, bright and splendid, sweet and of good savor. You will sail from Greenland to Norway and from there to Iceland and make your home in that country. There you two will live for a long time, and you will outlive him. You will go abroad and make a pilgrimage to Rome and return to your home in Iceland. There a church will be raised then, and there you will live and take the vows of a nun and there you will die. (chap. 6)

Like all other prophecies made in the sagas after the
fact, this one proved to be true. Among the three
bishops descended from Karlsefni and Gudríd was
Thorlák, son of Hallfríd, daughter of Snorri, son of
Karlsefni and Gudríd. (Snorri was the first European
child to be born on the North American continent.) No
doubt Bishop Thorlák recorded some of the family traditions about the adventures of his great-grandparents in
Greenland and in Vínland. Probably Ari did also, for
Snorri tells us in the Prologue of Heimskringla that
Ari "included also much other matter, both concerning
the lives of the kings of Norway and Denmark, as well
as of England, and also the notable events that had
occurred here in his own country." This no doubt
included Greenland, which Ari and the bishops Thorlák
and Ketil clearly considered to be an extension of
Iceland.

Morkinskinna and Fagrskinna

Although not compiled until about 1220-30, two additional synoptic histories must be considered here (44).
Morkinskinna originally covered Norwegian history
from about 1035 until 1177. Stylistically, Morkinskinna is more advanced and structurally more sophisticated than Ágrip and the earliest royal biographies.
The compiler was fond of humorous anecdotes, and in
its present form this synoptic includes a wealth of
excellent short stories about Icelanders, several of
which will be discussed in chapter 4. By contrast,
Fagrskinna ("Fair skin") contains few stories
intended to assert the importance of Icelanders at the
Norwegian court, but it has preserved numerous skaldic
stanzas in whole or in part. It is believed that
Fagrskinna was compiled by an Icelander for Hákon
Hákonarson. The oldest manuscript ends with the death
of Sigurd Jerusalemfarer (1130), a later one with the
Battle of Ré (1177). The compiler of this synoptic
made use of many written sources, and this accounts for
its uneven style and the sometimes awkward disposition
of its matter. Among these sources was Sæmund's
history, which supplied both the chronology and valuable information about Norwegian rulers until the death
of Magnús the Good. Whereas Fagrskinna is the most
significant synoptic history before Snorri's Heimskringla, Morkinskinna sheds more light on the development of saga literature.

Conclusion

In the early historical literature of the North, we note several significant developments. During the second half of the twelfth century, Latin yields to Old Norse. Just as skaldic poetry at an earlier period had become an Icelandic monopoly, so the writing of history is soon taken over by Icelanders. The dry recording of historical facts and traditions is gradually replaced by historical fiction. The emphasis shifts from the presentation of action to the delineation of character, which, as Hallberg expressed it, is the alpha and omega of saga literary art (45). Latinisms in vernacular narrative prose gradually diminish, but in typically medieval fashion, a distinction continues to be made between the simple, lucid language of narrative accounts and the more formal, complex periods of expository and laudatory passages. Structurally, too, the Latin heritage persists: the medieval excursus or ecbasis continues in the form of digressions, which remain characteristic of saga literature to the very end. A further development of style and composition takes place in the earliest biographies of Norwegian kings and Icelandic bishops, as we shall see in the following chapter.

Chapter Three
The First Biographies

Introduction

Even more intricate than the question of the extent of
Ari's authorship and of his influence on subsequent
historical writing is the problem of the relationship
among the various chronicles and biographies of Norwegian kings. The scholarly literature on this problem
is enormous, and the opinions set forth, to paraphrase
Jónas Kristjánsson, are almost as numerous as the
publications (1). In this chapter, as in the last one,
we shall follow the conventional relative chronology
(with occasional modifications) as it has emerged from
the painstaking research of philologists and literary
historians, even though our confidence in this chronology has been shaken somewhat by recent studies (2).

Biographies of Olaf Haraldsson the Saint

The Elzta saga Óláfs helga (Oldest saga of
Saint Olaf). The earliest extant biography of a
Norwegian king is the Elzta saga, which is believed
to have been composed about 1180 at Thingeyrar. The
six preserved fragments comprise 315 printed lines of
prose, six skaldic stanzas, and one line each of two
additional stanzas (3). The purpose of this biography
was the glorification of Saint Olaf, but the inordi-
nate amount of space devoted to the poets Ottar the
Black, Sighvat, and Thormód and to other Icelanders
reveals that the compiler also wished to underscore the
prominence of his countrymen at the Norwegian court.
The curious disposition of the material suggests that
the compiler was unable to harmonize his disparate
sources, including skaldic stanzas and independent
tales (þættir). Thus Ottar the Black recites several stanzas in fragment 1 but is not introduced into the
saga until fragment 3; the author gives two different
accounts of a major battle; and he relates two conflicting versions of the banishment of one of Olaf's
enemies, Thórir Hound.
How rich the traditions were from which the author

48

of the earliest biography worked can be seen from the following facts. One year and five days after Olaf's death, his grave was opened by Bishop Grímkel; the body, it was said, was uncorrupt, and beard, hair, and fingernails had grown just as though the corpse had been alive. The transformation of history into legend had begun. The following year, Thórarin Praise Tongue addressed a poem to Olaf's adversary, King Svein Knútsson, in which he urged his patron to invoke Saint Olaf's help in ruling Norway and described several miracles performed by Olaf. In such a short time, Olaf's cult had spread to his former enemies. About ten years later, Sighvat Thórdarson, one of Olaf's favorite skalds, in his Erfidrápa (Memorial lay), expanded on his miracles, recounted his battles, and vividly described his awesome presence at the Battle of Stiklastadir. His enemies dared not look into his piercing eyes, which were as keen as those of a serpent. Here for the first time, we find mention of the solar eclipse that is said to have occurred during Olaf's final battle: "Men relate the marvel that the sun in a clear sky could give no warmth. Remarkable were the forebodings of the king's death. The day did not grow bright. I heard tidings of the battle from Norway" (4). The cult of Saint Olaf spread far and wide. As early as 1056, his sanctity is mentioned in English sources, and Adam of Bremen reports that many miracles had been performed at Olaf's grave and that the saint's day celebrated in his honor was observed throughout all northern countries (5).

A high point in the cult of St. Olaf was reached in 1153 at Nidarós, some months after the establishment of the archiepiscopal see, when the Icelandic priest, Einar Skúlason, declaimed his commemorative poem Geisli (The sunbeam) in Christ Church before the archbishop and three coregents of Norway. This drápa mentions the solar eclipse as well as Olaf's vision of a ladder to heaven that portended his imminent death. Additional sources are the anonymous Translatio sancti Olavi, used by Theodoricus, and Archbishop Eystein's Passio et miracula beati Olavi, which, according to Svend Ellehøj, was based in part on Theodoricus's Historia (6). When we consider that in addition to written Latin sources and a veritable thesaurus of skaldic poetry there must have existed a myriad of tales about Saint Olaf, we are not surprised that the

compiler of the Elzta saga should have had difficulty
in arranging and articulating his material.

The style of the Elzta saga is somewhat more
fluent and the syntax, for the most part, less cumber-
some than that of Ari and the first grammarian. At
worst, it is repetitious and tedious; at best, it is
characterized by a certain lumbering dignity. The
portion of Þormóðar þáttr preserved in fragment 2,
for example, begins with this sentence: "And now when
the time came for Thormóð and Hárek to depart from
[King Knút's] retinue, the gifts that Thormóð thought
had been promised him were not forthcoming from the
king's hand." Reminded of this in a verse recited by
the skald, the king drew a gold ring weighing half a
mark from his arm and handed it to Thormóð. "'Thank
you very much, sir,' he said, 'and do not reprove us
for forwardness if we speak about this somewhat
further. You stated, sir,' he said, 'that we were to
receive a mark of gold from you in payment for military
service.'" King Knút acknowledged the correctness of
Thormóð's assertion and gave him a second ring.

Even acts of violence are described in unhurried,
circumstantial language. One time when Thormóð's
vessel was leaving its berth, Saint Ólaf's dragonship
bore down upon it. "And it is said that the forecastle-man on the dragonship drew his sword and struck
at Thormóð; and he did not wish to remain in his debt
but returned the blow and killed that man; he then
sprang from his ship onto the dragonship and, with his
shield before him, [ran] aft all the way to the raised
deck." Asked by Saint Ólaf why he had done this, he
replied with a verse: "I would think I had seized
heaven with my hands, bold, fortunate seafarer, if you
were to take me into your care and keeping. Let us
carry the shields out to the ships. Wise, powerful
warrior-king, my desire is to live and to die with
you."

The Helgisaga Óláfs konungs Haraldssonar. The
"Legendary saga of King Ólaf Haraldsson" seems to be
an abbreviated, interpolated version of the Elzta
saga and was probably compiled about 1190 at Nidarós.
Although the redactor copied some passages verbatim,
he abridged others, such as the anecdote about Thormóð
quoted above, by as much as 50 percent. Consequently
the portrait of the poet is radically reduced: his
audacity remains, but his courtly bearing in the pres-

ence of royalty has disappeared. Needless repetitions
seem more abrupt in the legendary saga than in the
original since the redactor--this is a typical scribal
practice--has suppressed the first-person explanatory
comment sem ek gat áðr ("as I have already stated").
The redactor improved the disposition of the material
somewhat. He interchanged the matter of fragments 1
and 3, for example, so that the poet Ottar is formally
introduced into the story before he recites his verses
to Saint Olaf. But he was not consistent in correct-
ing contradictions. Thus, for example, Hrút
Lodinsson, who is slain in chapter 85, appears as a
leader of Saint Olaf's adversaries in chapter 89. The
language of the legendary saga is simpler than that of
its presumed source.

Because the structural and stylistic weaknesses of
the Helgisaga are so obvious, it is easy to do the
redactor an injustice by overlooking his efforts to
create a complex character and to put together a
cohesive narrative. The chief device by which cohesion
is effected is foreshadowing, which is employed in
various forms. Olaf Haraldsson is portrayed as a
saint, a sage, a warrior, and a monarch, and as a
monarch he is both the secular and the spiritual leader
of his people. The initial chapters of the biography,
which seem disconnected at first reading, are actually
prognostications of these future roles that Olaf is to
play. This technique of anticipation and fulfillment,
probably borrowed from the Bible and from saints'
lives, is also the most prevalent rhetorical device
employed by writers of Íslendinga sögur.

The first hint of future sainthood occurs immediately after Olaf's birth, when a brilliant light appears
above an outbuilding in which the child has been abandoned. This portent, reminiscent of the star of Bethle-
hem, causes Olaf's grandfather to revoke his command
to let the child perish. As so frequently in saga
literature, the initial portent is reinforced by subsequent predictions. Some years later, for example, a
seeress, whom Olaf refuses to consult because she is
heathen, informs his followers that great dread will
emanate from their leader and that light and brightness
will hover over him. She adds, however, that if Olaf
should ever happen to make a slip of the tongue, his
life would soon come to an end.

Chapter 5 relates how Queen Sigríd the Haughty of

Sweden burned Ólaf's father and another undesirable
suitor to death. Only much later do we realize that
the purpose of this seemingly irrelevant episode was to
anticipate and motivate Ólaf's punitive incursions
into Sweden. To make certain that his audience understood the connection, the compiler commented that Ólaf
harried in Sweden "because of Sigríd the Haughty"
(chap. 15).

A hint of Ólaf's future sagacity is given in chapter 6, where Ólaf, sitting on his widowed mother's
knees, unwillingly takes part in a discussion of her
plans to remarry. When she asks him whether she should
marry the chieftain Gudbrand or King Sigurd Sow, he
replies with a counterquestion: "Would you prefer your
[future] son to be a king or a vassal?" We recall this
scene later on when Ólaf, at the age of fourteen,
devises a plan that enables King Knút (Canute the
Great) to conquer London after all previous strategies
have failed.

At the age of five, we are told, Ólaf is baptized,
with King Ólaf Tryggvason as his sponsor. Here the
compiler has retained Icelandic tradition despite the
fact that the official legend of Saint Ólaf, read
several times a year in all churches, correctly states
that Ólaf was baptized as an adult in Rouen (7).
Probably he did this in order to foreshadow Ólaf's
future role as the second missionary king of Norway.

Shortly afterward the future warrior is revealed
when Ólaf finds his father's sword and refuses to
relinquish it to his mother or to his stepfather,
Sigurd Sow. Ordered to saddle a mount for Sigurd,
Ólaf puts saddle and bridle on the king's largest
goat. He clearly feels that it is beneath the dignity
of a future warrior-king to perform a menial task for a
man whose byname stamps him as a farmer-king. This
interesting variant of the generation-gap theme, which
plays such an important role in saga literature, has a
close parallel in Grettis saga (chap. 14). Whereas
the father usually represents the savage marauder and
the son the more civilized farmer, the situation in
these two works (and in a few others) is reversed (8).
Thus these episodes also portend the tragic deaths of
the two heroes through the reversal of a normal social
situation.

At the age of twelve, Ólaf begins his viking
career, which the author based mainly on Sighvat's poem

Víkinga vísur (Viking verses) (9). After eight
years of marauding, Ólaf experiences a desire to
return to his native land. Before doing so, however,
he seeks information about his future from a prescient
hermit. In order to test the hermit's perspicacity,
Ólaf first sends one of his men dressed in his royal
garments, but the disguise is detected immediately.
The episode is an adaptation of the story about Saint
Benedict and the Gothic king Totila related by Gregory
the Great in his Dialogues, which were well known in
Norway and Iceland in the twelfth century. The prophecy made to Ólaf encourages him to proceed to Norway,
for he is told that he will gain the throne that is his
birthright and become not only temporal king but king
of Norway "eternally" (chap. 19).

After a stormy voyage, the king and his men land at
a small island named Sæla. This is regarded as a good
omen since sæla means "bliss." But when they go
ashore "the king slipped on the muddy beach so that he
sank down on one knee. Then the king said, 'Now I
fell.' Hrani replied, 'You did not fall, sir, but
rather, you gained a foothold on Norway.' The king
laughed and said, 'If it is God's will, we shall be
victorious'" (chap. 20). The closest parallel and a
possible source for this passage is the well-known tale
about William the Conqueror at the Battle of Hastings
(10). This portent occurs neither in Theodoricus's
Historia, which is a major source for this portion of
the saga, nor in the corresponding section of Ágrip
(11).

Ólaf is confronted with two major tasks, the first
of which is to secure his position as sole and rightful
ruler of Norway. An auspicious beginning is made when
Ólaf in a clever naval maneuver captures his kinsman,
Earl Hákon Eiríksson, and exacts a promise from the
earl not to oppose him. The successful climax of
Ólaf's military campaign comes with his victory over
Erling Skjálgsson, Kálf Árnason, and other powerful
chieftains in the Battle of Nesjar. When Ólaf permits
his adversaries to escape alive, Sigurd Sow predicts
that Ólaf's enemies will attack him again and that he
"will leave this world as a very saintly man" at the
time when his country will need him most (chap. 28).

Now Ólaf undertakes his second task, and that is to
enforce just laws on rich and poor alike and to recon-
vert those Norwegians who abandoned Christianity follow-

ing the death of Olaf Tryggvason. Not until this
crucial moment in Olaf's career does the author
present a full portrait of his hero (chap. 30), just as
Snorri Sturluson postpones his unforgettable description of Egil Skalla-Grímsson until the viking-poet
becomes the dominant figure of his saga (chap. 55).
Olaf's appearance and character are depicted in
flowery, highly alliterative language that is appropriate for the description of a saint. The panegyric ends
with the declaration that "the more he exalted God in
his life and humbled himself before both God and men,
the more God revealed his glory." The comment about
Olaf's humility seems just a bit ironic when we read a
few pages further on that the king gave his subjects
the choice of submitting to baptism or to the sword.

The most skillfully composed episode in this biography is the confrontation between Olaf and Dala-
Gudbrand, the leader of the farmers in Gudbrandsdal,
who have clung tenaciously to the customs of their forebears (chaps. 33-39). The scene of the action is
prepared in advance down to the finest detail, the king
and his bishop are cleverly played off against Gudbrand
and one of his henchmen, and the action progresses with
increasing intensity to a fitting climax. After
several days of discussion under lowering clouds, the
farmers, who have a richly gilded, jewel-encrusted
statue of Thór before them, promise to accept Christianity on the condition that Olaf cause the sun to
shine the following morning. As so often in the story,
Olaf wins the day with the aid of divine intervention.
As the sun gloriously shines forth, one of the king's
men with a single blow of his cudgel demolishes Thór's
statue, from which writhe adders and other serpents.
The bewildered farmers seek to flee, only to find that
their horses have been driven off and the keels of the
boats perforated. Conceding that Olaf's God is more
powerful than theirs, Gudbrand and his followers submit
to baptism and later erect a church at the site of
their conversion.

Olaf zealously pursues his missionary crusade to
the very end, but his brutal methods alienate and antag-
onize the farmers. His vassals rebel at the ignominy
of being subjected to his just laws and of being
compelled to receive in fief from the king the estates
they regard as their private possessions by right of
inheritance. King Knút, who has repeatedly asserted

his claims to tribute from Norway, now bribes the king's vassals to betray him. When Olaf's most powerful adversary, Erling Skjálgsson, is slain--contrary to the king's wish--the vassals and farmers, aided by King Knút, rise up against him and drive him out of the country. Olaf confesses that "in many respects we have ruled this realm with arrogance and obstinacy rather than with justice" (chap. 75).

As the end approaches, miracles and portents increase. Water is transformed into mead and wine, and the flesh of two oxen suffices to feed five hundred men. A vision prompts the king to return to Norway. In another vision the king sees a ladder leading up to heaven, and this is interpreted to mean that he will soon receive his heavenly reward for his missionary endeavors. Shortly afterward he makes a slip of the tongue, and this, as we know from chapter 18, signifies his imminent death. Before the Battle of Stiklastadir (1030), he donates a large sum of money for a requiem mass for his enemies who will be slain, and when he receives his first wound, "he cast his sword away and prayed for his enemies" (chap. 93). Immediately after his death, further miracles begin to be wrought, and Olaf is soon deemed to be holy. The oppression brought upon the Norwegians by the harsh rule of Queen Alfífa and her son Svein of Denmark soon cause them to regret their revolt against Olaf, and they make his son Magnús king of Norway. Thus they seek "to compensate his son for the wrongs they had committed against his father" (chap. 103).

One of the sources for the Elzta saga was Þormóðar þáttr, which was interwoven throughout the second half of the biography. Before the Battle of Stiklastadir, Thormód repeats the sentiment expressed in the first stanza cited in fragment 2 of the Elzta saga. When asked by Saint Olaf what reward he expects for having recited the poem Bjarkamál to entertain the troops, he replies, "I would like to be your protection [brjóst, "breast"] and to remain in your presence and not survive you" (chap. 88). After the king's death, Thormód is depressed until an arrow pierces his chest. "No one drew his bow in a better hour," he said. "Now I have hope that I shall not be separated from the king" (chap. 95). Appended to the biography are a series of miracles attributed to Saint Olaf.

Biographies of Olaf Tryggvason

The second royal biography to come from the monastery at Thingeyrar is Óláfs saga Tryggvasonar (Saga
of Olaf, son of Tryggvi), which was written in Latin
by the monk Odd Snorrason about 1190. This saga is
preserved in two versions of an Icelandic translation
and a fragment of a third one (12). The A version,
which is closest to the lost original, is almost
complete, and its lacunae can be filled from the somewhat abridged S redaction.

Finnur Jónsson assumed that the Elzta saga had
inspired Odd to write his biography of Olaf Tryggvason
—an assumption that grows more convincing with each
rereading of this work and the Helgisaga (13). Lars
Lönnroth has advanced reasons for believing that some
of the parallels between Odd's biography and the
Helgisaga represent a transfer of clerical traditions
about Saint Olaf to his namesake (14). There seem to
have been two reasons for this. Icelandic clerics
wished to magnify the accomplishments of the king who
had brought Christianity to their country, and clerics
from Trondheim sought to present the role of their
province in the conversion of Norway more favorably
than was actually the case (15). Many of the phrasal
similarities between the two works, however, are borrowings on the part of Odd or his translator.

Whereas the compiler of the Elzta saga had to
struggle with a plethora of material about his hero,
Odd seems to have had rather scant sources with which
to work. His lament in the Prologus that "people knew
of no miracles wrought after the death of the most
famous King Olaf Tryggvason" suggests a paucity of
clerical traditions. Odd twice mentions Sæmund and
Ari as authorities, and there is a specific reference
to Íslendingabók in S (chap. 31). The description
of the acceptance of Christianity by the General Assembly (chap. 41) is an expanded version of Íslendingabók (chap. 7), although this is a later interpolation. The vivid, skillfully constructed description of
the passing of Olaf's fleet, with each vessel larger
than the preceding one until the king's majestic Long
Serpent sails by, is modeled on the story of the Lango-
bard king, Desiderius, watching Charlemagne's army
march past a tower in Pavia (16). The saga contains
the Latin translation of one skaldic verse in a simple

meter (chap. 65); the remaining fifteen stanzas are later interpolations.

Odd interspersed his lean account with entertaining tales of various kinds. The king has encounters with Óðin, Thór, and trolls (chaps. 43, 59, 60), all of which are interpreted as the devil (or devils) in disguise. Here we come close to oral traditions, for edifying anecdotes like these—at which Snorri took umbrage in the Prologus of his Edda—were told by priests to demonize the pagan deities. Ólaf's severe punishment of heathen wizards (chaps. 36, 40), based partly on Sæmund's history, has been explained as a rebuttal of Adam of Bremen's assertion that Ólaf had renounced Christianity and reverted to pagan practices (17). Still another important insert is the so-called Íslendinga þáttr, which relates the swimming contest between the king and Kjartan Ólafsson, the hero of Laxdæla saga. Further padding is provided by the Märchen-like stories of Ólaf's first two marriages (chaps. 10-11, 17), an exemplum about the licentious Earl Hákon (chaps. 20-21), and an interpolation from Jómsvíkinga saga (chap. 18).

The technique of foreshadowing future events long before they occur, which we found in the Helgisaga, is also employed by Odd. In chapter 50, in which he describes King Ólaf's unusual athletic skills, he tells us that the king practiced removing his mailcoat while swimming under water. The purpose of this remains obscure until we come to the very end of the saga, where Ólaf, in his final sea battle, had to leap overboard. Just as the king's chief adversary, Earl Eirík of Hladir, was about to strike him down, Ólaf was surrounded by a "heavenly light," so that no one could see what became of him (chap. 73). Some people, Odd tells us, believe that he perished, but others maintain that he was able to divest himself of his mailcoat under water and swim to safety. Odd clearly inclined to the latter interpretation.

A more significant example of anticipation and fulfillment concerns Ólaf's relationship with Sigríd the Haughty, whom we encountered as the slayer of Saint Ólaf's father in the Helgisaga. Ólaf had been engaged to Sigríd, but when she refused to accept the true faith, he called her an old hag and slapped her on the cheek with his glove. The queen was so incensed that she spent many days devising schemes to entice

Olaf into an ambush (chap. 38). Years later Sigríd
threatened to divorce her husband, King Svein Forkbeard
of Denmark, if he failed to avenge Olaf's insult to
her by luring her enemy into an ambush (chap. 69). The
plan she outlined was successful, and King Olaf suffered defeat in the Battle of Svöld at the hands of
the combined forces of the kings of Denmark and Sweden
and the earls of Hladir. The Sigríd story seems to
have been derived from some version of the tragedy of
the Niflungs (18).

Odd's primary purpose was to honor Olaf Tryggvason
by portraying him as the "apostle of the Northmen"
(chap. 78). As a child, Olaf was sold into slavery,
"but God delivered him . . . as he had delivered Joseph
in former days" (chap. 7). Like his namesake, Olaf
Tryggvason went harrying at an early age, but he fought
only against pagans and evil marauders, nor did he ever
take part in pagan sacrifice. On his missionary cru-
sades he employed various methods of conversion. For
the most part, however, he resorted to armed force and
torture. He grew increasingly more fanatic and violent. Reprimanded by his bishop for having one of his
adversaries bitten to death by his dog, King Olaf
repented and wept. As the battle of Svöld neared its
end, Olaf at close range hurled three halbards at his
most formidable adversary, Earl Eirík, and all missed
their mark. "And when King Olaf saw that, he was very
astonished and said, 'Great is the earl's good fortune
(hamingja). It is now God's will that he have the
kingdom and possess the country'" (chap. 73). Even in
defeat, however, Olaf Tryggvason gained a victory, for
Earl Eirík had vowed to submit to baptism if he won
the battle and indeed, even before fighting began, had
replaced the idol of Thór on the prow of his ship with
the cross.

Appended to this saga are two chapters from an Icelandic translation of a lost Latin biography of Olaf
Tryggvason by the monk Gunnlaug Leifsson, which seems
to have been an amplified, more hagiographic adaptation
of Odd's book. In his final paragraph, Gunnlaug names
six informants, three men and three women, and states
that he "showed the book to Gizur Hallsson and corrected it according to his advice." Gunnlaug's biography was a major source for Kristni saga (The saga of
Christianity), which was compiled by Sturla Thórdarson
(19).

Sverris saga (Saga of King Sverrir)

In Óláfs saga Tryggvasonar, King Sverrir is said to have asserted that he had never heard of any other king who had exposed himself to danger as bravely as King Olaf did during his final battle. This suggests that Odd was working on his biography at the same time as Karl Jónsson was writing Sverris saga. Karl, who was abbot of Thingeyrar from 1169 to 1181 and from 1190 to 1207 and who died in 1213, eleven years after the death of his patron, spent the years 1185-88 in Norway, where the king, as we read in the Formáli (Prologue), "sat over him and decided what should be written" as he composed the first forty chapters, known as Gryla (Bugbear). The remainder of the book is based on eyewitness accounts, some of which were recorded "immediately after the events occurred, and they have not been changed since" (Formáli). It has often been maintained that Karl wrote only the first half of Sverris saga, but this biography is too consistent throughout in style not to be the work of one man (20). Styrmir the Learned is said to have revised it, but the extent of his revision cannot be ascertained.

Although Sverris saga comes from the same "school" as the Helgisaga and Óláfs saga Tryggvasonar, it far surpasses these two pioneering works in literary excellence. Since it is contemporary history, it possesses a wealth of vivid realistic detail that is lacking in the other two sagas. For the most part, Karl succeeded admirably in integrating and articulating his materials. Only fourteen extemporaneous stanzas and one from the Eddic Fáfnismál (Lay of Fáfnir) occur in this work, which is as long as the two Olaf biographies combined. That Karl's biography was highly esteemed by contemporaries is shown by the fact that Snorri Sturluson ended his Heimskringla with the year 1177, the year in which Sverrir first received the title of king from a band of raggle-taggle enemies of King Magnús Erlingsson named "Birchlegs," so called because they were so destitute that they had to tie birch bark around their legs when their clothing wore out. Snorri evidently felt no need to improve on Karl's book, as he had done with other sagas in his Heimskringla. Further proof of the popularity of Sverris saga is the fact that it has been preserved in four complete redactions, the longest and fullest of which comes closest to the original.

Karl began his biography with four prophetic dreams, designed to bolster Sverrir's somewhat dubious claims to the Norwegian throne, which were based entirely on his allegation that he was an illegitimate son of King Sigurd Haraldsson (21). Before Sverrir's birth, his mother dreamed that she had given birth to a white stone that glowed with a brilliant light—an elaboration of the dream of King Athelstan's mother before his birth. Sverrir dreamed that he went to Norway, where he turned into a bird whose "beak reached to the easternmost regions of the land while its tailfeathers extended northward to the territory of the Finns, and with its wings it covered the entire country" (chap. 2). This is a variant of a type of dream prophetic of kingship. In the third dream (chap. 5), Saint Ólaf appeared to him, called him Magnús (the name of his son), and entrusted his standard to him, exhorting him to bear it heðan í frá ("henceforth"). In the fourth dream "God's prophet" Samuel kissed him, assured him he would be king, and anointed his hands with these words: "May these hands be hallowed and strengthened for hatred against your enemies and adversaries and to rule over many people" (chap. 10). No doubt Abbot Karl and Sverrir collaborated to invent or to adapt these dreams, for the king too was a learned man and an ordained priest (22).

At the age of five, Sverrir had been given into the tutelage of his paternal uncle, Bishop Hrói, in the Faeroe Islands. Like many other saga heroes he was unruly in his youth "and did not adapt himself well to the priesthood" (chap. 1). At the age of twenty-four, he learned from his mother that his father was not her husband, Unas the comb-maker, but King Sigurd Haraldsson. This news filled Sverrir with great anxiety, for he realized how difficult it would be to contend for the throne with King Magnús and his father, Earl Erling. Not only were they themselves powerful; they also enjoyed the strong support of Archbishop Eystein. Yet he felt compelled to do so, and his dreams "aroused his desire for vengeance for his kinsmen" (chap. 4).

In the early chapters of his biography, Sverrir is portrayed as a sort of Hamlet figure. Finding little support at first for his campaign against Magnús and Erling, he vacillated and almost despaired in face of the seemingly insuperable odds against him. Almost

contrary to his own will, he was chosen king by the
Birchlegs. Gradually, however, he grew more resolute,
and with repeated divine intervention and through skillfully executed surprise attacks, he gained the support
of farmers and former followers of King Magnús. Finally, after years of struggle, Sverrir defeated first
Earl Erling and then King Magnús (1184), both of whom
were slain in battle. After the death of Eystein
(1188), King Sverrir asserted that the archbishop on
his deathbed had begged the king's forgiveness for the
wrongs he had done him (chap. 107). Ten years after
the fall of Magnús, Bishop Nikolás made peace with
Sverrir, and he and two other bishops consecrated
Sverrir king of Norway (chap. 123). Shortly before
this, Sverrir had been excommunicated by the pope.
Sverrir produced letters purporting to be official in
which the pope allegedly rescinded his ban. Various
insurrections followed, but Sverrir quelled them all
and remained in power until his death from illness in
1202.

Although Abbot Karl was writing on behalf of King
Sverrir, he maintained the appearance of strict objectivity, as did most of the authors of Íslendingasögur. The long struggle between Sverrir and Magnús
is related alternately from the viewpoint of the two
rivals. After the death of Magnús, his virtues as
well as his vices are recounted. In chapter 3 and
again in his necrology we read that he was bæði
vinsæll ok ástsæll við landsfólkit ("both popular
and beloved among his countrymen"). "This was the
measure [mark] of his popularity that however detri-
mental it was to follow him, he never lacked followers
as long as he lived" (chap. 98). In Sverrir's necrology, too, Karl, after listing the king's many good
qualities, adds that although the king presented an
imposing figure as he sat magnificently clad on his
throne, his legs were rather short (chap. 181).
Despite this apparent objectivity, however, there is
little doubt regarding Abbot Karl's sympathies. King
Sverrir ruled according to the laws of Saint Ólaf and
Grágás, the law code established by Ólaf's son
Magnús. The king and the farmers were to have jurisdiction over the churches they built and the priests
they appointed. Eystein, on the other hand, insisted
on the primacy of canon law, according to which the
pope had jurisdiction over the churches and priests

through the archbishop and the bishops. Magnús
claimed the right to the throne because he had been
consecrated and crowned by Archbishop Eystein, whereas
Sverrir argued that he had been chosen king by God and
Saint Olaf. Furthermore, Sverrir was the alleged son
of a king, whereas Magnús was only the son of an earl
and therefore ineligible to be king.

Perhaps the most striking innovation in Sverris
saga is the rather elaborate set speech, which Lee M.
Hollander attributed to influence from Livy (23). We
find eleven such orations in the first half of the
saga, five delivered by Sverrir, three by Magnús, and
three by others. In several of these, Sverrir exhorts
his troops to be courageous, upbraids his enemies, and
asserts his right to the kingship by the will of God.
In one of them--it reads almost like a sermon--he
inveighs against the evils of drunkenness and castigates German merchants for selling wine to his men and
the townspeople. More important from the standpoint of
literary history is the introduction of the stranded
plot, which Snorri perfects in his Ólafs saga and
which is employed with a greater or lesser degree of
skill in subsequent Íslendinga sögur, especially in
Eyrbyggja saga and Njáls saga. Typically medieval
digression, to be sure, is found in the Olaf biographies, but plot interlace seems to have been introduced
into saga literature by Abbot Karl. And polycentric
composition is, as Carol Clover expressed it, "prima
facie evidence of self-conscious literary authorship"
(24). This structural device, in turn, facilitated the
stance of neutrality or objectivity on the part of the
author by enabling him to tell his story simultaneously
from two or more points of view. And this appearance
of objectivity, as we know, is a characteristic feature
of the Íslendinga sögur.

In the sagas we often find nature descriptions,
usually quite brief, in which natural phenomena are
represented not as objects to be visualized by the
audience but as hostile forces to be endured and overcome by the saga characters. Nowhere is this type of
nature depiction treated so effectively as in Sverris
saga. On their many toilsome forced marches through
winter darkness over steep mountains covered with deep
snow and dense underbrush, Sverrir and his men repeatedly suffered from hunger, cold, and extreme weariness.
We can sense the utter desperation that on one occasion
drove the men to the point of mass suicide. Through

his eloquence, Sverrir managed to dissuade them, and as
soon as he finished his exhortation, the howling winds
died down and "at once there came bright skies and
sunshine and such balmy weather as though it had been
midsummer" (chap. 20).

Karl's narrative style is lucid and free-flowing.
Only in his speeches does he resort to long, complex-
compound periods with a rather heavy use of alliteration and antithesis. He makes little use of dialogue,
however; the confrontations between Sverrir and Magnús
or Eystein are not conversation but an exchange of
assertions and counterassertions in the form of short
speeches. The most striking aspect of Karl's style is
his predilection for "huntsmen's jargon" (Holm-Olsen),
which he uses in many variations throughout his book.
The men are described as "eager for the chase" and they
"hunt" their enemies or "set snares" for them.

Of the many literary connections between Sverris
saga and the Ólaf sagas I shall cite only two. Shortly before his death Magnús made a speech in which he
recalled that he had been consecrated and crowned king
at the age of five. At that time, he said, he "would
rather have played with other young boys than sit in
the midst of chieftains" (chap. 89). These words are
almost identical with those uttered by Saint Ólaf when
he counseled his mother to marry Sigurd Sow: "I would
rather play with other boys than talk about this
matter" (chap. 6). In Sverrir's funeral oration for
Earl Erling, the king scornfully referred to Archbishop
Eystein's assurance that the souls of all men killed
fighting for the earl "would be in paradise before
their blood was cold on the ground" (chap. 38).
Similar words were used by Saint Ólaf against the
chieftain Erlend of Gerd: "I can tell you truly that
you will be killed here and that your soul will be in
hell before your blood is cold on the ground" (chap.
90). Such verbal and motival similarities are not
surprising when we consider that the Elzta saga, the
two biographies of Ólaf Tryggvason, and Sverris saga
were all compiled in the same monastery during the last
two decades of the thirteenth century.

Biographies of Icelandic Bishops

Þorláks saga byskups (Saga of Bishop Thorlák).
Around the turn of the century, Icelandic church leaders, motivated in part by national pride and economic

considerations, felt a strong need for a saint of their
own. The obvious candidate was Bishop Thorlák, who
had received his education abroad, had served as abbot
of two monasteries, and had continued to lead the celi-
bate life of a monk as long as he lived. Also in his
favor was his fanatical advocacy of Archbishop
Eystein's ecclesiastical policies, despite their unpopu-
larity with chieftain-priests and other church proprietors. Even during his lifetime, Thorlák had wrought
minor miracles such as helping people find lost objects
and curing illnesses in humans and domestic animals.
After his death in 1193, stories about miracles brought
about through his intercession increased. These
stories were recorded in a book, which was read out by
Thorlák's nephew and successor, Bishop Pál Jónsson,
before the General Assembly in 1199, whereupon that
body declared Thorlák to be a saint. The "First
Miracle Book" was followed by two others, each longer
than the last. These miracle books, all of which have
been preserved, offer good insights into Icelandic
civilization; for although many of the tales are adaptations of "standard" international miracles, others
reflect beliefs and experiences of the Icelandic
people.

  Although _Þorláks saga byskups_ (ca. 1205) creates
the impression of being an objective biography, it was
obviously written by a friend of Thorlák and his
nephew Pál. The bishop's shortcomings are not concealed. Although he never drank to excess, he did not
always observe the dietary laws strictly, especially
when in bad health. He excelled as a teacher and
writer but had a poor singing voice and spoke halting-
ly. Thorlák's piety and devotion to the church are
stressed. He severely castigated drunkenness and moral
laxity but was generous to the poor and enjoyed poetry
and social gatherings. Thorlák not only read much but
was "constantly writing, and he always wrote sacred
books after the example of the Apostle Paul" (chap.
14).

  After completing his education, Thorlák decided to
get married, but during the night before his planned
proposal "a man of magnificent appearance and nobly
dressed" appeared to him in a dream with the pronounce-
ment that "a more exalted bride was intended" for him
and that he should take no other (chap. 5). Thorlák
subsequently entered the monastery of Kirkjubæ. Upon

his arrival at Nidarós, Thorlák was cordially welcomed by Archbishop Eystein, but King Magnús and Earl
Erling angrily denied permission for his consecration.
The anger, of course, was a reflection of the current
hostilities between Norwegians and Icelanders. Through
patience and humility, Thorlák eventually gained the
friendship of father and son, and, we are told, King
Sverrir often asserted that the king and the earl were
singularly successful in all their undertakings as long
as Thorlák remained in Norway (chap. 11). Even though
Thorlák had little success in promoting Archbishop
Eystein's ecclesiastical reforms, he faithfully dis-
charged his duties as pastor and administrator, as we
read in the laudatory words spoken over his grave by
the learned Gizur Hallsson (chap. 19).

For obvious reasons, the author of Þorláks saga
had omitted mention of the long, bitter conflict
between Bishop Thorlák and Bishop Pál's father, Jón
Loptsson, the leader of the church proprietors and the
most powerful chieftain in Iceland. A later redactor
added an account of this conflict because, as he tells
us in the prologue of his redaction, "the good man who
first compiled the saga" had not adequately related
"the hardships and offenses that Bishop Thorlák had
suffered from his adversaries." The first of the two
major confrontations has already been mentioned. The
second, of a more personal and acrimonious nature,
resulted from the fact that Jón Loptsson was living in
concubinage with the bishop's sister, Pál's mother.
When Thorlák threatened Jón with excommunication if
he did not terminate this illicit relationship, he is
said to have retorted as follows:

> Your interdict . . . is legitimate, and my guilt is
> sufficient. I shall comply with your request to the
> extent that I shall move to Thórsmörk or to some
> other place where people will not incur guilt from
> associating with me and live there with the woman
> for whose sake you are rebuking me. But neither
> your interdict nor the coercion of any other man
> will separate me from my impediments until God
> breathes into my breast that I should part from them
> of my own free will. (25)

Eventually Jón acceded to the bishop's demands. A
third and possibly violent confrontation was prevented

by a dense fog that "almighty God" caused to descend on
Jón and his armed followers, so that they were unable
to carry out their intended attack on the bishop. The
motif of the blinding fog became a popular one with
later saga writers, but it was usually attributed to
pagan wizardry. Jón is the central figure of this
episode, but the author's sympathies were clearly with
bishop Thorlák.

Jóns saga helga (**Saga of Saint Jón**). Two
years after the elevation of Thorlák, the people of
the North Quarter succeeded in having Jón Ögmundarson
declared a saint by the General Assembly, but unfortunately few people from outside the Hólar episcopacy
were willing to recognize his sanctity. It was probably for this reason that Bishop Gudmund commissioned
the monk Gunnlaug of Thingeyrar, a prolific writer, to
compile the saint's biography. The Latin original is
lost, but the biography has survived in a vernacular
translation that bristles with Latinisms--Latin quotations from the Bible (usually translated), loanwords
such as kumpánn ("companion") and dispensera ("to
manage"), dative absolutes, and especially participial
phrases. On one page we find nine present participles,
six of them in a single sentence (chap. 36).

In order to demonstrate the validity of Jón's sainthood, Gunnlaug began his account with three prognostications, each one more authoritative than the preceding
one. A certain Gudini, called "the Good," declared
that the infant Jón was "truly a mirror of holiness"
(chap. 3). While still a child Jón and his parents
were the guests of King Svein Ulfsson of Denmark and
his mother, Queen Astríd. At table Jón reached for
some dainties, whereupon his mother slapped his hand to
chastise him for his discourtesy. "Seeing this, the
queen was filled with a spirit of prophecy and said,
'Do not do that, dear Thorgerd, for the hands that you
have struck are the hands of a bishop.'" Saint Ólaf
had previously told Thorgerd's parents that she was a
woman of great good fortune, which her descendants
would also possess (chap. 4). Throughout the royal
biographies discussed in this chapter, the great good
fortune of kings (gipt, gipta, gæfa, hamingja,
lukka), which can be bestowed temporarily upon
favorite subjects to reinforce their own good fortune,
seems to be identical with the Christian concept of
divine grace (26). In Jóns saga helga, Gunnlaug

states this identity explicitly in speaking of the infant Jón: "At an early age God's good fortune [guðs gipta] was evident in him, which later was manifested in the performance of superhuman deeds and the working of miracles" (chap. 3).

Mention has already been made of Jón's endeavors to improve the education of priests. To this end he attracted several foreign scholars to the school he had founded at Hólar. One of these, Gísli Finnsson from Gautland, was a "learned . . . interpreter of divine writings." Whenever he preached, "he did not . . . trust his memory, but explained the writings of the holy fathers according to the book which lay on the lectern before him." He also wanted the people to see "that he took his sermons from sacred and noteworthy books and not merely from his own mind and heart" (chap. 22). Another foreign teacher was the Frenchman Rikini, who taught the art of singing and composition of poetry in Latin and in Icelandic. Among the native teachers was the virgin Ingunn, who "corrected many Latin books by having them read aloud as she sat sewing" (chap. 27). Jón seems to have supervised his pupils closely, for he once forbade Klæng Thorsteinsson to read Ovid's Ars amatoria, since "man's frail nature is all too eager for a life of lust and carnal love without inflaming his feelings with such unchaste and sinful poems" (chap. 24).

As Odd Snorrason had done, Gunnlaug interspersed his otherwise meager account with entertaining stories. According to one of these, Jón helped Sæmund the Learned to escape from an evil magician in France and to return to Iceland (chaps. 15-16). In a longer þáttr, Jón rescued a fellow Icelander in Norway by cutting him down from the gallows alive several days after he had been hanged (chaps. 9-14). This episode too reflects the hostilities of the years 1170-1220: the Icelanders are contemptuously referred to as "suet-landers" (mörlandar), and the king's steward declares that ten Icelanders should be killed to avenge the death of one Norwegian. Gunnlaug also employed dreams of a nonprophetic nature to round out Jón's portrait. In one such dream, Saint Jón heard King David playing the harp. Upon awakening he recalled the melody and played it perfectly to the great delight of King Svein of Denmark (chap. 7). On another occasion, Jón dreamed that someone gave him a book in which he read a remarkable but puzzling story: it was the well-known Flagellatio Crucis (chap. 36). A later redactor revised Jóns saga by omitting some of the tales, adding several miracles, and eliminating many of the Latinisms.

Páls saga byskups (Saga of Bishop Pál). Unlike the royal and episcopal sagas thus far discussed, Páls saga byskups, which was compiled shortly after the bishop's death (1211), begins with a brief genealogy and a thumbnail sketch of the central character:

> Pál was the son of the most illustrious Jón, the son of Lopt, the son of Sæmund the Learned. Jón's mother was Thóra, the daughter of King Magnús Bareleg, and Pál's mother was Ragnheid Thórhallsdóttir, the sister of Bishop Thorlák the Saint. . . . Pál was handsome, with fair and firm eyes and wavy blond hair. He had shapely arms and legs, small feet, a light skin, and a bright complexion. He was a man of average height and of most elegant manners. He was quick at learning and very learned at an early age and skillful at whatever he did, whether it was writing or something else. (chap. 1)

After spending some time with Earl Harald in the Orkneys, Pál studied in England for several years and was made bishop-elect the year after his uncle's death (1193), even though he was only a deacon in orders.

Páls saga is an even more personal biography than Þorláks saga. We are told that Pál was very fond of his wife and their four children. Like King Sverrir, he accepted the heavy responsibility of his office reluctantly and only because he believed it was God's will that he do so. His father's death deprived him of his strongest support, but "almighty God . . . caused his great good fortune [gipt ok gæfa] always to increase from day to day and never to decrease" (chap. 7). Bishop Pál was reluctant to believe in his uncle's sanctity, but once convinced of it, he promoted it at the General Assembly. The author several times states that Pál "preached the same message" as Thorlák, but these words can be accepted only in a narrow literal sense. Like his father, Pál was a conservative national chieftain. The conflict between Bishop Brand, Thorlák's successor as champion of canon

law, and Pál's friends and kinsmen, who led the struggle for the retention of private church ownership, was
distressing to him. His most grievous experience was
the loss of his wife and one of their daughters by
drowning.

Páls saga is remarkably free of the Biblical quotations and Latinisms that abound in the biographies of
Jón and Thorlák. Yet the style of Páls saga is
decidedly Latinate, for the well-balanced periods are
excessively long and intricate. Only in Pál's
necrology, however, did the author resort to flowery
rhetoric. Quoting Ari's statement that Iceland
"drooped" after the death of Bishop Gizur, the anonymous author of Páls saga declared that

> the whole earth quivered and trembled with fear, the
> sky and the clouds wept, so that a great part of the
> fruit of the earth was spoiled, and the heavenly
> bodies showed manifest tokens of death as the final
> life-days of Bishop Pál drew near, and the sea
> burned before the coast. In the region over which
> he had had episcopal jurisdiction, almost all the
> elements seemed to show signs of sorrow. (chap. 18)

Despite Bishop Pál's great learning, his contribution to his diocese seems to have been less scholarly
than esthetic in nature. He had the cathedral beautified through the installation of large glass windows;
he had an imposing tower erected to house the bells;
and he had a large gold-and-silver shrine encrusted
with jewels made for the relics of Saint Thorlák.

The fact that Thorlák and Jón were never canonized
in no way lessened the Icelanders' pride in their
national saints. For many it was a source of consola-
tion to be able to invoke their help in times of adversity. Since the cult of Thorlák had spread throughout
Scandinavia and the British Isles, gifts from abroad
began to pour into the episcopal coffers at Skálholt.
Without these monies, it is doubtful that Bishop Pál
would have been able to have the cathedral beautified
or to have his uncle's relics so magnificently enshrined.

Conclusion

Although neither great literature nor reliable histo-

ry, the Ólaf biographies are important as models and
sources for later saga writers. As we study them, we
can visualize their compilers and redactors struggling
to harmonize their diverse sources and to mold their
obstinate material into cohesive narrative. The most
effective rhetorical device employed to achieve narrative cohesion is foreshadowing. The episcopal sagas
afford glimpses into life in Iceland at the time when
the earliest stories about Icelandic poets and farmers
were being compiled. All these works clearly reveal
the relevance of saga literature for contemporary
times--in this case the fateful years 1170-1220. The
first of the royal biographies to be officially commissioned, <u>Sverris saga</u> is also the first literary
masterpiece of its genre. Here we find for the first
time the consistent use of plot stranding, a structural
device that enables the author to advance two or more
related plots simultaneously and from more than one
point of view. It would be difficult to assess the
importance of this work for Snorri Sturluson and other
saga writers. Like the earliest historical writings,
these biographies must be carefully studied by anyone
who is seriously interested in the genesis of saga
literature and the development of saga style and
structure.

Chapter Four
Early Stories about Icelanders

Introduction

As their external circumstances worsened, the Icelanders turned to the literary creation of their heroic age when Icelandic farmers had been, in retrospect, the peers of foreign kings. It seems reasonable to assume that their first efforts took the form of short tales and that these þættir, as Anthony Faulkes expressed it, "facilitated the transition from the writing of stories about the kings of Norway to the treatment of purely Icelandic subjects" (1). Many þættir are strongly nationalistic in tone, their purpose being to assert the importance of Icelandic poets, warriors, and farmer-diplomats at the Norwegian court. The heroes of several of these stories are national leaders or sons of national leaders. Some þættir also serve to illuminate certain character traits of Scandinavian monarchs through their various confrontations with pertinacious Icelanders, and it was largely for this reason that many of them were inserted or incorporated into royal biographies and chronicles. The þættir found in the Elzta saga must have been among the earliest prose narratives to be composed in Iceland.

More than one-third of the fragmentary Elzta saga is devoted to Saint Ólaf's skalds and his dealings with them. As we have seen, the Helgisaga contains excerpts from tales about Sighvat and Óttar the Black as well as substantial portions of Þormóðar þáttr. In this biography, the þáttr of Egil, son of Hall of Sída, tells how this young warrior aroused the fury and later won the admiration of Saint Ólaf through his compassion and steadfastness (chaps. 53–55). One passage in this tale, rendered meaninglses by the redactor's thoughtless pruning of his source, contained Ólaf's prediction that Egil's grandson would become a saint, as we know from Jóns saga helga (chap. 4). When Saint Ólaf's quarrels with his namesake, King Ólaf of Sweden, over tribute from certain territories

had reached an impasse, the Norwegian king appealed to
Hjalti Skeggjason to negotiate a peace treaty between
them (chaps. 42-44). Hjalti and Hall of Sída had been
two of the most enthusiastic advocates of Ólaf
Tryggvason's missionary endeavors in their home
country. Chapter 63 of the Helgisaga is an inco-
herent summary of part of a þáttr about Stein, the
son of Skapti Thóroddsson. It is regrettable that
this tale was so badly mutilated, for its theme is
especially appropriate to a legendary saga. The
þáttr tells how Stein incurs the disapproval of
Saint Ólaf and King Knút and finally brings about his
own destruction through his avarice and arrogance (2).
These vices figure prominently in saga literature from
the time of Theodoricus monachus, for whom cupiditas
and ambitio were the chief causes of misfortune in
the history of Norway (3).

Since Odd Snorrason drew heavily on ecclesiastical
traditions and legendary motifs, he had less need to
use tales about Icelanders to construct his Ólafs
saga. Both of the þættr he included in his book
have already been referred to. It is surprising that
Odd had so little to say about Hallfred, since he was
one of the king's favorite poets and the most reluctant
and troublesome of his converts to Christianity--whence
his sobriquet vandræðaskáld ("troublesome poet").
It is also surprising that Odd does not mention Stefnir
Þorgilsson, one of whose stanzas he translated into
Latin (chap. 65). According to the þáttr, Ólaf
sends Stefnir and a certain Bishop Fridrek to convert
the Icelanders. The missionaries are treated badly,
especially by Stefnir's kinsmen. Stefnir retaliates by
destroying idols and places of pagan worship. Because
of this, a law is established making Christianity a
frændaskömm, that is, a disgrace to one's family,
and Stefnir is banished from Iceland, his kinsmen
acting as prosecutors. After the death of Ólaf,
Stefnir makes a pilgrimage to Rome. On his return journey he composes the stanza mentioned above, in which he
castigates Earl Sigvaldi for treachery against Ólaf.
Although the stanza mentions no name, the earl "thought
he recognized his brand on it," and he had Stefnir put
to death (4).

Some Early Tales

To judge from its archaic language, Hreiðars

þáttr must be one of the earliest short stories in Old Norse literature (5). It is also one of the most highly sophisticated and realistic. Hreidar, an uncouth bumpkin who pretends to be an idiot, inveigles his pompous brother into taking him abroad so that he can broaden and deepen his human experience. At the Norwegian court, the gentle, good-natured man learns the feeling of rage when tormented and threatened with death by the courtiers of Harald the Harsh (d. 1066). He later admits that it was not a pleasant experience. Hreidar insults Harald by fashioning a gold and silver sow for him (his father was Sigurd Sow) and cleverly manipulates his nephew Magnús the Good (d. 1047). There is little action in the story, which consists largely of finely honed dialogue. The emphasis is on character analysis and portrayal, which is effected primarily through contrast between the two brothers, between the two kings, and especially between Hreidar and the coregents of Norway.

Near the end of the story, Hreidar asks King Magnús for permission to recite a poem he has composed about him. The poem, which is not quoted (and probably never existed), is described as beginning oddly but improving greatly toward the end. King Magnús perceptively interprets the poem as a symbol of Hreidar's life. The payment Hreidar receives matches the poem. The king first gives him an island off the coast of Norway--an odd reward for a laudatory poem--and then buys it back at a handsome price. Hreidar returns to his farm in Iceland, becomes a great man, and lives to old age. His state of life continues to improve "in accordance with the king's conjecture," for he rids himself of "the outlandish behavior he took upon himself in his earlier years." The essential difference between simple oral tales and the deliberate, sophisticated art of Old Icelandic prose literature becomes apparent when we compare the anecdotes about trolls and pagan deities related by Odd in his Óláfs saga with the subtle analysis and gradual revelation of human personality in this þáttr.

Another study of the human heart is the charming tale about Ívar Ingimundarson, the author of a laudatory poem about Sigurd slembidjákn, two stanzas of which are quoted by Snorri in his Heimskringla (6). Ívar's brother Thorfinn visits the poet at the court of King Eystein (d. 1125) but soon returns to Iceland

because he resents being less highly esteemed by the
king than Ívar. Ívar gives his brother a message to
his sweetheart Oddný, asking her to remain unmarried
until he returns to Iceland, but instead Thorfinn sues
for her hand and marries her. When Ívar learns of his
brother's deceit, he is plunged into despair. All of
this is related in a few sentences. The remainder of
the story consists of dialogue between the king and the
poet. In a series of probing questions, King Eystein
unveils the cause of Ívar's despondency. He thereupon
suggests various remedies--money, estates, power, beautiful women, all of which he is willing to give Ivar--
but his suggestions are rejected. Finally the king
recommends that Ívar talk to him about his troubles
whenever he is not occupied with urgent affairs of
state. The poet thankfully accepts this offer, and
gradually his cares disappear and his cheerful nature
returns.

The redactor who inserted Ívars þáttr into
Morkinskinna states that its purpose was to show what
a glorious man King Eystein was and how he endeavored
to assuage the grief of his dearly beloved friends.
But it is clear that the author also, and doubtless
primarily, intended to enhance his hero by having the
king of Norway devote his free time to helping the Icelander overcome his despondency. As in so many
þættir, the scene here is pleasingly incongruous:
instead of being entertained by his court jester, the
king serves as his jester's analyst.

A personality of a different kind is revealed in a
series of clashes between Halldór, son of Snorri the
Chieftain, and Harald the Harsh in Halldórs þáttr
(7). A wily military commander, Harald is prone to
pettiness. Halldór, his most intrepid and trustworthy
warrior, is blunt and taciturn. He interprets the
king's chicaneries as personal affronts and usually
responds by threatening to quit his service. When paid
by the king in coins that contain more copper than
silver, he scornfully dumps them on the floor. The
king is later persuaded to pay him his wages in pure
silver. When compelled to drink a sconce horn for
being late for a Christmas festivity, he insults the
king by declaring that Snorri the Chieftain could not
have been bullied into drinking the penalty horn by
Sigurd Sow. The king turns livid with rage but remains
silent.

In contrast to Ívars þáttr, the verbal exchanges

between the obstinate protagonists in this tale are few and brief. Much of the interplay is carried on through an intermediary, who maintains an uneasy armistice between them. On one occasion they do not speak to each other but past one another. As the king's ship approaches a harbor, Halldór commands the steersman to veer. The king countermands the order. A second order to veer is countermanded. The ship strikes a submerged rock, the keel is ripped out, and the crew are taken aboard other ships of the fleet. Although Halldór says nothing to Harald, he interprets the king's action as a deliberate attempt to dishonor him. To prevent Halldór from sailing off to Iceland in high dudgeon with a merchant ship anchored nearby, the king provides him with a ship, formerly commanded by a Norwegian nobleman named Svein. When Svein objects to being replaced by an Icelander, the king replies, "His family is no less distinguished in Iceland than yours here in Norway, and not a very long time has passed since those who now live in Iceland were Norwegians" (chap. 3). The king now buys back the ship he has given Halldór, but does not pay him the full price. Finally Halldór tires of Harald's repeated excuses for not completing payment. With drawn sword he bursts into the royal bed-chamber and accepts a golden ring from the terrified queen as payment in full. Thereupon he sails to Iceland, where he lives to old age on his farm Hjardar-holt. Years later, at the king's request, Halldór sends "the old rooster" some foxskins to keep him warm.

The most frequently translated of the early tales is Auðunar þáttr, the story of a young Icelander who spends his meager means in Greenland to buy a polar bear for King Svein of Denmark (8). King Harald of Norway offers Audun a handsome price for the bear, but he insists on taking it to King Svein. Harald gives him permission to do so even though the two countries are at war with each other. After delivering the bear in spite of serious obstacles, Audun makes a pilgrimage to Rome. Upon Audun's return to Denmark as a half-starved pauper, King Svein rewards him handsomely for his gift. Later, in Norway, King Harald has to admit that Svein is more generous than he is since Svein gave Audun two more gifts than he would have given him. But in the end the Icelander is perceived to surpass both kings in generosity and is declared to be a man of great good fortune.

The salient features of this genre are irony and

what has been called "the art of the half-sung song."
Harald the Harsh admits that Icelandic farmers are the
peers of Norwegian noblemen, but the author of
Halldórs þáttr demonstrates that at least one
Icelander surpassed in audacity and craftiness the king
who, according to his biography, blinded the Byzantine
emperor and in 1066 almost succeeded in conquering
England. The authors of þættir seldom tell us too
much and sometimes not quite enough. We rather suspect, but cannot know for certain, that King Eystein
gradually came to realize that he was being duped by
Hreidar but could not graciously disentangle himself
from the Icelander's little game until it had been
played out. However that may be, at a time when the
Icelanders were becoming increasingly dependent on the
Norwegian crown for essential commodities and even for
transportation abroad, it must have been a source of
pride and comfort to them to read or hear tales about
their self-assertive, independent forebears who outwitted, outmaneuvered, and outbluffed Scandinavian
monarchs and enriched themselves at their expense. The
combination of subtle irony, shameless exaggeration,
and understatement that makes the þættir so enjoyable is also the hallmark of the best of the
Íslendingasögur.

Fóstbræðra saga (Saga of the sworn brothers)

The oldest sagas about Icelanders are transitional
works. They are so similar to the Ólaf biographies in
structure, spirit, and use of skaldic poetry that
Thorkil Damsgaard Olsen aptly defined them as "off-
shoots of the enlightening and entertaining anecdotes
about . . . Icelanders in the service of foreign kings"
(9). Fóstbræðra þáttr, for example, seems to have
been inspired by Þormóðar þáttr, by Thormód's
drápa in honor of his sworn brother Thorgeir, and by
his poem praising his sweetheart Thorbjörg (if,
indeed, this flokkr ever existed).

Fóstbræðra exists in two redactions, one of
which is characterized by learned digressions and
poetic passages in an ornate style with extended metaphors, personification, and kennings. Vera Lachmann
seems to have been the first scholar to consider the
ampler recension as the original one. Sigurður Nordal,
who agreed with Miss Lachmann on this point, regarded

Fóstbræðra saga as one of the oldest examples of
the genre, and his early dating of the work was generally accepted by scholars. Einar Ólafur Sveinsson, however, demonstrated on the basis of linguistic evidence
that the extant redactions cannot be as old as Nordal
believed them to be. Largely on stylistic grounds,
Jacoba M. C. Kroesen developed the theory of dual
authorship. Passages written in a simple, paratactic
style are survivals of the older saga, whereas passages
in a hypotactic, rhetorical style represent additions
and amplifications made by the second "author." Jónas
Kristjánsson went one step further than Einar Ólafur
Sveinsson and, in a comprehensive study, endeavored to
demonstrate that the "story of the sworn brothers" was
composed during the last decades of the thirteenth
century. Many of his arguments are persuasive, and yet
certain features of the saga suggest that the work as
we have it may be a reworking of an older saga, as
Klaus von See has convincingly argued (10). Furthermore, Fóstbræðra is similar in spirit and structure
to the Helgisaga and to Hallfred's biography. For
this reason, and because Fóstbræðra is so closely
associated with sagas about Saint Ólaf, it will be
discussed here.

The first part of the saga, which consists of disconnected, poorly motivated episodes, tells about two
young warriors, the poet Thormód and the arrogant
killer Thorgeir, who become sworn brothers, harass and
intimidate people in the northwestern fjords, and
commit sundry slayings. At first the slayings are
justifiable according to the ethical code of that time,
but gradually Thorgeir's killings become more and more
wanton. When Thorgeir asks Thormód who would be
victorious if they were to fight each other, the latter
terminates their partnership. Thorgeir, who has
already been outlawed for homicide, now goes abroad
after killing two more men on his way to the ship. He
joins the court of Saint Ólaf but sails back and forth
between the two countries six times. On one visit to
Iceland, he kills three more men and during the last
one kills still another, at the king's prompting, to
avenge an injury to one of Ólaf's retainers. This
leads to his own death, and one of his slayers rides
away with Thorgeir's head tied to his saddle. His
other assailant, named Thorgrím, sails to Greenland.

The love-triangle theme is handled differently and

more lightly in this story than in the other skáldasögur ("stories about poets"). Thormód becomes
enamored of two young ladies, Thordís, the daughter of
the sorceress Gríma, and Thorbjörg Kolbrún ("Coal-
brow"), who lives with her mother Katla at Arnardal.
During a two-week sojourn at Arnardal, Thormód
composes a poem about Thorbjörg that he calls
Kolbrúnarvísur, and for this Katla gives him the
byname Kolbrúnarskáld. Sometime later, Thormód
"recalls the friendship he had had with Thordís" and
pays her a visit (chap. 11). Gríma is happy to see
him, but Thordís, who has heard about his poem in
honor of Thorbjörg, turns him a cold shoulder. Thereupon Thormód recites the Kolbrúnarvísur, changing
the poem so that it praises Thordís. Shortly thereafter, Thorbjörg appears to the poet in a dream and
threatens to repay him for his lausung ok lygi
("falsehood and lying") by inflicting such fierce pains
upon him that his eyes will spring out of his head
unless he makes public confession. He awakes with
unendurable pains in his eyes that persist until he
confesses before many witnesses and restores the poem
to its original form. Neither Thorbjörg nor Thordís
is mentioned again in the story, nor does the author
quote any of the stanzas of the poem that brought
momentary heartache to the skald's two lady friends.

Like Thorgeir, Thormód becomes a retainer of Saint
Ólaf. Upon hearing of Thorgeir's slaying, he sails to
Greenland to avenge his sworn brother on Thorgrím.
The scene in which he slays Thorgrím is skillfully
prepared and vividly described. Thorgrím is sitting
on a chair outdoors, boasting about killing Thorgeir.
A sudden heavy downpour causes the audience to seek
shelter. Thormód drives his axe into the killer's
head, conceals the weapon under his cloak, and calls
out that Thorgrím has been wounded. In the general
confusion he makes his escape. A series of exciting
adventures and violent encounters follow, and Thormód
is severely wounded.

Although several scenes of this story are vividly
described, it is obvious that the author had never been
in Greenland. The juxtaposition of Christian and pagan
motifs reflects the Icelanders' belief that the Greenlanders were somewhat backward. Three times Saint
Ólaf intervenes to save Thormód's life (once in a
vision), but on one occasion the poet is saved by pagan

sorcery, which is usually a source of tragedy in the
sagas. Disabled by his wounds, Thormód is nursed by
the old witch Grima. The witch Thordís, whose son
Thormód has killed, discovers his hiding place by
riding a magic wand in a dream. Sensing the approach
of Thordís and her followers--likewise in a dream--
Grima renders Thormód invisible by having him sit on
a chair on which the figure of Thór is carved. After
failing to find Thormód, the witch Thordís accuses
the witch Grima of not having given up her pagan ways.
To this Grima replies: "I seldom get to church to
hear the teachings of priests, for I have a long way to
travel, and there are few people here. But it occurs
to me, whenever I see the likeness of Thór carved in
wood, which I can break and burn whenever I wish, how
much greater he is who has created heaven and earth and
all things visible and invisible and has given life to
all beings and whom no man can overcome" (chap. 23). A
captious, pious utterance from the lips of a heathen
sorceress! Soon afterwards Thormód recovers suffi-
ciently to return to Norway.

The conclusion of Fóstbræðra saga is similar to
that of the Helgisaga but is more fully and effectively related. The basic tenor of the final scenes seems
more solemn in Fóstbræðra than in the Helgisaga,
especially in the version preserved in the codex
Flateyjarbók. When Thormód declares before the
battle that he does not wish to be parted from the
king, living or dead, he adds, "I wish to share the
same quarters with you tonight." The king promises to
grant him his wish if they both leave the battlefield
alive. Thormód repeats that he does not wish to
outlive the king. Ólaf, however, is not quite certain
that they are both equally prepared to share the same
abode in the world beyond, "and yet I will promise you
that you will come to some place of repose after your
death." To Thormód's third declaration that he never
wishes to be separated from the king, Ólaf replies,
"All of us will travel together if my will prevails."
There can be little doubt that this scene was inspired
by Christ's words to the thief on the cross.

Thormód deliberately fights without a shield, and
after Ólaf has fallen, the poet appeals to the king:
"Holy King Ólaf, do you not intend to keep the promise
you made that you would never forsake me if your will
prevailed?" At that moment he hears the twang of a bow

string, and an arrow pierces his chest. Sitting down beside Olaf's body, he breaks off the arrow shaft. Later, after a physician has failed to draw the arrowhead out, Thormód seizes the tongs and does so himself. "There were barbs on the arrow, and heart fibres adhered to them, some red, and some white, yellow, and green. And when Thormód saw that, he said, 'The king has fed us well. There is whiteness [i.e., fat] around the heart roots of this fellow.'" Leaning against a wall-partition, Thormód declaims his last stanza. But before he can utter the final word, he dies and falls to the ground. The poem is later recited to Saint Olaf's half-brother, Harald the Harsh, who immediately supplies the missing word svíða ("to burn, to smart"), thus honoring the Icelander by completing his poem. Jónas Kristjánsson is correct in dating the extant versions of this story to the last decades of the thirteenth century, but even in this modernized form, it belongs to the transitional sagas in regard to structure and spirit.

As already mentioned, the two extant redactions differ markedly in style. The language of the version preserved in Hauksbók, a codex written for, and partly by, Sir Hauk Erlendsson, is simple and fluid. By contrast, the language of the redaction preserved in other codices has been characterized as "baroque" by Hallberg (11). Two examples will suffice to demonstrate this verbose, florid style. Thorgeir commits his first homicide to avenge the slaying of his father. When he received word of his father's death, "he did not give a start at the news. He did not redden, for anger did not flow into his flesh. He did not pale, for fury did not penetrate his breast. He did not turn black, for anger did not enter his bones. Rather, his demeanor remained unchanged in every way, for his heart was not like the gizzard of a bird. It was not full of blood so as to tremble with fear, but it was tempered in every activity by the highest chief builder [i.e., God]" (chap. 2).

When Thormód deceives Thordís by reciting the revised Kolbrúnarvísur, her anger and jealousy melt away. "And as a dense fog rolls in from the sea and dissipates, and bright sunshine returns with balmy weather, so the poem drew all dislike and darkness from Thordís's heart, and all the brightness of her heart flew to Thormód with gentle warmth" (chap. 11) (12). Although striking, the stylistic differences between the two redactions are rather superficial. Both versions share unique turns of phrase that make the style of Fóstbrǽðra distinctive (13). Like several other saga writers the author of this story takes pains to stress differences between contemporary times and life in the saga age. In the olden days, for example, swords were not commonly used as weapons, and methods of bailing bilge water out of ships were more primitive. And as other authors did, he attributes lingering traces of paganism in Iceland and Greenland to the fact that Christianity was still "young and imperfect" (chap. 9).

In this saga too, there are discrepancies between stanzas and the episodes they are intended to authenticate. According to the story, the sworn brothers come to the parting of the ways because of Thorgeir's excessive arrogance and competitiveness. The stanza quoted to substantiate this, however, tells a different story. "Thormód refers to this discord in this stanza of Þorgeirsdrápa," the author asserts. "People have learned that there were traitors enough who bore calumny between us. I long enjoyed the warrior's counsels. Henceforth I shall remember nothing about Thorgeir except our good friendship. I had to suffer the hatred of men" (chap. 7). The stanza does, indeed, refer to the discord between the sworn brothers, but it flatly contradicts the prose. The two sworn brothers were the victims of malicious mischief, as Thormód discovered after they had dissolved their partnership. This fact helps explain the poet's grief at Thorgeir's death and his readiness to risk his life to avenge the slaying of a man whose friendship he still cherishes.

Like most stories, Fóstbrǽðra saga has its good and bad points. Individual scenes and dialogue are handled well. Motivation, however, is sometimes obscure, and there are superfluous characters and occasional blind motifs. Its most glaring weakness, however, is in character portrayal. In saga literature, heroism frequently borders on, and sometimes degenerates into, heroics. Both Thormód and Thorgeir are overdrawn. It was this weakness that prompted Laxness to parody the sworn brothers in his novel Gerpla, the English translation of which bears the apt title The Happy Warriors.

Hallfreðar saga vandræðaskálds

The "saga of Hallfred the troublesome poet," the
author of which made copious use of stanzas by Hallfred
and others, is the most obvious example of a transitional work. Most of the action involving the hero takes
place abroad, and the protagonists are the troublesome
poet and his revered patron, Ólaf Tryggvason, whose
personality dominates Hallfred from their first encoun-
ter until the skald's death. At first glance the
author of Hallfreðar saga seems to have handled the
verses more skillfully than the compiler of the
Helgisaga. A closer reading of the story, however,
shows that this is not always true. According to the
saga, Hallfred composes his first stanza about his
sweetheart Kolfinna while preparing to go abroad. The
content of the poem, however, does not bear this out:
"I still desire to kiss Kolfinna, though the surging
sea grows billowy--the ship is about to capsize--for I
now desire to enjoy the well-born woman almost more
than if she were betrothed to me" (chap. 5).

In his very first stanza, Hallfred berates a fellow-
countryman for conducting pagan sacrifices and drinking
the blood of sacrificial animals at a time when the
poet is still a staunch and enthusiastic pagan (chap.
4). And in chapter 9, he quotes a series of seven
stanzas, largely gross invective against Kolfinna's
husband Grís, with little or no meaningful comment.
In these stanzas he depicts Grís as a pot-bellied,
stinking sea gull waddling up to Kolfinna's bed. His
hot sweat drips heavily on his wife while "the disconso-
late woman droops . . . like a swan on the water."
Hallfred also found other lovely metaphors and similes
to praise the woman he craved--but did not want to
marry. One day, when he saw Kolfinna out walking, he
composed this verse: "It seems to me, when I glimpse
the goddess of gauzy kerchiefs, as though a ship were
gliding over the water between two islands. But when
the goddess of needlework appears among a bevy of
ladies, it is as though a warship with golden gear were
sailing forth in its glory" (chap. 10). What could
appear more graceful and splendid to a seafaring people
than a fully rigged ship gliding over the water?

When Kolfinna's father marries her to Grís to put a

stop to the fickle poet's dalliance with her, Hallfred
sails to Norway, where he takes service with the pagan
Earl Hákon of Hladir. On his next visit to Norway, he
learns that Ólaf Tryggvason has come to power with a
new religion. He appeals to his pagan gods to help him
escape, but adverse winds hold him back. The king
summons Hallfred and demands that he submit to baptism.
Hallfred counters with several conditions, the last of
which is that the king become his sponsor. During the
confrontations between Hallfred and the king, which are
the most entertaining and most skillfully composed part
of the entire story, the skald's kennings grow less and
less pagan. Finally the king commands that he compose
a drápa on the Resurrection as proof of his piety
(14).

On an expedition to Sweden, Hallfred marries a woman
named Ingibjörg, and in that pagan country, his Christianity dwindles to such a degree that he no longer
sings hymns but merely blows over his horn in the form
of a cross before drinking. At this point, as at other
crucial moments in his life, King Ólaf appears to the
poet in a vision, and he returns to Norway, where he is
shriven and Ingibjörg and their two children are
baptized.

After his wife's death, Hallfred returns to Iceland
with the children. Here he and his men come upon
Kolfinna and some other women at a mountain dairy.
Hallfred sleeps with Kolfinna, and all of his men do
likewise with the other women. Because Hallfred continues to compose scurrilous verses about Grís, Grís
challenges him to a duel, but Ólaf again appears in a
vision and admonishes his poet to refrain from further
evil. Hallfred is deeply grieved at the death of his
lord at the Battle of Svöld, and he expresses his
grief in a memorial drápa that contains these telling lines as a refrain: "All lands in the North have
grown desolate since the death of the king. All peace
is confounded because of the fall of the stout-hearted
son of Tryggvi." The poet is so grief-stricken that he
wanders about aimlessly from land to land. He now
resolves to avenge Ólaf by killing his slayer, Earl
Eirík, but Ólaf appears in a final vision and urges
him not to kill Eirík but rather to compose a laudatory poem about him. Just before the poet dies at sea
of injuries suffered during a storm, he composes his
final stanza: "I would now die free of care if I knew

that my soul would be saved. When young I was harsh of
tongue. I know I should not be afraid--all men must
die. I fear only hell. May God rule over where I
shall pass my life [in the world beyond]." Hallfred's
coffin drifts ashore at the Holy Isle in the Orkneys,
where the poet is given honorable burial. "A chalice
was made from his ring, an altar-cloth from his cloak,
and candlesticks from his helmet."

Despite its shortcomings as literature, Hallfreðar
saga is important for the stanzas it has preserved
describing the skald's conversion. As Dag Strömbäck
has shown, these stanzas afford insights into the
spiritual conflict many Icelanders must have
experienced in renouncing the beliefs of their
ancestors (15). This struggle must have been
especially critical for skalds, since their poetic
diction, their kennings, were rooted in pagan
mythology. It has been suggested that Hallfred's
"conversion was not easy, and perhaps not deep" (16).
This is the impression we gain from one redaction of
the story, but the stanzas--assuming they are genuine
and not the fabrication of the author and of later
scribes, as Bjarni Einarsson maintains--tell a
different story (17).

Kormáks saga

In Kormáks saga, which seems to have been the
model for Hallfreðar saga, the discrepancies between
verse and prose are even more startling. Indeed, the
sparse prose creates the impression of being "a
free-hand sketch without any appreciable support in
Kormák's numerous stanzas," as Hallberg expressed it
(18). Two examples will suffice to demonstrate the
author's misunderstanding, or disregard, of Kormák's
poetry. In one episode, Kormák and his brother rescue
Steingerd from a viking ship anchored near some islands
off the coast of Sweden (chap. 26). The situation in
this puzzling passage, which seems to be a badly
garbled interpolation from Tristrams saga, is difficult to understand (19). Although the brothers have
first rowed out to the ship and then boarded it a
second time by the gangplank, they choose to swim
ashore with the heroine. "As Kormák approached the
shore, eels twisted around his arms and legs so that he
was close to being pulled down." While struggling for

his life, the poet composes and recites a stanza in which he says that díkis bokkar ("goats of the dike") swam against him in herds. The kenning is a perfect periphrasis for porpoises, but cannot possibly mean "eels" (20).

In his final battle Kormák mortally wounds a "Scottish blótrisi." The wounded "sacrifice giant"--the word occurs only here--seizes Kormák, breaks his ribs, and falls down on top of him so that he cannot get up-- we are reminded of the battle between the giant Hrungnir and Thór in Snorri's Edda. As Kormák lies dying on his ship, he composes four verses, in one of which he declares that it was not like having Steingerd in his arms when he wrestled with the "steerer of the rope stallion," that is, the steersman of the enemy vessel. The author here mistranslated a simple kenning for "viking" as blótrisi, whatever that may mean.

The differences between this story and Hallfred's biography are as remarkable as their many major and minor similarities. Kormáks saga is as strongly pagan as Hallfreðar saga is Christian. The love triangle, which is a secondary theme in Hallfreðar saga, is dominant in this story. Kormák is even more irascible, fickle, and violent than Hallfred, and his derisive stanzas directed against Steingerd's two husbands are more scabrous that Hallfred's. Kormák is defeated in two duels with Steingerd's first husband, Bersi, and is victorious in a duel with her second one, Thorvald. He becomes engaged to Steingerd, makes no effort to attend the wedding, and even fails to achieve union with her when the opportunity arises. All of this is attributed to witchcraft by the author, who describes various acts of sorcery at length. Modern critics have suggested other reasons for Kormák's perplexing behavior, such as psychological impotence, mother fixation, overidealization of his sweetheart, and so on, which are perhaps more appealing but no more satisfactory than the one advanced by the author.

Whereas Kolfinna is docile and apathetic, Steingerd is vigorous and self-willed. When her first husband receives a humiliating wound in a duel, she asserts that his name will be changed from Duel-Bersi to Arse-Bersi and declares herself divorced since she does not want to be married to a maimed invalid. After the divorce, a digression of several chapters of the saga deals with Bersi's feuds. When Kormák and his brother

go abroad, Steingerd insists that she and her second
husband Thorvald follow them. Off the coast of Norway,
their ships come so close to each other that Kormák is
able to knock Thorvald down with his tiller, whereupon
Steingerd steers their vessel into Kormák's and cap-
sizes it. After Kormák has rescued Steingerd from
vikings for the second time, as described above,
Thorvald offers to relinquish her to him, but she
declares she will not be traded like a piece of merchandise. Kormák dolefully agrees that she should remain
with Thorvald, since "evil spirits . . . or ill fate"
from the very beginning has made their union impossible.

Surprisingly this story of violence and jealousy and
unrequited love has a few light touches. Before sailing to Norway, Kormák steals two kisses from
Steingerd, for which he must pay compensation to
Thorvald. In a stanza he wryly laments the high cost
of the kisses. In Norway he seizes Steingerd while she
is out walking, but King Harald wrestles her away from
him and chides the Icelander for his unseemly behavior.
On another occasion in Norway, Kormák steals four
kisses from Steingerd. King Harald is summoned to
mediate between the poet and the wronged husband. One
kiss, he decides, can count as a greeting and one as a
reward for Kormák's first rescue of Steingerd and her
husband from vikings. For the other two kisses, he
must again pay compensation. "Kormák recited the same
stanza that has already been written" (chap. 24).

Despite the stiff form of the dróttkvætt stanza
and the uninspired kennings for "woman," Kormák's
erotic poetry is regarded as the best produced by Icelandic skalds. Whatever else we may say about the
saga, we should, to paraphrase Einar Ólafur Sveinsson,
be grateful to the author for having preserved so much
of this poetry.

Bjarnar saga Hítdælakappa

The "saga of Björn, the Hítadal champion," which
may be the oldest of the sagas about poets, has not
been well preserved. The missing initial chapters have
been replaced by a somewhat abridged insert in one manuscript of Heimskringla, and there is a sizable lacuna
at the end of chapter 14. The biography is episodic,
and motifs and situations are needlessly repeated,

evidently because the author wished to make use of all available skaldic stanzas. The antagonists, Björn and Thórd, are both poets, and much of the story consists of vulgar, invidious stanzas that they direct at each other. The characterization is inferior to that of the best sagas. Thórd is cast from the beginning as a deceitful, cowardly villain, while Björn is initially too courageous and conciliatory to be quite credible. With all its weaknesses, however, this story, like all the transitional sagas, contains several impressive and enjoyable scenes.

The dominant theme of Björn's biography, like that of Kormák, is the love triangle. Björn's fiancée Oddný is won by Thórd through deception in a manner so similar to that of Ívars þáttr that this tale is regarded by some scholars as the inspiration and model for the beginning of the saga (22). The dissimilarities between them illustrate the differences between the two genres, between the compendious mode of the þáttr and the more leisurely, detailed manner of the saga. The beginning of the story is the statement of the theme, the body of the saga is an excessive elaboration on it, and the conclusion is the inevitable outcome of the increasingly more violent clashes between the two antagonists. The saga conception is excellent, but the execution is uneven.

Like many other saga heroes, Björn goes abroad to win fame and fortune. In Russia he gains the appellation kappi ("champion") by defeating Kaldimar, a kinsman of King Valdimar and pretender to his throne, in a duel. When Björn learns of Oddný's marriage, he loses all desire to return to Iceland. In England he takes service for two years with King Knút, on one occasion slaying a flying dragon. After several years of marauding, he intercepts Thórd as he is returning to Iceland after collecting an inheritance in Denmark. Björn despoils him of ship and cargo but spares his life because Thórd has recently enjoyed the hospitality of Saint Ólaf.

Björn and Thórd both visit the king, who offers to mediate their dispute. He declares the disgrace suffered by Thórd through the loss of his goods to be equal to the disgrace inflicted on Björn through the loss of Oddný, brings about a reconciliation between the two rivals, and admonishes them always to remain at peace with each other. Björn now remains with the

king, and his reverence for Saint Ólaf is as boundless
as that of Hallfred for Ólaf Tryggvason. One day
Björn inadvertently puts on the king's leg thongs
after bathing, and Ólaf graciously permits him to keep
them. At this point, the author makes use of a form of
foreshadowing that is unusual in saga literature:
"Björn always wore these thongs on his legs as long as
he lived, and he was buried with them. And much later,
when his bones were disinterred and taken to another
church for burial, these same thongs on Björn's legs
were undecayed although all else was decayed. They are
now [used as] a cincture in a priest's vestment at
Gardar on Akranes" (chap. 9).

When Björn returns to Iceland, Oddný bitterly
rebukes Thórd for having led her to believe that he
had died of wounds in Russia. She vigorously objects
to his inviting Björn to spend the winter with them,
but Thórd alleges that his action is meant as a token
of his complete reconciliation with Björn and of his
penitence for having wronged her. At first both men
try to heed Saint Ólaf's admonition, but soon they
begin to chide and deride each other in increasingly
invidious stanzas, and by the time Björn leaves in the
spring, they are completely at odds. Björn's reason-
ableness and conciliatoriness have completely disappeared. He carves a scorn pole depicting Thórd in the
act of sodomy and boasts of being the father of one of
Oddný's sons. The exchange of insulting stanzas leads
to repeated litigation, with Thórd usually the loser,
and finally to violence, with Thórd's henchmen and
hired assassins always the losers. Thórd himself is
too cowardly to face his enemy. But now public opinion
begins to turn against Björn. His killing has become
excessive, and among his victims are the sons of two
influential farmers. And when Björn kills one of
Thórd's sons, Thórd has no other recourse but to
muster the strength of all of Björn's enemies for
final retaliation.

At this point in the story, Björn's moral rehabilitation begins. An influential man named Thorstein,
caught in a blizzard while on his way to spend Yule
with one of Thórd's henchmen, is obliged to seek
shelter for several days at Björn's farm. On the
first day, Björn behaves boorishly, but after that he
treats his guests cordially. When Thorstein volunteers
to act as arbiter in the controversy, Björn accepts

his offer immediately, but Thórd is less eager to do
so. During the negotiations he demands that all the
shameful stanzas that have passed between them be
recited once more and counted. When the count shows
that Björn has recited one more verse than he has,
Thórd insists on evening the score. Björn retaliates
in kind, and the meeting breaks up. Convinced that
Thórd wanted the negotiation to fail, Thorstein now
turns his allegiance to Björn. The two men solemnly
agree that in case one of them is slain, the survivor
will demand the right of being sole arbiter in the
prosecution or else wreak vengeance on the slayers as
though the two were blood brothers. Only blood
vengeance is ruled out by Thorstein since that does not
befit Christians.

Thórd now devises a plan and assembles forces to
kill Björn. Despite ominous dreams and the fearful
objections of his wife, Björn sets out one morning
with a young farmhand to trim the manes of his horses.
As they approach the pasture, the boy catches sight of
riders in the distance and urges Björn, who has not
yet seen them because of his weak eyesight, to turn
back. Instead, Björn sends the boy to fetch the
horses. Soon Björn is surrounded by twenty men, who
attack immediately. Björn defends himself manfully
but is soon so seriously wounded that he has to fight
from a kneeling position. Björn derides Thórd for
being among the last to arrive. "'And yet I will stand
close to you today,' said Thórd, 'and deal you a shameful blow (klækkishögg).' 'Those are the only kinds
of blows you will ever deal,' said Björn, 'as long as
you live.' Thórd had made a slip of the tongue. He
had meant to say he would deal him a shaming blow
(klámhögg)" (chap. 32). When his sword fails him,
Björn continues to defend himself with his shears, but
he is finally overborne and killed.

Thórd strikes off Björn's head and shows it to
Björn's wife and then to his mother. When he asks her
whether she recognizes it, she retorts: "I recognize
the head, and you must recognize it too, since you ran
away from it in terror often enough when it was
fastened to a body. Take it to Oddný. She will like
it better than the miserable puny head that bobbles on
your neck" (chap. 33). The news of Björn's death af-
fects Oddný so deeply that she pines and wastes away.
Thórd often places her on a horse and leads it to and

fro, for this is the only way Oddný can find temporary
relief from her affliction.

Björn is buried at the church he had built and dedicated to the apostle Thomas, about whom he had composed
a drápa. Thorstein keeps the solemn promise made to
Björn. He banishes some of the attackers and assesses
enormous penalties against Thórd.

Stylistically, Bjarnar saga is more interesting
than the biographies of Kormák and Hallfred. For the
narrative the author used a simple, paratactic style,
connecting clauses with ok ("and") or en ("but").
In passages of exposition and speeches, however, he
resorted to a more formal style characterized by
compound-complex periods that sometimes run to eight or
ten lines. Although the work as a whole is episodic
and quite a few chapters consist largely of exchanges
of abusive stanzas with brief comments, the story
becomes more coherent toward the end. The storm that
drove Thorstein to seek shelter with Björn and his
subsequent sojourn there are well described, and
Björn's last stand against overwhelming odds is unforgettable. The only source mentioned is a priest named
Runólf Dálksson. The author, who may have been connected with the monastery at Hítardal, seems to have
constructed his story on the stanzas of the two poets
and on local anecdotes about them. Björn's adventures
abroad are probably the author's own creation.

Heiðarvíga saga

The "saga of the battle on the moor," the story of a
battle that took place in 1014 on a desolate moor between men from the Húnavatn district of the north and
the Borgarfjord district in the west of Iceland, is generally considered to be the oldest of the extant
Íslendinga sögur. The language of Heiðarvíga is
so awkward that it is sometimes difficult to distinguish between narrative and direct or indirect discourse. Unnecessary details are mentioned, and characters who take no part in the story are described. A
typical example is the following paragraph taken from
the clumsy description of planning for the battle on
the moor: "In Langadal there is a farm called Audólfs-
stadir. There lives that man whose name is Audólf.
He is a noble-minded and important man. His brother is
Thorvald, and he is not mentioned in connection with

the expedition. He lives at a place called Sléttadal.
That is up from Svínavatn. There are two farms of
that name. He was the strongest man in physical
strength in the north [of Iceland]. 'You are not to
choose him for the expedition, and the reason for this
is his disposition'" (chap. 16). The entire paragraph
is disconnected if not irrelevant.

The first half of the story is dominated by Víga-
Styr ("Killer Styr"), who prides himself on having
killed thirty-three men without ever having paid compensation for them. Víga-Styr is, as Andersson has aptly
labeled him, "a paradigmatic example of an
ójafnaðarmaðr," that is, a brutal killer with no
sense of pity or justice (23). Among his victims are
two berserkers given to him by his brother Vermund.
One of them is suffocated in an overheated sauna, the
other one is cut down as he slips on a fresh oxhide
while attempting to escape from the bath (chap. 4).
The idea of disposing of the berserkers in this manner
was probably suggested to the author by the fact that
saunas were still a novelty in Iceland at the time the
saga was composed. The detail of the raw oxhide seems
to stem from a lost Eddic poem (24). This episode is
well told, no doubt because it occurs also in
Eyrbyggja saga, which Jón Ólafsson could use to
refresh his memory (25).

In creating the character of Víga-Styr, the author
had no lack of models, for many of his contemporaries
manipulated the law as Styr did to misappropriate the
property of others. Even building a large church on
his estate for the sake of self-aggrandizement fits the
picture of the Sturlung Age: "At that time a good
event occurred here in this country. The ancient
religion was laid aside, and the true faith was taken
up. Many powerful farmers had churches built on their
estates. One of them was Styr, and he had a church
erected at Hraun. In those days people believed that
whoever had a church built would have the right to
select as many followers to go to heaven as could stand
within his church" (chap. 8).

Styr meets an ignominious end when Gest, the youth-
ful son of his last victim, strikes him in the head
with an axe and escapes. Snorri, Styr's son-in-law,
takes the body to the church at Styr's farm Hraun for
burial. But the evil of such ójafnaðarmenn lives on
even after death--a common and significant theme in the

sagas. Snorri and his men stay overnight at the home
of a farmer, whose daughter is curious to see the
corpse of the wanton killer. When she catches sight of
him in the dark room, it seems to her that the corpse
rises and speaks a verse. "She was so mad with fright
that four men could scarcely restrain her. Her shrieks
and convulsions did not abate all night long until
daybreak, when she died" (chap. 9).

Styr's son pursues Gest to Norway and even to
Constantinople for the sake of blood vengeance, but
each time his own life is saved by his intended victim.
Finally he returns to Iceland after Gest has promised
never again to come to the North. Saga writers seldom
moralize, but the moral is nearly always clear: Styr
slaughters an innocent man and then offers his son Gest
"compensation" in the form of a sickly lamb; by contrast, Gest three times spares the life of his would-be
killer. Jan de Vries, in commenting on this passage,
declared that Heiðarvíga saga has "a distincly
Christian stamp" (26).

Snorri now decides to avenge Styr by killing
Thorstein Gíslason, one of Gest's protectors. Before
setting out, he attends divine services—a common practice in the Sturlung Age.

> Snorri went to the church that he had had built.
> The sun shone from the east. And when he entered,
> he met [his son] Gudlaug. He was just leaving, and
> he had been at prayers after his custom. Snorri
> asked whether he did not wish to go along to avenge
> his grandfather. Gudlaug replied that Snorri had
> such a large force that he did not need his help,
> and that he had never taken part in killing. His
> father might decide, but he would prefer to remain
> at home. . . . Snorri said he had never seen such a
> human countenance like that of his son Gudlaug when
> he met him in the church. His face had been as red
> as blood, and it had seemed to inspire terror.
> Several years later Gudlaug went to England. His
> father gave him money for the voyage. There he
> entered a monastery, led a virtuous life, and was
> regarded as an excellent cleric until his dying day.
> (chap. 12)

Snorri and his men now proceed south to Thorstein's
farm and early on a Sunday morning lure Thorstein and

two sons out of the house and slaughter the unarmed
men. At this point, Thorstein's youngest son, a child
of nine, appears in the doorway, sleepily rubbing his
eyes. "Snorri said to his son Thórd kausa ["Cat"],
'Does the cat see the mouse? The young shall attack
the young.'" But Thórd furiously refuses to kill the
boy, and Snorri spares his life. Nowhere else does the
ubiquitous Snorri appear so callous and brutal as in
this episode. Without comment the author condemns
Snorri'a actions through the skillful use of contrast
and irony.

Despite the legal settlement of these killings, the
sons of Hárek decide to exact blood vengeance for
Thorstein by killing Kolskegg, a kinsman of Snorri who
took part in the slaughter. Hall Gudmundsson helps
Kolskegg escape, and so they kill him instead. The
killers perish in a shipwreck. The prosecution is
undertaken by Hall's brother Bardi, who now becomes the
central figure of the story. On the advice of his
foster father Thórarin, he seeks to arrive at a peaceful settlement at the General Assembly three years in
succession and thus wins public approval for his
patience and restraint. Finally there remains no other
resort but blood vengeance.

Thórarin now advises Bardi whom to select for his
expedition south to the Borgarfjord and prescribes the
strategy for the attack. Crucial to the success of the
undertaking is swift withdrawal to a certain defense
position in anticipation of the counterattack. After
completing his minutely detailed instructions, the wise
old man admits doubts about the complete success of
their venture: "And yet I suspect that you will not
succeed because of the ferocity of your followers"
(chap. 24). The attack itself proceeds according to
plan: Bardi comes upon Gísli Thorgautsson unawares in
a hay meadow, cuts him down, and urges quick withdrawal
to the prescribed defense position. But Thórarin's
prophecy fulfills itself. On the pretense of being
ravenously hungry, his men insist on first eating a
leisurely breakfast. Consequently, they are able to
reach only the alternative, greatly inferior defense
position before they have to fend off the first of
three onslaughts.

In three attacks, nine men from the Borgarfjord and
five of Bardi's men are killed. When the northerners
see a fourth band of attackers approaching, so large

that it is "like looking into a forest," they withdraw.
Under cover of darkness, they join a caravan without
being recognized, and Bardi secretly apprises Snorri of
their difficult situation. Snorri now plays the role
of mediator, as he so often does in saga literature.
After flattering one of the men into reciting the truce
formula, which is binding on all present, Snorri
divulges the situation and presses for a composition.

The fragile truce holds until the matter can be
brought before the General Assembly. Here Bardi exchanges insults with Tind, whose major accomplishment
was chopping the head off of one of Bardi's men as he
lay dying after the battle.

> Then an old man stood up, and it was Eid Skeggjason,
> and said, "We are very concerned that men should use
> abusive words here, whether it be our men or others.
> That leads to no good, and often evil comes of it.
> Men should say only that which will bring about
> agreement. We think that no one has a greater right
> to seek redress than I, and no one has suffered deep-
> er grief. And yet it seems advisable to us to come
> to terms. Therefore we will not forgive those who
> rant against each other. It is most likely that, as
> usual, evil will result if men speak shamefully to
> each other." He received loud acclaim for his
> speech. (chap. 35)

Although he has lost both of his sons in the battle on
the moor, Eid is more concerned about the common good
than he is about personal recompense. He is thus the
first of several magnanimous characters in the
Íslendingasögur who are willing to make a personal
sacrifice in order to reestablish peace in the community. A settlement is finally reached through the mediation of Snorri and other men of good will and common
sense. The author, who maintains an air of detachment
and neutrality, states his own position through the
words of Eid and through the comment that Eid "received
loud acclaim for his speech."

Despite its angular style and disproportionate structure, Heiðarvíga saga contains several unforgettable
scenes, one of the best of which immediately precedes
the battle. Because of Bardi's seeming dilatoriness in
exacting redress for his brother's slaying, his enemies
in Borgarfjord get into the habit of asking derisively,

"Don't you think that Bardi will come?" As Bardi and his men approach the hay meadow where Gísli and his two brothers are working, one of them thinks he can distinguish Bardi. Gísli says to his two brothers, "You have been acting all summer long as though you expected Bardi to leap out from behind every little bush, but he still hasn't come." Ketil replies, "It won't turn out to be false that Bardi really has come." The brothers run for the buildings, but Gísli slips while trying to climb over the stone fence, and Bardi kills him with a blow that almost sheers off his face. Ketil carries him to the forge where his father, Thorgaut, is working. Thorgaut says jestingly, "There is certainly a lot of noise. Hasn't Bardi come?" Ketil steps inside and casts his brother down at his father's feet with the answer: "Your son Gísli found out that he has come" (chap. 27).

Although the action of the story evolves from the temperaments of the characters, the author fails to develop any meaningful interplay between them, such as the lifelong quarrel between Björn and Thórd. Most of the victims have no real personal relationship to their killers. They are slain in lieu of those against whom the attacks should have been directed. As already suggested, Snorri's brutal murder of Thorstein and his sons seems inconsistent with his role as mediator in the story. Bardi's behavior too is inconsistent. He cruelly taunts two of his enemies, and this seems out of character with the remarkable patience and self-control (hóf) he displays earlier in the story. He also divorces both his wives in a pique. Bardi's mother Thuríd is memorable, but she comes to life only momentarily in her role as the female inciter to vengeance.

After the peace settlement, Bardi goes abroad. He pays a visit to Saint Ólaf, but the king refuses him hospitality because he has heard that the Icelanders have not completely abandoned their pagan practices. After a visit to Iceland, Bardi goes to Constantinople, joins the emperor's bodyguard, and takes part in many battles. "And there Bardi fell with good repute, and had manfully wielded his weapons until his death."

Conclusion

The transitional sagas have much in common. Some of

the characters are well drawn, the dialogue is often
skillfully handled, and individual scenes and episodes
are effectively related. But with few exceptions Icelandic writers had not yet learned to integrate their
disparate materials and to maintain a consistent level
of excellence throughout an entire saga. In all these
stories, only one of the protagonists, Björn, dies a
heroic death, and he is the only one who is avenged.
In these works, many skaldic stanzas are quoted, but
the startling discrepancies between stanzas and the
prose in which they are embedded lends little support
to the belief that skaldic stanzas served as nuclei for
the preservation of oral tales. Skaldic poetry did
preserve old traditions, but the poems were frequently
misinterpreted by the authors who inserted them piece-
meal into their stories. With the exception of
Kormáks saga, the transitional sagas reveal a strong
preoccupation on the part of their authors with Christianity or with the conflict between Christianity and
paganism during the time of Ólaf Tryggvason and Saint
Ólaf.

Egils saga is also classified among the transitional sagas by Thorkil Damsgaard Olsen. For Jónas
Kristjánsson, however, the biography of the viking-
poet Egil marks the beginning of the Íslendinga
sögur as a genre distinct from the konunga sögur
(27). There is something to be said for both points of
view, but it will be more appropriate to discuss Egils
saga in the following chapter.

Chapter Five
Major Sagas about Icelanders

Introduction

Snorri Sturluson. From what little is known about his life, Snorri Sturluson seems to have been a perfect embodiment of the vices and virtues of the Sturlung Age (1). Ambivalent and enigmatic, Snorri both courted the favor and feared the power of the Norwegian crown. Like many of his contemporaries, he was ruthless and relentless in his pursuit of wealth and prestige. At the same time he was one of the most significant and influential writers of medieval Europe. Snorri is generally believed to have written his _Edda_, _Óláfs saga hins helga_, _Heimskringla_, and _Egils saga_ in that order between the years 1220 and 1235.

Although the internal and external evidence for Snorri's authorship of _Egils saga_ is cogent, some scholars still hesitate to acknowledge it (2). A recent stylistic-statistical analysis of _Egils saga_ and _Heimskringla_, however, has established so close a lexical and stylistic affinity between the two works that rejecting Snorri's authorship of the one is virtually tantamount to denying his authorship of the other--and that is what one eminent scholar seems to have done (3).

Snorra Edda. Snorri's _Edda_ consists of four parts, which were composed in the reverse of their present order. As we know, Snorri completed his _Háttatal_ after returning to Iceland from Norway in 1220. With this tour de force--masterful in technique but vapid in content--Snorri clearly hoped to ingratiate himself with King Hákon and Earl Skúli. The present annotated form of the poem reveals a second, didactic, purpose: Snorri hoped to revitalize a moribund art by providing poets with examples of a wide variety of correctly composed stanzas. As a record of history, oral poetry had long since been supplanted by Latin and vernacular chronicles and biographies. As court entertainment, the intricate, esoteric art of the

skalds had had to yield to the simpler ballads of
wandering minstrels. Furthermore, allusions to pagan
mythology in kennings were no longer fully understood.

Snorri therefore wrote Skáldskaparmál (Poetic
diction) as a commentary on skaldic poetry. He interspersed his definitions and illustrations of metaphorical compounds and other poetic figures with well-told
stories about ancient gods and heroes that explain the
meanings of many kennings.

Skáldskaparmál was supplemented by Gylfaginning (Beguiling of Gylfi), which takes its title from
the framework of this section of the book. A Swedish
king named Gylfi comes to Ásgard ("abode of the
Æsir") in order to secure information about the
ancient gods. Here he is conducted into the presence
of a pagan trinity: High, Equally High, and Third. In
answer to his questions, they tell him about the creation and the destruction of the world--Ragnarök
("doom of the gods"). They relate tragic and comical
stories, based on Eddic poems (and perhaps also on
popular tales) about Thór, Baldur, Frigg, and other
deities. In the end Gylfi heard a tremendous crash on
all sides. "And when he looked about, he was standing
outdoors on a level field. He saw there neither hall
nor citadel. He then went his way and came home into
his kingdom and related the events that he had seen and
heard, and these tales have been passed on as he told
them from one man to another." Gylfi's entire experience with the gods was an illusion.

Finally Snorri provided his handbook for poets with
a Prologus in which he presented a euhemeristic
explanation of the origin of the pagan deities: they
had been powerful kings who in the course of time came
to be revered as gods. In this way, he safeguarded
himself against possible accusations by the clergy that
he was promoting heathenism. In Jóns saga (later
redaction, chap. 12), we read that Saint Jón expunged
the names of pagan gods from the designations of the
days of the week, so that Þórsdagr ("Thór's day,"
i.e., Thursday) was changed to Fimmtudagr ("Fifth
day"), and so on. We also recall Ólaf Tryggvason's
fury at Hallfred's use of pagan kennings in his poetry.
Similar thirteenth-century reflections of antipagan
sentiment are found throughout saga literature (4).

Snorri's treatise did not achieve its intended purpose. Skaldic court poetry expired during the

thirteenth century, two of its last practitioners being
Snorri's nephews, the grammarian Ólaf Thórdarson (d.
1259) and the historian Sturla Thórdarson (d. 1282).
Nevertheless, his Edda exerted an enduring influence
on Icelandic literature. Traditional meters and poetic
figures continued to be used in religious poetry, of
which Lilja (The lily, ca. 1350) is the most splendid
example. No doubt later saga writers who composed
skaldic stanzas to embellish their stories in imitation
of older sagas about kings and poets also benefited
from Snorri's treatise. It is furthermore believed
that Snorri's Edda inspired the collection of mythological and heroic poems found in the Codex regius--
Icelandic Konungsbók (The king's book)--now housed
in the Arna-Magnæan Foundation of Iceland. The
importance of Eddic lays for saga plots has already
been noted. Snorri's handbook was also of importance
for authors of rímur, ballad cycles employing
alliteration and kennings, which have been composed in
Iceland since about 1350. And Gylfaginning and the
narrative portions of Skáldskaparmál, known as the
Prose Edda, have remained popular reading until the
present day (5).

Óláfs saga hins helga. As a literary work
Snorri's biography of Saint Ólaf far excels all previous konungasögur in structure, style, psychological
realism, motivation, and character portrayal. In this
work Snorri exhibits a mastery of the stranded plot,
which he elaborated by skillfully intertwining three or
even more plot strands (6). In the use of finely honed
dialogue, both to advance the story and to reveal emotions and aspects of character, Snorri was surpassed by
only a few of the greatest authors of Islendinga
sögur.

The fact that Snorri made use of many sources is
reflected in his style. Sometimes he copied almost
verbatim and sometimes he treated his sources more
freely and creatively. In general, however, his style
is clear and is usually adapted to the situation.

We recall that in the Helgisaga Ólaf's future
sainthood was revealed immediately after his birth and
that he was attended by miracles and other divine mani-
festations throughout his life. Snorri omitted some
miracles, rationalized others, and postponed still
others until shortly before or after--sometimes long
after--Ólaf's death. Whereas the compiler of the

Helgisaga had Ólaf miraculously sail his ships through the isthmus Agnafit, Snorri has the king and his men dig a channel through it, thus, to paraphrase Jan de Vries, replacing a miracle with an impossibility (7). Snorri first presents Ólaf as a fierce marauder, then, following his conversion, as an equally fierce missionary king, and finally as a martyr and saint. Ólaf's actions and those of his adversaries—primarily the powerful warlords and regional rulers of Norway— are carefully motivated, and Ólaf's enemies are more objectively and sympathetically characterized than in earlier biographies of this king.

Heimskringla. With only minor changes, Óláfs saga was incorporated into Heimskringla. Snorri expanded the introductory and concluding matter of Óláfs saga into a synoptic history beginning with the mythical and legendary kings of Sweden and ending with the arrival of King Sverrir in Norway. The first part of this comprehensive history, Ynglinga saga (Saga of the Ynglings), is largely based on the poem Ynglinga tal (Enumeration of the Ynglings) by the Norwegian skald Thjódólf of Hvin and on Skjöldunga saga. For the remainder of the work, Snorri employed a wide variety of written sources and many skaldic stanzas, over six hundred of which he quoted. No doubt he also made use of oral tales, the nature and extent of which cannot be determined, and much of his work is the product of his own creative imagination. The most detailed of the individual biographies are Óláfs saga Tryggvasonar and Haralds saga hins harðráða (Saga of Harald the Harsh).

Snorri succeeded in integrating his disparate materials into a unified history by overlapping and interweaving the matter of the individual sagas. Thus Harald Fairhair is introduced as a future successful military king in the preceding biography, Hálfdanar saga svarta (Saga of Hálfdan the Black), and certain events in this saga prefigure events in later biographies. In Hálfdanar saga, Queen Ragnhild experiences a variant of the tree dream, which is interpreted in Haralds saga to presage the greatness of Harald and his progeny. This prediction is reinforced by a parallel dream experienced by King Hálfdan (8). Harald Fairhair is pictured by Snorri as a virtuous heathen, and in this capacity he adumbrates the conversions of Ólaf Tryggvason and Ólaf Haraldsson. Saint

Olaf's hair, beard, and fingernails continue to grow and to be trimmed until his body is finally enshrined by Harald the Harsh in 1066. Miracles are wrought through Saint Olaf's intervention throughout Heimskringla until 1161.

Heimskringla is not history in the modern sense, nor did Snorri follow the aims and methods of Ari Thorgilsson, whose veracity he praised highly in the prologue of his work. Rather, it is an imaginative re-creation of the past colored by Snorri's own concept of history and his personal experiences with royalty. For Snorri, the course of history was determined by powerful, self-willed men. As in the Íslendinga sögur, action is generated in Heimskringla by the temperaments of the characters. The major conflict is between kings who endeavor to unify Norway and local chieftains who seek to preserve their traditional way of life. Snorri's descriptions of Norwegian conditions and institutions are correct but anachronistic, since they are back projections based on personal observation and on his study of Sverris saga.

It would be difficult to assess the full extent of the influence of this imposing work. Heimskringla was the model for the anonymous Knýtlinga saga (Saga of the Knýtlings), a history of the kings of Denmark from the tenth century until 1186, which has been attributed to Olaf Thórdarson by Sigurður Nordal (9). There can be little doubt that Snorri's work both inspired Sturla Thórdarson to compose Íslendinga saga (History of the Icelanders), which comprises a major part of Sturlunga saga, and also influenced him in his composition of Hákonar saga Hákonarsonar (Biography of Hákon Hákonsson), which was commissioned by Hákon's son and successor Magnús. According to Lee M. Hollander, no other medieval work "has exerted such broad and pervasive influence on Scandinavian life, literature, the arts as Heimskringla" (10). On the eight hundredth anniversary of the author's birth (1979), new editions of Heimskringla appeared in Norway and Iceland, and in the same year, the first major work about the author in the English language, Marlene Ciklamini's Snorri Sturluson, was published in this series.

Why did Snorri devote years to compiling this comprehensive work of eight hundred printed pages? It is possible that Heimskringla, like Sverris saga and

Hákonar saga, was officially commissioned. It seems
more likely, however, that Snorri undertook this enormous task to win favor and fortune--that is, to ingratiate himself with the Norwegian court and at the same
time to collect a fitting reward, as Icelandic skalds
had done for over three centuries.

Egils saga Skalla-Grímssonar

The first of the major Sagas of Icelanders, Egils
saga bears a superficial resemblance to Hallfreðar
saga. The protagonists are skalds, their antagonists
are Norwegian kings, the major part of the action takes
place outside of Iceland, and neither one of the bellicose warrior-poets dies by the sword. Despite these
obvious similarities, however, there are essential
differences between the two biographies. Whereas
Hallfred, the reluctant Christian, lives and dies in
the shadow of Ólaf Tryggvason, Egil stubbornly maintains his stance as the peer of the kings he serves or
defies and remains a reluctant adherent of the treacherous god Óðin. Furthermore, Egils saga has a political dimension that is missing in Hallfreðar saga and,
for that matter, in all other Íslendinga sögur.
The conflict here is not between individuals but
between the Norwegian crown--Harald Fairhair and his
sons--and the descendants of the Norwegian warlord
Kveld-Úlf ("Evening Wolf"). The two powerful dramas,
Egils saga and Heimskringla, are performed on the
same panoramic stage.
The scene of action for the first third of Egils
saga is Norway. Kveld-Úlf and his elder son Skalla-
Grím refuse to support Harald against a rival king,
but his younger son Thórólf joins Harald and wins
fame and fortune in his service. Upon the death of
Thórólf's kinsman Bárd, Thórólf inherits all his
goods including his wife Sigríd. Thórólf rejects
the claims of Bárd's two half brothers to a share of
the properties on the questionable grounds that their
mother Hildiríd was not legally married to their
father. The sons of Hildiríd retaliate with a
campaign of insidious slander, to which the king finally succumbs. Harald attacks Thórólf on his estate
and sets his house on fire. Thórólf and his men
break out of the blazing building and counterattack.
"Thórólf ran forward, hewing to right and left. He

pressed forward toward the king's banner. . . . And
when Thórólf reached the shield-wall, he thrust his
sword through the standard-bearer. 'I am three strides
short,' he said. He was pierced with swords and
spears, but it was the king who gave him his death-
blow, and Thórólf fell forward to the king's feet"
(chap. 22).

Thórólf's death is avenged by a kinsman, Ketil
hæng, who kills the sons of Hildiríd and then
emigrates to Iceland. Further vengeance is wreaked by
Kveld-Úlf and Skalla-Grím, who kill two of the king's
henchmen before following Ketil to Iceland. Úlf dies
at sea, but Grím makes land in western Iceland and
sets up house at Borg, where his father's coffin has
drifted ashore. He and his wife Bera have several
children, but all die in infancy except two daughters
and two sons, Thórólf and Egil.

Although this introduction to Egil's biography
(chaps. 1-27) seems at first glance to be excessively
long, it is remarkable in two respects. It is the most
skillfully composed part of the book, probably because
Snorri was unencumbered here by skaldic stanzas and
local anecdotes. Consequently, he was able to create
an exciting story that is well rounded and complete
within itself and simultaneously functions as an almost
perfect prefiguration of the main part of the saga.

The conflict between Harald Fairhair and Kveld-
Úlf's sons anticipates the conflict between Harald's
sons and Egil. There is a close correspondence between
the contrasting personalities of Skalla-Grím and
Thórólf on the one hand and those of Skalla-Grím's
two sons on the other. Like his father, Skalla-Grím
is dark, ugly, huge, and demonic, whereas Thórólf is
blond, handsome, popular, and courtly. Egil inherits
his father's physique and temperament, while his
brother Thórólf is a replica of his uncle. And finally, as we shall see, the questionable legitimacy of
Hildiríd's birth, which leads to the enmity between
Harald and Thórólf, has a parallel in Egil's relationship to King Eirík Bloodaxe.

At this point Snorri introduces what seems to be a
digression. Björn, the son of a Norwegian warlord,
elopes with Thóra to Shetland, where they marry without her guardian's consent. Outlawed by King Harald,
Björn takes his bride to Iceland, where they are welcomed by Skalla-Grím, since Thóra is the sister of

his foster brother Thórir Hróaldsson. Thórólf persuades his father to bring about a reconciliation between Björn and Thóra's brother Thórir, after which Thórólf accompanies Björn and Thóra to Norway. Their daughter Ásgerd remains in Iceland and is fostered by Skalla-Grím and Bera.

In Norway Thórólf wins the friendship of King Harald's favorite son, Eirík Bloodaxe, by giving him a ship. An even closer friendship develops between Thórólf and Eirík's wife Gunnhild, who is notorious in saga literature for her fondness for men. On a brief visit to Iceland, Thórólf brings his father an axe as a gift from Eirík. When Skalla-Grím cuts the heads off two oxen with the axe, the edge of the axe breaks. Just before Thórólf returns to Norway, his father hands him the ruined axe with a comment in verse containing the words fox es illt i øxi ("there is evil deception in the axe"), which is intended to characterize the giver of the gift.

Like several other saga heroes, Egil matures early. At age three he composes his first skaldic stanzas and at age seven commits his first manslaughter. A few years later he slays his father's foreman to avenge a friend whom Kveld-Úlf has killed in a berserk rage. When only thirteen or fourteen years old, he persuades Thórólf to take him along to Norway.

Here Thórólf marries Ásgerd, whom he has taken to her parents on a previous voyage, and Egil wins the friendship of Ásgerd's cousin Arinbjörn. Egil loses no time in incurring the wrath of Gunnhild by killing her steward. This leads to further killings, and Thórólf and Egil must leave Norway to escape the queen's fury. After a viking expedition to the Baltic, they sail to England, where they lead King Athelstan's troops to victory over the rebellious Scots. Thórólf is slain in battle at Vínheid (Brunanburh). From this point on Egil dominates the story.

At the victory banquet, Egil is assigned the seat of honor opposite the king. He sits down and casts his shield before his feet.

He had his helmet on his head and laid his sword across his knees. He kept drawing his sword halfway out of the scabbard and thrusting it back in again. He sat upright, but his head was bowed. Egil had coarse features, bushy eyebrows, and an extremely thick nose. His long beard covered much of his face, and his chin and jawbone were terribly broad. His neck was so thick and his shoulders so wide that he stood out from all other men. His expression was harsh and grim when he was angry. He was of great stature, being taller than anyone else. His hair was gray and thick, but he became bald quite young. But as he sat there, as was written above, he alternately pulled one of his eyebrows down to his cheek and the other one up to his hairline. His eyes were black, and his eyebrows joined in the middle. He would not drink even though he had been served but continued to raise and lower his eyebrows. (chap. 55)

After observing Egil for a while, King Athelstan silently handed him a gold armband. Egil laid down his sword and put on the armband. His tortured features relaxed, and he began to drink with the others.

The king further gave Egil two chests of silver for his father and other kinsmen as compensation for Thórólf's death, but Egil never parted with this treasure. In this passage Snorri points up one of Egil's (and his own) besetting sins: avarice--an everrecurring theme in saga literature from Theodoricus until Gull-Þóris saga (Saga of Gold-Thórir, ca. 1400).

Egil sails to Norway, marries Ásgerd, and brings her back to Iceland. Upon learning of Björn's death, he returns to Norway to claim Ásgerd's patrimony. Only now do we realize the significance of the Björn-Thóra episode (chaps. 32-35): Berg-Önund, another son-in-law of Thórir, claims the entire inheritance for his wife Gunnhild on the questionable grounds that Thóra was not legally married to Björn at the time of Ásgerd's birth. With the help of his friend Arinbjörn, Egil appeals the case to the Gulathing, but the court is broken up at Queen Gunnhild's instigation. Before returning to Iceland, Egil kills Berg-Önund and Eirík's son Rögnvald and erects a scorn pole against the king and queen.

On the scorn pole, he carves runes imploring the gods and the guardian spirits of the land to drive Eirík and Gunnhild from Norway. Soon afterward the royal couple are forced to leave the country, and they go to England, where King Athelstan appoints Eirík

ruler over Northumbria. Magnus Olsen has shown that
stanzas 28 and 29 of the saga can both be transliter-
ated into seventy-two runes each and has therefore
concluded that these verses represent the inscription
carved on the scorn pole (11). This suggests that
Snorri rather than Egil composed the stanzas, since
they could not possibly have survived three centuries
of oral transmission intact.

Upon Egil's return to Iceland, his father asks him
for the silver entrusted to him by King Athelstan, but
Egil refuses the request with the comment that Skalla-
Grím has no need for the money. Shortly before his
death, Skalla-Grím secretly buries his own considerable treasure, which is never recovered. Egil takes
over the estate Borg but is restless and depressed, and
people attribute this to Queen Gunnhild's sorcery.

Egil sets out to visit his friend King Athelstan but
is blown off course and shipwrecked near York, the
residence of King Eirík. Arinbjörn, who has accompanied the royal couple into exile, persuades the king
to listen to a poem in his honor, which Egil, according
to the saga, composed during the course of a single
night. Eirík hears the poem and grants Egil permission to leave unharmed despite Gunnhild's shrill
insistence that he be killed. The poem is appropriate-
ly entitled Höfuðlausn (Head ransom). Arinbjörn
thanks the king and accompanies Egil to King Athelstan.

Hákon Adalsteinsfóstri ("foster son of Athelstan")
has succeeded his brother Eirík as king of Norway.
Egil again presses his claim to Ásgerd's patrimony,
and Hákon reluctantly accedes to Egil's demands
because of Egil's friendship with his foster father.
In two duels Egil kills a berserker named Ljót and
Berg-Önund's brother Atli. Again Snorri emphasizes
Egil's boundless cupidity. Ljot's wealth has been
legally confiscated as royal property. Egil, however,
importunes Arinbjörn to claim it for him from the
king. Arinbjörn reluctantly does so, but Hákon
furiously refuses his request. Thereupon Arinbjörn
offers to compensate Egil personally, and Egil, despite
his enormous wealth, accepts the money.

On his final visit to Norway, Egil magnanimously
undertakes a dangerous mission in place of Arinbjörn's
nephew Thorstein, whom King Hákon wishes to have slain
in retaliation for Arinbjörn's support of Hákon's
rival, Harald gráfeld: he collects overdue royal

taxes in Värmaland. On this expedition he cures a farmer's sick daughter with rune magic and single-handedly slays twenty-one assailants. After this super-human feat he retires to Iceland.

Following the death by drowning of his son Bödvar, Egil determines to starve himself to death but is persuaded by his daughter Thorgerd to compose a memorial poem for his drowned son:

Hard it is to stir my tongue and to draw forth song from the recesses of my heart. For sorrow oppres-ses: not happy is the man who bears his kinsman's corpse from his house. My kin have almost come to an end, like storm-lashed trees in the forest. . . . Rán [goddess of the sea] has bereaved me of much. Could I take vengeance with my sword, it would be the death of Ægir [Rán's husband]. But for this I have no strength; the old man's forlornness is clear as day. I have not been able to hold my head upright since the fever of sickness snatched away my other son. Still do I remember when Odin took the support of my clan up to the abode of the gods. I was on good terms with Odin and put my trust in him before the god of victory sundered our friendship. Reluctantly do I pay homage to him. Yet he has given me redress, a noble gift: the unfailing art of poetry and a heart that turns false friends into frank foes. Now I am sad. Yet I shall gladly await Hel [goddess of the underworld], ungrudging and serene of heart. (chap. 78)

"Egil gradually recovered strength as the poem progressed, and when it was finished, he recited it for Ásgerd and Thorgerd and his household. Then he got out of his bed and once more took his place in the high seat. He called his poem Sonatorrek" (12). Sonator-rek (Loss of sons) is an intensely personal poem. It is less a memorial to Bödvar, however, than an expres-sion of the poet's grief and rage and pride in his poetic art. This poem is followed in the same chapter by the first stanza of a drápa for Arinbjörn and a discussion of poetry, interspersed with occasional stanzas, between Egil and a young poet named Einar. In one of these stanzas, Egil boasts of once having slain eight and twice eleven assailants single-handedly.

In contrast to the introduction, the final chapters

lack cohesion--perhaps, as Andersson has surmised, because the author was handicapped by a plethora of information about his hero (13). The aging viking's sole feat in Iceland is his high-handed arbitration of a dispute between his son Thorstein and a neighbor. Blind and infirm, he is teased and tormented by the maidservants. Dissuaded from his plan to scatter the silver entrusted to him by Athelstan at the National Assembly for the purpose of embroiling the chieftains in confusion and conflict, he secretly buries his treasure shortly before his death, as Skalla-Grím has done.

Egil's son Thorstein, for whom the viking-poet had little affection, resembles his uncle Thórólf in appearance and temperament. Thorstein submits to baptism, has a church built at Borg, and dies of old age. But the conflict between the descendants of Harald Fairhair and Kveld-Úlf has not quite run its course. Thorstein's son Skúli takes over the estate at Borg, but only after serving as Earl Eirík's forecastle-man in the battle in which Olaf Tryggvason is killed.

Laxdæla saga

Like Egils saga, the "story of the people of the Laxárdal" begins at the time when Harald Fairhair is extending his dominion over the whole of Norway, and the picture of the king is similar in both sagas. The introduction is equally long in both works, although considerably more intricate in Laxdæla. Greed for money and power, which motivated most of Egil's deeds and misdeeds, is also a major theme in this work. Otherwise the two stories are very dissimilar. Laxdæla relates the story of a family, the descendants of Ketil flatnef, for several generations. Whereas Snorri derived much of his information from skaldic poetry and konungasögur, the anonymous author of Laxdæla derived his inspiration from Eddic lays, from a wide variety of sagas and chronicles, and from current events (14).

The nucleus of the story is the love triangle involving Kjartan Olafsson, his cousin and foster brother Bolli Thorleiksson, and Gudrún Osvifrsdóttir, all of them descendants of Ketil. W. P. Ker characterized this story as "a modern prose version of the Niblung tragedy, with the personages chosen from the life of

Iceland in the heroic age, and from the Icelandic traditions" (15). The question that formerly occupied students of this saga is to what degree the author was
indebted to Eddic poetry on the one hand and to oral
traditions on the other. Einar Ólafur Sveinsson represented what might be called the older conservative
view. According to him, the nucleus of the story
existed as a coherent oral tale, and "the events as
they occurred were seen in the light of the heroic
lays" (16). What little information we have about the
historical personages whose names are borne by the saga
characters suggests, however, that many of the crucial
events of the story could not have happened as there
described. A. Margaret A. Madelung demonstrated in her
literary analysis of Laxdæla that the work is "of
one piece." Heinrich Beck has recently shown that the
Niflung tragedy provided a design that embraces not
just the nucleus but the entire saga. And Rolf Heller
has furnished cogent evidence that Laxdæla is an
artistic creation of the thirteenth century (17).

On a trading voyage to Norway, Kjartan's grandfather
Höskuld buys a slave named Melkorka, who pretends to
be mute. One day Höskuld overhears her speaking to
their son Ólaf pái ("Peacock") in Irish. She now
reveals that she is an Irish princess and some years
later sends Ólaf to visit her father Mýrkjartan. Off
the coast of Ireland, the ship runs aground, and a band
of hostile natives approach and demand ship and cargo
as stranded goods. At this point, the author describes
the young hero. "Ólaf walked forward to the prow, and
he was dressed thus. He wore a coat of mail and had a
gilded helmet on his head. He was girded with a sword,
and the guard and pommel were adorned with gold, and in
his hand he carried a barbed spear, chased and finely
inlaid. He held a red shield before him, on which a
lion was traced in gold" (chap. 21).

Mýrkjartan chooses Ólaf over his own sons to succeed him, but Ólaf wisely declines the honor, declaring it better to have "brief honor than lasting shame."
In Norway he is welcomed warmly by King Harald
gráfeld and even more warmly by Gunnhild, who offer
him any office he wishes if he will remain at the
Norwegian court. But Ólaf insists he must return to
his "noble kinsmen" in Iceland, and in parting the king
gives him a merchant ship. Upon his return to Iceland
with precious gifts from two kings, Ólaf marries

Thorgerd Egilsdóttir, to whom, according to _Egils saga_, we are indebted for the poem _Sonatorrek_. Their son is Kjartan, the central figure of the story. On his deathbed Höskuld tricks his legitimate sons into agreeing to a large inheritance for Olaf. In order to placate his enraged brother Thorleik, Olaf offers to foster Thorleik's son Bolli. Thus Kjartan and Bolli grow up together and become inseparable companions. Both are tall, handsome, strong, and dexterous, but Bolli is described as "second only to Kjartan in all skills and accomplishments" (chap. 28).

Like other saga writers, the "_Laxdæla_ artist" (Heusler) employed foreshadowing to strengthen the cohesion of his story, to maintain suspense, and to create the illusion that the fate of the major characters was inevitable. When still unmarried Gudrún has four dreams, which the sage Gest interprets as predictions of her four marriages. Gest further foretells the slaying of Kjartan by Bolli and the death and burial of himself and his friend Osvíf. When Kjartan begins to visit Gudrún at her home at Laugar, Olaf has forebodings that their friendship will not bring good luck to them or their families. Kjartan does not share his father's pessimism. "Kjartan continued his visits in his usual way, and Bolli went with him" (chap. 39).

Before going abroad, Kjartan asks Gudrún to remain unmarried for three years, but Gudrún refuses, declaring that his decision to leave the country is rash. In Norway Kjartan competes with Olaf Tryggvason in an aquatic contest, which the king barely wins. The role played and the lines spoken by Hallfred vandræðaskáld in Odd's biography (chap. 40) are here assigned to Bolli (chap. 39). The king, depicted in this story as benign and benevolent, patiently persuades Kjartan to submit to baptism (after he has threatened to burn Olaf in his hall), and Bolli and the crew follow his example. When the ban on sailing to Iceland pending acceptance of Christianity by the General Assembly is lifted, Bolli returns home, but Kjartan remains for another year at the Norwegian court. Bolli convinces Gudrún that Kjartan plans to marry the king's sister Ingibjörg and with the support of her kinsman persuades her to marry him. This episode seems to have been influenced by _Bjarnar saga_.

Upon returning to Norway, Kjartan marries a woman

named Hrefna. Gudrún's love for him turns to jealousy and hatred. Olaf's forebodings are fulfilled. Insults are exchanged between the two families. Kjartan bluntly refuses Bolli's gift of a stud of beautiful horses. At Gudrún's instigation, Kjartan's sword, the gift of Mýrkjartan, and Hrefna's precious headdress, a gift from Ingibjörg originally intended for Gudrún, are stolen. Kjartan retaliates by forcing the cancellation of a land sale to Bolli and by besieging the house at Laugar for three days to prevent the inhabitants from using the outdoor privies.

Like Brynhild in the Niflung tragedy and Sigríd the Haughty in Óláfs saga Tryggvasonar, Gudrún now demands that her husband kill her former lover or else lose her favor. Bolli reluctantly accompanies Gudrún's brothers to ambush Kjartan but remains aloof from the fighting as long as possible. When Bolli finally makes his attack, Kjartan throws away his sword with the crushing words, "It is truly a dastardly deed, kinsman, that you are about to do, but I think it far better to receive death from you, kinsman, than to give it to you" (chap. 49). Without speaking a word, Bolli deals Kjartan his death blow, and he holds him in his arms as he dies.

When Bolli arrived at Laugar, Gudrún asked him what time it was, and Bolli replied that it was about three o'clock (nón).

> Then Gudrún said, "Morning tasks are of different kinds. I have spun yarn for twelve ells of cloth, and you have killed Kjartan."
> Bolli replied, "That luckless deed would not soon leave my mind even if you did not remind me of it."
> Gudrún said, "I don't regard that as a luckless deed. It seemed to me that you enjoyed greater esteem the winter Kjartan was in Norway than now, when he has trodden you underfoot since he returned to Iceland. But last but not least, what seems best to me is that Hrefna will not be laughing when she goes to bed tonight."
> Then Bolli said, and he was very angry, "I think it unlikely that she will pale more than you at this news. And I suspect that you would have been less shocked if we were lying dead on the field and Kjartan had brought you the news."
> Gudrún now saw how angry Bolli was and said,

"Don't say such things, for I am very grateful to
you for the deed. I feel certain now that you will
not do anything to displease me." (chap. 49)

Ólaf protected Bolli as long as he lived, but after
his death Bolli was killed. In due course, counterven-
geance was taken by his son Bolli Bollason, so named
because he was born after his father's death. Gudrún
became a nun, and when she was quite old, her son
Bolli asked her which man she had loved the most.
Gudrún tried to evade the question by listing the good
qualities of three of her former husbands but at last
had to admit, "I was worst to him I loved the most."
This classical quotation from the sagas is "a paradoxi-
cally pointed formulation of tragic human experience"
(18).
Turville-Petre characterized Laxdæla saga as "in
some ways, the richest" of all the Íslendinga
sögur, and Andersson commented on the "generosity" of
both narrative and personal dimension (19). The
language is fuller than that of many sagas, and the
author took pains to describe and explain emotions. He
made skillful use of antithesis and parallelism. Until
recently, strong lexical and stylistic influence from
the riddarasögur has been assumed, but Rolf Heller
has demonstrated that earlier konungasögur were the
chief models for Laxdæla. Although we find no
demonic, superhuman vikings here, the characters are
larger than life, and they stride majestically through
the pages of the book. The men characters are somewhat
overdrawn in that their descriptions sometimes are more
impressive than their deeds. The women characters,
however, are superb, from the matriarchal Unn (Aud) the
Deepminded to Gudrún. Enigmatic, imperious,
passionate, Gudrún is one of the most fascinating
women in saga literature.
More than any other saga writer, the Laxdæla
artist had an eye for visual beauty, for pomp and
pageantry. His description of Bolli Bollason upon his
return from Constantinople, where he had served in the
emperor's bodyguard, may serve as one example for many:

He was dressed in clothing made of silk wrought with
gold, which the king of Miklagard [Constantinople]
had given him, and over this he had a scarlet cloak
with a hood. He was girded with the sword Fótbít
["Leg-biter"], of which the guard and pommel were

inlaid with gold and the hilt bound with gold. He wore a gilded helmet on his head, and at his side he carried a red shield adorned with a knight inlaid in gold. In his hand he carried a lance of a kind that is popular abroad, and wherever he and his followers took lodging, the women paid heed to nothing else but to gaze at Bolli and at the finery of himself and his men. With such courtly splendor Bolli rode through the countryside with his retinue until he came to Helgafell. Gudrún was very happy to see her son Bolli. (chap. 77)

Laxdæla has been ascribed to various men including Sturla Thórdarson, Ólaf Thórdarson, and Snorri Sturluson (20). Snorri must be eliminated on lexical and stylistic grounds. Whoever the author was, it is certain that he was a member or a close acquaintance of the Sturlung family (21).

Eyrbyggja saga

Like the author of Laxdæla, the compiler of Eyrbyggja made use of a wide variety of sources including thirty-four skaldic stanzas. In general he summarized, and sometimes corrected, pertinent matter that had already been treated in detail elsewhere. A typical example is his three-line reference to Víga-Styr's burial: "Snorri godi had gone south to that place for the body. At Hrossholt he had to restrain Styr in the women's workroom after Styr had sat up and seized the farmer's daughter about the waist" (chap. 49). Two notable exceptions are the story of Víga-Styr's slaying of the berserkers, which he improved upon, and an episode from Gísla saga, which he augmented in such a way as to anticipate the future dominant role of Snorri the Chieftain (chaps. 13-15) (22).

The initial chapters of Eyrbyggja are a chronicle of the settlement of the peninsula Snæfellsnes; the remainder of the story is a biography of Snorri. Unlike the Laxdæla artist, the author of Eyrbyggja was an antiquarian with a predilection for ghost stories, one of which inspired Robert Louis Stevenson's "Waif Woman." His description of a pagan temple and pagan worship (chap. 4), adapted from Snorri Sturluson's Hákonar saga góða (Saga of Hákon the Good, chap. 14), is so convincing that it was long regarded as authentic (23).

Structurally, Eyrbyggja is so intricate that the
reader is obliged to leaf backward and forward repeatedly in order to appreciate the significance and relationship of the seemingly disjointed episodes. Individual
scenes are vivid, the dialogue is pithy, and the character delineation masterful. The action is briskly
narrated, but in expository passages the author tends
to employ complex and compound-complex periods. The
author was fond of litotes and ironic understatement.
In the first chapter, for example, Harald Fairhair sent
Ketil flatnef out to rid the Hebrides of vikings.
Instead, he made himself master of those islands and
sent the crew back to the king. They reported this,
"but they did not say that they had observed that he
was furthering the power of King Harald in those
parts." Like all the major sagas, Eyrbyggja was
probably designed primarily for private rather than for
public reading (24).

The precise topographical descriptions, the realistic portrayal of individuals, and the sober relation of
events--even supernatural ones--combine to create the
impression that the author intended his work to be
accepted as history. In contrast to the portraits of
the invincible superman Egil and the courtly fashion
plate Bolli Bollason, the picture of Snorri has a
semblance of probability. This description is part of
the Helgafell episode, in which Snorri tricks his stepfather into selling him the estate Helgafell at a
ridiculously low price.

> Snorri was a man of average height and rather
> slender. He was of handsome appearance, with regu-
> lar features, a fair complexion, blond hair, and a
> red beard. He was usually of an even disposition.
> It was not easy to detect whether something pleased
> or displeased him. He was a shrewd man and foresee-
> ing in many things. To his friends he gave good
> counsel, but his enemies rather thought they felt
> the coldness of his counsels. He now had the
> custody of the temple and was therefore called
> Snorri godi. He became a great chieftain but was
> rather envied for his prestige since there were many
> who felt they were not inferior to him as to birth
> and believed they were better men in regard to
> strength and proven hardihood. (chap. 15)

This introductory picture satisfies our curiosity about

Snorri's appearance and prepares us for the manner in which he will conduct himself in future clashes with his peers.

Snorri's first major contest is with a chieftain named Arnkel. In a series of lawsuits brought about by quarrels between kinsmen and followers of the two chieftains, Arnkel usually had the upper hand. The feud between Snorri and Arnkel receives added significance through the injection of the father-son conflict (25). Arnkel's father Thórólf, an avaricious, unregenerate viking, commits a series of outrages against his neighbor Úlfar, for which Arnkel exacts compensation. When Thórólf incites his slaves to kill Úlfar, Arnkel has them intercepted and hanged. Thórólf thereupon bribes Snorri with the gift of a wooded tract to prosecute Arnkel, but the outcome of the trial is unsatisfactory to both sides. Thórólf has Úlfar slain, and this involves Arnkel in disputes about Úlfar's property. Thórólf now tries without success to enlist his son's aid in the recovery of his forest land from Snorri. Thórólf dies of rage and frustration, and his evil spirit haunts the region until near the end of the saga. Finally Snorri has to have Arnkel slain in order to maintain his prestige among his followers.

Arnkel's necrology clearly reveals the author's sympathies: "His death was lamented by all, for he was in every respect one of the best and wisest men in the ancient faith. He was composed, stouthearted, and as daring as anyone; determined, yet with a good hold on himself. He was generally successful in litigation with whomsoever he contended. For this reason he provoked envy, as was shown here" (chap. 37).

A less serious conflict, which is related in rather widely separated segments, involves Snorri's sister Thuríd. Because she is both attractive and flirtatious, Snorri marries her to a wealthy farmer named Thórodd. As soon as Thúrid comes to her new home at Fródá, Björn Breidvíkingakappi ("Champion of the people of Breidavík") begins to pay regular visits there, "and the general opinion was that there was some dalliance between him and Thuríd" (chap. 29). Thórodd and four other men set an ambush for Björn, but he kills two of them and puts the rest to flight. Sentenced to banishment for three years, Björn joins the Jómsvikings. Thuríd gives birth to a boy and names him Kjartan. Upon returning to Iceland, Björn resumes his relationship with Thuríd. To end this disgrace to Thórodd and himself, Snorri sets out with a band of followers to kill Björn.

As Snorri rides across Björn's hay meadow, Björn seizes him by the cloak and holds a knife against his chest. Snorri is thus obliged to offer Björn a truce, and Björn agrees to leave the country. He takes passage with a ship that is never heard of again. Many years later, shortly after Thórólf's spirit has committed its final atrocity, an Icelandic ship is wrecked off the coast of a strange country, and the crew are threatened with death or enslavement by the hostile natives. They are rescued through the intervention of a white-haired man who has their ship repaired and sees them off with gifts of a sword for Kjartan and a gold ring for Thuríd. When asked by the Icelanders who they shall say sent the precious gifts, the white-haired man replies, "Say that he sent them who was a better friend to the mistress of the house at Fródá than to her brother, the godi at Helgafell" (chap. 64).

Snorri survives his numerous feuds by outmaneuvering his adversaries and by never letting his henchmen kill to excess. His greatest virtue is the one most highly esteemed by saga writers: hóf, that is, moderation. Snorri dies of natural causes at the age of sixty-five, but his biography tells us nothing about him for the last two decades of his life. It has been suggested that the author omitted his later exploits because they had been related in Laxdæla saga. This seems to be a reasonable suggestion, but the debate on the relative dates of composition of these two sagas continues (26). Jan de Vries was doubtless correct--and this is one of his most perceptive observations on saga literature--in interpreting Eyrbyggja as an exemplum for the age of excess, the Sturlung Age (27). The author is believed to have been a monk in the Benedictine monastery that was moved from the island Flatey to Helgafell in 1184. Here the author would have had access to written sources as well as to skaldic poems and anecdotes about Snorri and other characters in his story. The historical Snorri died in 1031. His daughter Thuríd was one of Ari Thorgilsson's most highly esteemed informants (28).

Brennu-Njáls saga

Brennu-Njáls saga (The story of Njál of the burning) is the longest, the most profound, and the most powerful of the Íslendinga sögur. It is a trilogy with a preface of twenty chapters in which the author introduces several main characters and adumbrates one of the major conflicts of the saga. The first part is the story of a remarkable friendship between Njál, a wise and gentle, albeit devious, lawyer who has never wielded weapons, and Gunnar, a formidable warrior who is reluctant to kill. This story ends with the slaying of Gunnar in a heroic stand against an overwhelming number of assailants. The second part relates the conflict between Njál's sons and Thráin Sigfússon and Njál's constant but vain endeavor to make and preserve peace following Thráin's slaying. This story culminates in the death by burning of Njál and his family in their home. The final part of the saga relates the relentless quest of Njál's son-in-law Kári for vengeance against the burners and concludes with a reconciliation between Kári and Flosi, the leader of the burners.

A century ago A. U. Bååth declared that the author of Njála had the final words of his saga in mind before he set the first ones down on parchment (29). This coherence and tightness of composition were achieved through the structural device of complex plot interlace and the rhetorical technique of foreshadowing, which is employed with greater skill, variety, and density in Njála than in any other saga. Dreams, visions, warnings, predictions, premonitions, omens, portents, taunts and introductory character sketches are artfully used to anticipate the future, heighten suspense, and connect widely separated events.

In the first chapter, for example, Hallgerd is introduced as a tall, beautiful child with long, silken hair. When her father Höskuld asks his brother Hrút whether he does not think she is beautiful, he replies, "That girl is beautiful enough, and many will suffer because of it. But I cannot understand how thief's eyes have come into our family." In chapter 48, Hallgerd sends a slave to steal cheese from a neighbor, and the ensuing feud eventually leads to her husband Gunnar's destruction. Hallgerd's first two husbands were killed by her foster father for slapping her face. When Gunnar slaps her for instigating this theft, she says that she will remember the slap and repay it if possible. During Gunnar's last stand—he is in his

home at Hlídarendi with Hallgerd and his mother
Rannveig--his bowstring is cut asunder.

> He said to Hallgerd, "Let me have two strands of
> your hair, and you and mother twist them into a
> bowstring for me."
> "Does it mean something to you?" she asked.
> "It means my life," he said, "for they will never
> overcome me as long as I can use my bow."
> "In that case," she said, "I shall remind you of
> the slap on the cheek. I do not care at all how
> long you hold out."
> "Each earns fame in his own way," said Gunnar.
> "You will not be asked again."
> Rannveig said, "Your behavior is evil, and your
> shame will long endure." (chap. 77)

No less remarkable than the tight structure and complex texture of Njála are the memorable characters
the author has created. Einar Ólafur Sveinsson
devoted over two-thirds of his monograph on this saga
to a discussion of these fascinating men and women and
to an analysis of the author's techniques of character
delineation and development (30). A few of the characters are painted in black and white, but most of them
are complex, being portrayed in various shades of gray.

More than most saga writers, the author of Njála
expressed his own opinion of his characters through the
technique of having one individual pass judgment on the
behavior of another. After Gunnar has slain a man
named Thorgeir Otkelsson, Njál succeeds in bringing
about an arbitration, according to which Gunnar and his
brother Kolskegg agree to go abroad for three years.
When at the last minute Gunnar unexpectedly decides to
remain in Iceland and urges Kolskegg to do likewise,
his loyal brother declares, "I shall not act basely
(níðast) in this or in any other matter in which
people trust me" (chap. 75). Kolskegg goes abroad,
never to return; Gunnar rides home to Hlídarendi, thus
giving Hallgerd the opportunity of repaying him for the
slap on her cheek.

It is not surprising that a work of such magnitude
as Njáls saga should have been subjected to differ-
ing interpretations. An older generation of scholars
believed firmly in its historical veracity, and some
went so far as to declare Ari Thorgilsson in error when
his sober recording of facts differed from the literary

treatment of them in the saga (31). It is clear that the author made use of historical sources. In Landná-mabók we read that a man named Njál was burned to death with seven other persons in his home at Bergthórshvol, and there is archaeological evidence to support this statement. Landnámabók also records Gunnar's death at Hlídarendi as well as a fight between Gunnar and some farmers at Knafahólar and Gunnar's killing of two enemies named Otkel and Skammkel (32). A surprisingly large number of major characters, however, are not mentioned in historical sources, and some of them, at least, must be regarded as fictitious.

A comparison of the sparse historical records with the treatment of them in Njála is revealing. The historical Njál appears to have been an obscure farmer whose name was remembered only because of the horrible manner of his death. The author of Njála imaginatively embellished the meager historical account of this event with details borrowed from descriptions of burnings recorded in Sturlunga saga. In the skirmish at Knafahólar, Gunnar and his band (lið) killed an Icelander and two Norwegians, and Gunnar's brother Hjört and a manservant were slain. From this event, the author created three fights, in which Gunnar himself dispatched over twenty men. In his final battle, Gunnar was aided by another man; in the saga, he has to fight unaided, as is proper for saga heroes. It is obvious that the author dealt freely with his materials for the purpose of expanding the dimensions of his heroes, and some readers will doubtless feel that he went too far in this. Even greater distortion is found in his treatment of Skapti Thóroddsson. We recall that Skapti around 1005 improved the constitution by establishing the appellate court known as the fimmtardómr and making it difficult for chieftains to blame their crimes on henchmen. In the saga, credit for this is given to Njál, and Skapti is denigrated and degraded into a ridiculous figure who is taunted at the General Assembly. By contrast, Gudmund the Mighty, who appears in a dubious light in the earlier works, is portrayed very favorably in Njála (33).

More recently there has been a tendency to regard Njáls saga as a roman à clef, in which the author thinly disguised contemporary happenings and prominent persons, including himself (34). Certain events and individuals in Njála, it is true, have close corres-

pondences in Sturlunga saga, and the author did de-
rive inspiration and information from that history.
Furthermore, the significance of the saga for contemporary times was so great that, according to Heusler,
copies were made of it before the author had had time
to eliminate minor errors in a final revision (35).
The careful development of two central themes in the
work, however, indicates that Njála is much more
than a mere literary reflection of the contemporary
scene.

There is better reason to interpret Njáls saga as
a homily as, among others, Magnus Magnusson and Hermann
Pálsson have done (36). In the first part of the saga
(chaps. 21-81), which takes place during pagan times,
there is much talk about fate and honor. Early in the
second part (chaps. 82-132), the author inserted a
digression in the form of a detailed description of the
conversion (chaps. 100-105), after which the pagan
concept of fate, at least in Njál's mind, is transformed into the Christian belief in providence. Three
years after the conversion, Ámundi the Blind, illegitimate son of Höskuld Njálsson, miraculously has his
sight restored long enough to wreak vengeance on his
father's slayer (chap. 106). We are reminded of the
skaldic stanza by Earl Rögnvald about the slaughter of
Saracens in Orkneyinga saga ("This was God's doing")
and of the prophet Samuel's anointment of King
Sverrir's hands for hatred against his enemies.

A deeper understanding of Christianity is demonstrated by Njál's foster son Höskuld. After the killing
of Thráin by Njál's sons to avenge indignities suffered because of him in Norway, Njál fosters Thráin's
son Höskuld in the hope of averting further killing.
When Höskuld is fully grown, the villain Mörd, who
plotted Gunnar's death, through insidious slander
convinces Njál's sons and Kári that Höskuld intends
to kill them all in vengeance for Thráin's death. As
Höskuld goes out to sow grain on a spring morning,
they attack him from ambush. Without attempting to
strike back, Höskuld sinks to his knees with these
words on his lips, "May God help me and forgive you."
"This was the only thing," the author tells us, "that
grieved Njál so deeply that he could never speak about
it without being moved to tears" (chap. 111). These
words are an echo of a passage in Snorri's Prose Edda
describing the grief of the gods, and especially of
Óðin, at the slaying of the innocent god Baldur (37).

Njál, who has long known the manner of his own
death (chap. 55), now reveals that Höskuld's slaying will bring disaster to his wife and their sons
as well, and Flosi ominously declares that "seeds
of evil have been sown, and they will yield evil"
(chap. 115). Höskuld's widow Hildigunn implores
her uncle Flosi in the name of his Christ to exact
blood vengeance for her husband or else be called a
"vile wretch (níðingr) by all men" (chap. 117).
From this point on, the author presents a crescendo
of pagan portents interspersed with Christian
sentiments until the tragedy reaches its climax.
When all efforts at arbitration fail, Flosi rides
to Bergthórshvol with 120 followers. Despite the
fact that Njál's people can hold them off out of
doors, Njál insists that they enter the house.
Reluctantly, Flosi orders the building to be set on
fire, "for this," he says, "is a great responsibility
before God, since we are Christian men ourselves"
(chap. 128).

Soon the roof is ablaze, and Njál consoles the
frightened women: "Take heart and speak no words of
despair, for this will be only a brief storm, and it
will be long before another one like it comes. Have
faith in God's mercy, for he will not let us burn in
both this world and the next" (chap. 129). The reason
for Njál's insistence that his people enter the house
is now clear: inexorable pagan fate in his mind has
been transformed into benign Christian providence, and
he regards the destruction of himself and his family as
an act of penance for the slaying of his spiritual son
Höskuld (38).

The women, children, and servants are now permitted
to leave the house. Flosi, who feels obligated to kill
only Njál's sons and Kári, begs Njál and his wife
Bergthóra to come out also. Njál refuses because, he
says, he is too old to avenge his sons and unwilling to
live in shame for not doing so. Bergthóra, who has
often been strong-willed and abrasive, replies to Flosi
with quiet dignity, "I was married to Njál when young.
I promised him that we should endure the same fate."
They lie down, cross themselves, commend their souls to
God, and calmly await death. After the fires have died
down, it is found that their son Skarphédin, the
fiercest of warriors, has burned two marks of the cross
on his body, and Hjalti Skeggjason declares that
Njál's countenance and body "have a radiance such as I

have never seen before on a dead man's body" (chap. 132). All present agree that that is so.

The prosecution of the burners ends in a mistrial, and a bloody battle breaks out at the General Assembly. With the help of several other chieftains, Snorri godi separates the two sides and later initiates arbitration. The turning point in the bitter wrangling comes when Hall of Sída, whose son Ljót was killed in the fighting, in a spirit of Christian humility and magnanimity foregoes compensation for his son and yet pledges peace to his adversaries. Heavy fines are imposed on Flosi and all the other burners, and they are ordered to leave the country, some for three years and some for life. Kári, who alone has escaped alive from the burning, excludes himself from the settlement and launches a fearful campaign of vengeance, during which he kills twenty of Flosi's men, the last one in Wales. Flosi makes no attempt to retaliate.

At this point the author inserted a second digression into his story. In the Battle of Clontarf, which is fought on Good Friday, fourteen of Flosi's remaining fifteen followers are killed while fighting against the Christian King Brján of Ireland. Although the king himself is slain, his army is victorious. This dramatic interlude, preceded by portents and attended by marvels, is one of the finest examples of the medieval digression ad aliud extra materiam, that is, to something outside the story proper (39). Just as the conversion episode marked the beginning of the conflict between paganism and Christianity, the Battle of Clontarf signifies its conclusion (40).

The second theme in Njáls saga is stated by Njál himself in the form of a well-known proverb: "With laws shall our land be built up, but with lawlessness laid waste" (chap. 70) (41). The author, who probably completed his book about 1290, had lived to see Njál's prophecy fulfilled. The barbarous cruelty and the disregard for and subversion of the law during the Sturlung Age doubtless whetted his curiosity about legal problems and procedures. From a lawbook, he filled page after page with minute descriptions of intricate legal moves and countermoves. Occasionally he was so intent on copying legal formulae correctly that he failed to substitute the names of his characters for the name Jón (that is, N.N.) in the codex (see chap. 141). Despite all the legalistic rigamarole, however, not one lawsuit is carried to a successful conclusion in this saga. Settlement of quarrels is usually achieved by extralegal means through arbitration, but powerful individuals thwart such settlements by refusing to abide by the terms imposed (Gunnar) or by excluding themselves from the agreement (Kári). Ironically the prosecution of the burners fails in the appellate court established (according to the story) by Njál himself, the wisest lawyer of his day (for the purpose of securing a chieftaincy for his foster son Höskuld in order to facilitate Höskuld's marriage to Hildigunn). The second theme of Njáls saga can thus be defined as an indictment of the legal system of medieval Iceland and a condemnation of the ruthless men who subverted it for selfish reasons.

Gunnar lived and died by the sword in accordance with the pagan heroic code of his day. Njál failed because he relied entirely on his own finite wisdom and on his cleverness in manipulating the law. As in Heiðarvíga saga, final reconciliation in Njála can be achieved only through the practical application of Christian ethics. Just as he skillfully brought together the many strands of his convoluted plot, the author of Njála thus neatly combined the two main themes of his story. After receiving absolution of their sins in Rome, Kári and Flosi too are reconciled. The reconciliation is sealed and symbolized by a marriage between Kári and Hildigunn.

From a cursory reading of Njála, we might gain the impression that the author was trying to imitate the simple language of oral tales. His style is more lucid and fluent than that of most sagas, but its cadences and nuances, as Einar Ólafur Sveinsson has emphasized, are not those of everyday speech (42). Unfortunately, the simple but sophisticated language of Njála cannot be reproduced in English because of its inflexible word order. The style of Njála can be approximated in German, but some Icelanders feel that only Latin is adequate for the satisfactory translation of this and other sagas.

Grettis saga Ásmundarsonar

The "saga of Grettir, son of Ásmund," is believed to have been composed about 1320. This approximate date is supported by a statement in the work itself

about a spearhead lost by Grettir: "The spear that
Grettir had lost was not found until within the memory
of persons still alive. This spear was found in the
latter days of Lawman Sturla Thórdarson in the bog in
which Thjorbjörn was killed and is now called
Spjótsmýr ["Spear Bog"]. And people regard that as
evidence that Thorbjörn was killed there, although it
is stated in some sources that he was killed at
Midfitjar" (chap. 49).

Grettis saga has long been associated with Sturla
Thórdarson (d. 1280). Árni Magnússon (d. 1730), the
great collector of old Icelandic manuscripts, recalled
reading a fragment of Sturla's "saga," and Sigurður
Nordal has adduced further evidence that the original
Grettis saga was composed by Sturla (43). The fact
that Sturla was a friend of Priest Halldór Oddsson, a
descendant of Grettir's sister Rannveig, would thus
help to account for the unusually large number of what
seem to be genuine traditions in this late work as well
as for Sturla's omission from his Landnámabók of
the statement by Styrmir the Learned, retained by Sir
Hauk, that the historical Grettir had murdered Orm, the
son of Thórir of Gard (44).

Grettla consists of a prologue (chaps. 1-13), the
biography of the hero (chaps. 14-91), an epilogue
(chaps. 86-92), and a concluding statement attributed
to Sturla (chap. 93). The prologue is an imaginative
chronicle of Grettir's ancestors spun from Sturla's
Landnámabók. Its dual purpose is to relate the
story to Norwegian and Icelandic history and to make
the hero more credible to readers (45). The main part
of the story is based on a wide variety of written
sources, about half of which are cited. The epilogue
is a concoction of motifs from Tristrams saga, a
story about King Harald the Harsh in Morkinskinna,
and the Disciplina clericalis (46). The conclusion
derives from some piece of writing by Sturla, whether
or not it was actually a saga, as Árni Magnússon
believed.

The theme of Grettis saga is the progressive isola-
tion of the individual from society, the tragedy of a
romantic hero in a postromantic, unheroic world. As in
the Helgisaga, the tragedy is foreshadowed through
the reversal of roles in the generation-gap theme.
Like Saint Ólaf, Grettir considers normal tasks
assigned to him by his father dull and demeaning.

Whereas Ólaf (and Grettir's male ancestors) found opportunities to prove their mettle in viking expeditions, however, Grettir is frustrated by the lack of challenge to his strength and bravery in the constrictive society of Iceland.

At the age of sixteen, Grettir is exiled for three years for the slaying of a young shepherd--his only unprovoked killing. In Norway he begins his career of performing services to society that bring him fame and misfortune. He opens a grave mound, protects his host's wife by killing twelve berserkers, and rids the countryside of a ravaging bear. This exploit, however, leads to friction between Grettir and a man named Björn ("bear"). Grettir is forced to kill Björn, his two brothers, and their followers, and for these killings, he is banished from Norway. The two banishments adumbrate his later outlawry for life.

In a significant interlude in Iceland, Grettir volunteers to accompany Bardi Gudmundarson on his expedition to avenge his brother, but the sage Thórarin advises against it because of Grettir's choleric temperament. Grettir returns to his home at Bjarg. "He thought it a great hindrance that he could nowhere test his strength, and he inquired if there might not be something that he could grapple with" (chap. 31). He soon learns about Glám, a pagan revenant that has killed a shepherd and driven people and livestock mad. Grettir's uncle Jökul tries to dissuade him from challenging the monster, and when Grettir insists on doing so, utters the prophetic words: "Good fortune and great deeds are two different things" (chap. 34).

The battle between Grettir and Glám is one of the most vivid and memorable passages in saga literature. Glám drags Grettir out of the building, and Grettir succeeds in throwing him down on his back. "Outside there was bright moonlight, and there were heavy clouds with rifts in them. Sometimes they covered the moon and sometimes they cleared away. At the moment when Glám fell, the clouds cleared away, and Glám glared upward. Grettir said that this was the only sight he had ever seen that frightened him" (chap. 35). Grettir slays the monster, but Glám puts a curse on him: from this time on all Grettir's accomplishments will bring him misfortune, and he will live in constant fear of the dark. Grettir's temper worsens, he finds it more difficult not to flare up at the slightest offense, and he is plagued by phantoms after nightfall.

Upon hearing that Saint Olaf welcomes men of great accomplishments, Grettir travels to Norway in the hope of taking service with him. The merchant ship is driven ashore in a storm, and Grettir swims a sound in order to fetch fire for his freezing shipmates. On the following morning, it is seen that the house from which he brought the fire has burned to the ground. Grettir proceeds to the court of Saint Olaf, only to find that the merchants have spread the malicious rumor that he deliberately burned the house and all its occupants, including two sons of Thórir of Gardar. Grettir volunteers to clear himself of the charge through the ordeal of the hot iron, but he strikes a boy (later called an evil spirit) for taunting him in church. Because of this, Saint Olaf declares Grettir to be a man of great misfortune, calls off the ordeal, and orders him to return to Iceland the following summer.

Grettir spends the winter with his half-brother Thorstein. One morning Thorstein expresses admiration for Grettir's muscular arms, and Grettir declares that Thorstein's slender arms can be no stronger than a woman's. Thorstein admits that this may be true, but predicts that they will avenge Grettir's death "or else you will never be avenged" (chap. 41). In the spring they part in friendship, never to meet again.

Upon returning to Iceland, Grettir learns that his brother Atli has been slain and that he has been outlawed for life on the suspicion that he deliberately killed Thórir's two sons. Grettir avenges Atli's death and begins his outlawry. He is hounded from place to place for sixteen years. During this time, he has encounters with persons known from earlier sagas, including Gudmund the Mighty, Snorri godi, Björn the Hítadal Champion, and Lawspeaker Skapti. Skapti, who was reviled by the author of Njála, undergoes a complete and deliberate character restoration in Grettla, and Gudmund is almost as imposing in this story as in that one (47). It is Gudmund who directs Grettir to a safe refuge on the island Drangey off the north coast of Iceland. Some of these episodes, to be sure, have only a tenuous connection with the plot, but saga plots are secondary to character delineation. The episodes serve to reveal facets of Grettir's ofttimes puzzling character and to increase the dimensions of the story through allusion to other sagas--a technique apparently borrowed from <u>Njáls saga</u>.

Two of these episodes are of especial importance for the literary historian. The first relates Grettir's battle with a giantess and later on with a giant in a cave behind a waterfall. This is an analogue to Beowulf's battle with Grendel and her son, but the exact relationship between the two episodes is not clear (48).

The second is an erotic adventure between Grettir and a servant girl during his stay on Drangey. Grettir swims to the mainland to fetch fire—a comic parallel to the feat for which he was outlawed. Tired from the long swim, Grettir takes off his wet clothing and lies down to rest on the dais in an outbuilding. He falls asleep, and his cover slips to the floor. When the farmer's daughter and a maidservant come to the building, the maidservant makes disparaging remarks about Grettir, saying that he is big enough in the chest but small farther down. Grettir seizes her and pulls her up on the dais. "The maidservant shrieked loudly, but they finally parted in such a way that she had no complaint about Grettir" (chap. 75). This passage reveals influence from contemporary European farcical literature. According to R. J. Glendinning, the closest analogue is Boccaccio's story about Masetto and the nuns in the <u>Decameron</u> (day 3, tale 1) (49).

After three years on Drangey with his faithful brother Illugi and a lazy, cowardly slave as companions, Grettir is overcome and slain through pagan witchcraft. Because of this, his adversary, Thorbjörn öngul, is banished from Iceland. Like several other saga characters, Thorbjörn joins the Varangian guard in Constantinople.

Grettir's brother Thorstein now fulfills his own prophecy by following Thorbjörn and exacting blood vengeance. Thrown into a dungeon for this killing, Thorstein literally sings himself to freedom—and now we understand why his powerful voice was described in his introductory character sketch in chapter 13. Charmed by Thorstein's splendid singing, a wealthy townswoman named Spes (Latin for "hope") has him released and brought to her apartment. Accused of adultery by her feckless husband, Spes turns the tables on him through an ambiguous oath, declares herself divorced, and lays claim to all his possessions.

In Norway Thorstein and Spes live happily for many

years. Eventually they repent of their former frivoli-
ty. After providing for the care of their children and
giving much money to the church, they make a pilgrimage
to Rome, where they receive absolution and do penance
for their transgressions. There they live out their
lives in separate stone cells "so that they might
better enjoy eternal life together in the world to
come. . . . Most people said that in their judgment
Thorstein . . . and his wife Spes were regarded as
persons of the greatest good fortune" (chap. 92).

The character of Grettir is one of the most complicated in saga literature, partly because he plays contradictory roles. He is both a cruel, outrageous, and
sardonic trickster and a generous, benevolent, albeit
arrogant, hero. Kathryn Hume has pointed out a rather
consistent pattern in Grettir's behavior: a favorable
context seems to evoke the best in him, whereas an
incompatible one provokes his base qualities (50).

The only woman character described in detail and in
depth is Grettir's mother Ásdís. Even Thórir of
Gardar treats her with respect and consideration. The
author completes his touching picture of her by letting
her give dignified expression to her deep grief in her
farewell to her sons. She dreads the thought of letting her young son Illugi accompany Grettir to Drangey,
but does so in the hope that this will lessen Grettir's
distress. She has a foreboding that neither will leave
the island alive. Her final words are prophetic: "You
will be slain with weapons. I have had strange dreams.
Guard yourselves against witchcraft. Few things are
more powerful than heathenism" (chap. 69).

Most of the seventy-three skaldic stanzas quoted in
Grettis saga are demonstrably spurious. Of the two
genuine skaldic poems cited, five stanzas allude to
matters not related in the story (55-56 and 66-69).
Stylistically, Njála and Grettla are at opposite
poles. The author of Grettis saga favored complex
sentences with two or more dependent clauses and
compound-complex periods, many of them containing six
or more clauses.

Conclusion

The five major sagas have several features in
common. Their authors, who were well read, borrowed
freely from older sagas, Ari's Íslendingabók,

Landnáma, and various other medieval sources. These
sagas resemble Heimskringla in that they all have
stranded plots. The interweaving of plots is most
obvious in Eyrbyggja and most sophisticated in
Njála, in which as many as five synchronic plot
lines are intertwined. Digressions of various kinds
are also common to all of these sagas. Because of
their convolutions, the plots of these stories are
difficult to remember, but they all contain unforgettable vivid scenes and memorable complex characters.
The most effective rhetorical device is foreshadowing,
the most intricate and variegated forms of which are
found in Njáls saga. All five authors excel in
character portrayal and in the creation of finely honed
dialogue, and they all have a penchant for irony and
understatement. For the most part they maintain a
stance of neutrality and detachment, only occasionally
making subjective comments about characters and events.
   The authors of these stories, however, had widely
different predilections and pursued divergent goals.
The conflict between Norwegian kings and (Norwegian
and) Icelandic chieftains, for example, which is
central to Egils saga, is treated symbolically in the
aristocratic Laxdæla saga: Kjartan competes with
Ólaf Tryggvason in an aquatic contest, and Gudrún's
fourth husband, Thorkel, vies with Saint Ólaf in
church building. The conflict between paganism and
Christianity, which is virtually absent from Egils
saga, is a major theme in both Njála and Grettla.
Hóf (moderation and self-control), a virtue that is
foreign to Egil and Grettir, is embodied in Snorri godi
and in his opponent Arnkel, ideal chieftains who
restore and preserve peace in the countryside with a
minimum of force. The portraits of these two men are
symptomatic of Eyrbyggja: we find here little of the
exaggeration that is typical of character portrayal in
the other four sagas.
   Stylistically, these five works are strikingly different. Short sentences and parataxis are characteristic of Njáls saga. The Laxdæla artist prefers
longer, ampler sentences with more descriptive adjec-
tives, and he explains the moods and motives of his
characters more often than most saga writers. The
compiler of Eyrbyggja frequently makes use of complex
and compound periods, although they tend to be less
long and complicated than those favored by the author

of _Grettis saga_. The individual sagas also differ
markedly from one another in the employment of alliteration,
antithesis, and parallelism, as well as in use of
skaldic stanzas.

Andreas Heusler, the free-prose advocate, characterized
Njáls saga as _Dichtung_ ("work of literature"),
spoke of the "_Laxdæla_ artist," and unconditionally
attributed _Egils saga_ to Snorri Sturluson
(51). The combination of diverse and long-range
foreshadowing, intricate plot convolution, sophisticated
character delineation, individuality of style,
and thematic design stamps the major sagas unmistakably
as carefully planned and artistically executed literary
creations.

Chapter Six
Shorter Sagas
about Icelanders

Introduction

In addition to the ten Íslendingasögur already
discussed, twenty-nine sagas have been preserved in
whole or in part. These stories vary greatly in age,
length, style, and literary merit. The oldest is from
about 1220 and the latest from about 1500. Several of
these stories are so short that they are sometimes
classified as þættir, whereas one is almost as long
as Eyrbyggja. Two of the minor sagas display an
extraordinary degree of craftsmanship in character
delineation, crisp dialogue, and incisive narrative,
whereas one is incredibly ungainly, repetitious, and
replete with blind motifs.

Sagas from Northeastern Iceland

Ten sagas, whose total length is considerably less
than that of Njála, deal with people from north-
eastern Iceland. The contrast between the stories of
this group and the sagas already discussed is so
striking that Kurt Schier has suggested the possibility
of a separate genesis for them (1). Only one saga in
this group contains skaldic stanzas--six in number--
four of which are attributed to the same characters in
a later expanded and augmented version of the story.
Only one of these six stanzas is appropriate to the
prose passage in which it is embedded.

Droplaugarsona saga. The "story of the sons of
Droplaug" is one of the oldest of the group. It has
been preserved in entirety only in Möðruvallabók
and like all sagas in this codex has been subjected to
compaction. The language has been reduced in places to
the point of obscurity. The saga is well constructed,
but characters are sometimes ineptly introduced and
motivation is not always clear.

The widow Droplaug is maliciously slandered by a
follower of the chieftain Helgi Ásbjarnarson. Her

sons Helgi and Grím, thirteen and twelve years old,
kill the culprit, thus initiating a feud between Helgi
Droplaugarson and his namesake. Droplaug remarries,
but Helgi disapproves and with the connivance of his
mother has his stepfather killed, whereupon Droplaug
sails to Norway. Helgi so consistently defeats his
namesake at litigation that the discountenanced chieftain finally has him killed.

Helgi's last stand is one of the two best constructed episodes in the story. The killing is foreshadowed
by dreams, omens, and premonitions, including an itch-
ing on Helgi's lower lip. Before succumbing to an
overwhelming force of attackers, Helgi delivers himself
of two caustic gibes of the kind uttered by doomed
heroes to belittle their victorious assailants. When
his lower lip is sliced off by a sword stroke, he
remarks, "My face never was handsome, and you have done
little to improve it." Shortly afterwards he is
pierced by a spear thrust. Helgi struggles forward to
strike his assailant, but he quickly jabs the end of
the spear into the ground, leaving Helgi impaled on the
shaft. Helgi's dying words are "I tarried, but you
hurried."

The second memorable episode relates Grím's vengeance for his brother. Thought dead by Helgi's enemies, Grím hides out, biding an opportunity to kill
Helgi Ásbjarnarson. The scene of action is prepared
to the smallest detail. With the aid of two companions, Grím ties the tails of Helgi's cows together to
impede pursuit from that exit from Helgi's house. Then
he enters the house under cover of darkness, wakes Helgi, thrusts a sword through him, escapes, and bars the
door from the outside. Exiled for the killing, Grím
takes passage to Norway, where he dies of wounds inflicted by a viking and poison administered by a witch
called Gefjon—the name occurs in Snorri's Edda.

Grím's vengeance is based on old tradition, since
it is mentioned in Hauk Valdísarson's Íslendingadrápa (Poem about Icelanders, ca. 1200) (2). The
fact that this poem refers to Helgi as heathen may
account for the unusual ending of the saga: "Helgi
Droplaugarson was killed one year after Thangbrand the
Priest came to Iceland," that is, two years before
Christianity was accepted by the General Assembly.

Vápnfirðinga saga. Although the "saga of the
people of Vápnafjord" has been poorly preserved, it

is skillfully designed and artistically constructed. As Heller has shown, the story is built on the principle of contrastive parallelism (3). The chieftains Brodd-Helgi and Geitir have a Norwegian merchant murdered in the hope of seizing his cargo. In this, however, they are thwarted by the merchant's Icelandic partner, Thorleif the Christian, who delivers the cargo to the murdered man's heirs in Norway. Since Helgi and Geitir suspect each other of having filched certain of the Norwegians' valuables, their friendship turns to enmity. Brodd-Helgi divorces his ailing wife, Geitir's sister, and commits increasingly serious outrages against Geitir's liegemen. Finally Geitir succumbs to their demands that he kill Helgi.

Helgi's son Bjarni is goaded by his stepmother into killing Geitir, but immediately regrets the deed, and his uncle dies in his arms. (This scene is regarded as the model for the slaying of Kjartan in Laxdæla.) Geitir's son Thorkel returns from Norway and makes repeated attempts to avenge his father's death. Bjarni remains patient and conciliatory, and Thorkel is finally persuaded by his wife, who is in his own words "wise and kind," to accept honorable terms of settlement. In old age Thorkel moves to Bjarni's farm, where he remains for the rest of his days. Thus the Christian virtues of forgiveness and reconciliation prevail over the pagan ideal of blood vengeance. Among Thorkel's descendants, the author lists Bishop Pál and Saint Thorlák. Jan de Vries has suggested that the elevation of Thorlák inspired the author of Vápnfirðinga to create this story (4). This assumption is supported by the fact that the author greatly ennobled the character of Bjarni, who in real life was a killer and troublemaker (5).

Þorsteins saga hvíta. A similar spirit of conciliation is found in the brief "story of Thorstein the White," which was written about 1240 as an introduction to Vápnfirðinga saga. The beginning of the story is modeled on Bjarnar saga: a villain named Einar spreads rumors that Thorstein fagri ("the Fair") has died of scurvy in Norway and then wins the hand of Thorstein's fiancée Helga. When Einar refuses compensation, Thorstein kills him. In the ensuing feud, Thorgils, son of Thorstein hvíti, is killed, and Thorstein fagri is banished.

Upon his return to Iceland five years later, he im-

mediately goes to Thorstein hvíti's farm to offer him
redress. Thorstein hvíti, who is blind, "recognized
the smell of seafarers and asked who had arrived."
Thorstein fagri identifies himself, but his namesake is
unwilling "to carry Thorgils, his son, in his purse."
When Thorstein fagri lays his head on his knees, however, he relents with the comment, "Ears are most seem-
ly where they have grown" (chap. 8). He agrees to
reconciliation on the condition that Thorstein fagri
assume the duties of his slain son on the farm.

Thorstein fagri now marries Helga, and they live
with Thorstein hvíti for ten years. Thorgils' son,
Brodd-Helgi, is now eighteen years old and can be
expected to avenge his father's death. On the advice
of Thorstein hvíti, Thorstein fagri and Helga go
abroad to avert further bloodshed.

Þorsteins saga stangarhöggs. The "story of
Thorstein Staff-struck," a sequel to Vápnfirðinga
saga, was composed about 1270. Thorstein's father
Thórarin, a superannuated viking with many weapons and
little money, goads his son Thorstein, an excellent
farmer, into avenging a blow on the head by killing
three servants of the chieftain Bjarni. In return,
Bjarni's wife incites him to kill Thorstein in order to
maintain the respect of his liegemen.

During the duel, in which powerful blows and compli-
mentary words are exchanged, Thorstein refrains from
treacherously killing his opponent despite repeated
opportunities to do so. Finally Bjarni suggests that
Thorstein compensate him for his three servants by
working on his farm. Bjarni informs Thórarin that he
has killed his son and offers to let him live at his
place for life as compensation. Elated that Thorstein
has preserved the family "honor," Thórarin tries to
kill Bjarni with a sword concealed under his tunic.
Bjarni calls him an "old stinker," and he and Thorstein
ride off to Hof, Bjarni's farm. With the advent of
Christianity, Bjarni and Thorstein submit to baptism;
Bjarni undertakes a pilgrimage to Rome and dies abroad.

This story, which is sometimes labeled a þáttr,
is one of the most obvious illustrations of the generation-gap theme in saga literature. Like Thórólf in
Eyrbyggja, Thórarin embodies the bloody, unsocial
code of the viking, whereas Bjarni and Thorstein are
similar to Thórólf's son Arnkel in that they exempli-
fy the ideal chieftain and farmer-liegeman in post-

viking rural society (6). It seems obvious that, like
Eyrbyggja, these three sagas were intended as exempla
for contemporary times.

Þorsteins saga Síðu-Hallssonar. The "story of
Thorstein, son of Hall of Síða" is not well preserved.
The beginning and the end are missing, and there are
several lacunae in what remains of the text. The
author favored long sentences with one subject and a
series of parallel predicates and complex sentences
with several dependent clauses. The disposition is
awkward: the death of the villain and his equally
villainous sons is preceded by twelve sequentially
related dreams and their interpretations. Trouble
begins when Þórhadd refuses to relinquish Thorstein's
goðord, over which he has exercised custody during
Thorstein's absence. It is exacerbated when Þórhadd
and his sons spread libelous rumors about Thorstein
including allegations of sexual deviance. Thorstein's
killing of Þórhadd is mentioned by Hauk Valdísarson
in his Íslendingadrápa. The chronology of this saga
is quite confused. Thorstein, for example, participates in the Battle of Clontarf (1014), known from
Njáls saga, and then takes service with King Harald
the Harsh. The historical Thorstein was a member of
Harald's bodyguard, but that was in 1046-47.

Hrafnkels saga Freysgoða. The "story of
Hrafnkel, priest of Frey," which was composed about
1270-80, relates the humiliation of a domineering chieftain and his ruthless recapture of his former power and
supremacy. Hrafnkel swears an oath to kill anyone who
rides his horse Freyfaxi, which he has dedicated to the
god Frey, and he fulfills that oath by slaying his shepherd Einar. He offers Einar's father generous compensation, but Thorbjörn, old and poverty-stricken, stubbornly insists on mediation. When Hrafnkel refuses,
since Thorbjörn is not his equal socially, the old man
persuades his nephew Sám to undertake litigation
against the chieftain at the General Assembly. With
the help of two chieftains from the Westfjords, he wins
the case, overcomes Hrafnkel in a surprise attack,
tortures and humiliates him, confiscates his estate
Aðalból, and banishes him from the district.

Hrafnkel regains wealth and authority in his new
home. When Sám's brother Eyvind returns to Iceland
from Constantinople, Hrafnkel kills him and all his
companions and then drives Sám from Aðalból. Sám

appeals to the chieftains from the Westfjords for support against Hrafnkel, but they decline risking another clash with him since Sám clearly lacks the qualities of a leader. "Hrafnkel remained on his estate and maintained his honor. He died of illness, and his burial mound is in Hrafnkelsdal near Adalból" (chap. 20). Because of an unfortunate editorial emendation (land, "lands," was changed to lund, "mind, temper"), many scholars have believed that Hrafnkel's character was improved through humiliation and adversity. But his character was not improved, as can be seen by his heartless slaughter of Sám's brother Eyvind and all his followers, whose deaths, like that of Einar, remained unatoned. The author cynically transformed the ruthless ancient Frey worshiper into an equally merciless pragmatic chieftain of the Sturlung Age (7).

The disposition and style of Hrafnkatla are excellent. The author skillfully employed stylistic and motivational parallelism, alliteration, antithesis, and contrastive character delineation. Over half of the story consists of pithy, finely honed dialogue. The cast of characters is small, there are virtually no genealogies, and psychological motivation is superb. In the detailed functional description of nature, the author of Hrafnkels saga is the equal of Abbot Karl. His employment of the cinematic technique of describing the approach of a body of men from afar until they are recognized as enemies is unsurpassed in saga literature.

Gunnars saga Þiðrandabana. In the "saga (or þáttr) of Gunnar, the slayer of Thidrandi," the Norwegian merchant Gunnar is incited by a woman servant to kill Thidrandi in vengeance for the slaying of his host (8). He is sheltered first by a farmer named Steinki, then by Helgi Ásbjarnarson and his wife Thórdís, and finally by Gudrún Osvífrsdóttir, the heroine of Laxdæla saga. In the end he escapes to Norway, where he is joined by Sveinki. Although the style of this story is quite good, the disposition of the material is awkward. The author obviously was not well acquainted either with the geography of eastern Iceland or with the relationships of leading families there. He seems, however, to have been well acquainted with both the topography and the people of western Iceland. Similarities between this story and Laxdæla on the one hand and Droplaugarsona saga on the other

hand can be explained as influences from <u>Gunnars</u>
<u>saga</u>. All this lends support to Jón Jóhannesson's
hypothesis that the story was composed at Helgafell and
that it stimulated saga writing in eastern Iceland when
it became known there. If that is so, it is not necessary to posit a separate genesis for this group of
sagas, as Schier has done.

Sagas from Northern Iceland

<u>Reykdæla saga ok Víga-Skútu</u>. The elegance
of style and the sophistication of character portrayal
that make <u>Hrafnkatla</u> so enjoyable are completely lacking in "the story of the people of Reykjardal and of
Killer-Skúta." As the title indicates, this saga
combines two stories that in turn consist of series of
loosely connected episodes. That the author was aware
of the disjointedness of his narrative is evident from
his closing words: "We now bring to an end these tales
(<u>frásagnir</u>)." There is a plethora of characters,
none of whom comes to life except the chieftain
Áslák, an incredibly kind and benevolent peacemaker,
and his son Skúta, a grim and cunning killer. The
style is clear but tedious. Instead of crisp, dramatic
dialogue, we find here long, dreary passages of
indirect discourse. The author repeatedly intrudes,
often in the first person, with admissions of uncertain-
ty about the correctness of contradictory sources, and
he frequently explains otherwise obscure motives of his
characters and foretells coming events, some of which
he fails to relate.

The first part of the story deals largely with the
malicious acts of several scoundrels, the most vicious
of whom bears the name Vémund. His chief adversary is
a farmer called Steingrím. Áslák is kept busy medi-
ating petty quarrels, most of which involve theft.
Like one other noble peacemaker in saga literature,
Áslák receives his fatal wound while trying to mediate a quarrel, and like his saga counterpart, Áskel
conceals his wound in order to avert further bloodshed.
As he lies dying, he enjoins his kinsmen to renounce
blood vengeance for him and to come to peaceful terms
with their adversaries. Áskel's final instructions
are all related by the author in indirect discourse in
a single sentence ten lines in length.

Although Thorstein abides by his dying father's

wishes, his brother Víga-Skúta, who was abroad at the
time of Áslák's death, does not feel bound by the
conditions of the settlement. The second part of the
story relates Skúta's killings to avenge his father.
The most skillfully narrated part of the story is a
þáttr dealing with a feud between Víga-Skúta and
Víga-Glúm, which also occurs in Glúm's biography.
Ironically Áskel, the peacemaker, dies by the sword;
Vémund, the troublemaker, dies of illness; his doughty
and honorable adversary Steingrím drowns; and Skúta,
the ferocious avenger, is treacherously stabbed to
death in his underground bedroom.

Knut Liestøl maintained that Reykdæla is a
recording of orally told stories (9). Neither structure nor rhetoric supports that contention. The characteristic feature of oral tales is the short but well-
developed scene (10). There are very few such scenes
in this saga. The individual episodes are not so much
related as they are reported. Furthermore, we find
here simple forms of foreshadowing and an example of an
extraneous excursus (the þáttr). Björn Sigfússon has correctly characterized Reykdæla as
single stranded, yet the author does occasionally
present his story from alternative perspectives (11).
All this is evidence of deliberative, albeit clumsy,
composition. And the long-winded style is certainly
not that of an oral tale.

We may assume that the author was a cleric, for he
portrayed Áskel, a pagan chieftain, as an embodiment
of Christian virtues. Note, for example, Áskel's
response to the suggestion that men should swear an
oath to contribute money to the heathen temple, kill
old people, and expose children to die in order to
secure relief from the severe cold. Áskel considers
that outrageous (ómælilegt) and declares that it is
"more advisable to honor their creator by supporting
the old people and contributing money to bring up the
children" (chap. 7). The unusual structure and style
of the saga can perhaps best be understood if we regard
Reykdæla not as a finished work but as a preliminary
draft. This assumption would account for both the
indirect discourse--later to be turned into dialogue--
and the frequent repetitions and references to future
events, some of which have the appearance of parenthet-
ic notes by the author for his own use.

Víga-Glúms saga. Although the biography of

"Killer-Glúm" is far more skillfully constructed than Reykdæla, it is more difficult to understand, partly because of its severe abridgement in places--the work is preserved in Möðruvallabók--partly because of the complex character of the protagonist, and partly because of the obscurity of allusions to mythology and to contemporary events (12). In the first six chapters, we note clear reverberations of the Norwegian-Icelandic tensions that reached their second climax about 1220, roughly two decades before the saga was composed. The introduction foreshadows the beginning of the main part of the story, and an omen in chapter 9 adumbrates its conclusion.

In order to protect the family farm Thverá from encroachment, Glúm is obliged to kill a neighbor named Sigmund, whereby he comes into conflict with Sigmund's in-laws, the powerful family of Espahól. In a dream Glúm sees the guardian spirit (fylgja) of his grandfather, a worshiper of Óðin, approach in the form of a huge woman. Since Glúm already possesses three protective Odinic gifts from his grandfather, he interprets the dream as an omen of his future predominance in the region. Sigmund's brother Thorkel cites Glúm for manslaughter, but Glúm quashes the case on a technicality and forces Thorkel to sell him his lands at half price. Before giving up his farm, however, Thorkel sacrifices an ox to his patron deity Frey with the request that "Glúm be forced to leave Thverá no less unwillingly than I leave now" (chap. 9). Although Óðin was never widely worshiped by Icelanders, he was known to them through Eddic and skaldic poetry as the god of poets and warriors as well as of perjurers, murderers, and other lawbreakers. Frey, on the other hand, was the patron deity of farmers and the guardian of the fertile field Vitazgjafi ("Certain giver") at Thverá.

In the course of his feud with the men of Espahól, Glúm grows ever more unscrupulous. He has a man cited for a killing he himself committed, illegally harbors an outlaw near the temple of Frey, and commits perjury by swearing an ambiguous oath in that god's sanctuary. Shortly afterward he gives away the Odinic talismans. When Glúm inadvertently betrays his guilt of the manslaughter charge of which he has been cleared on the basis of his ambiguous oath, the case is reopened. Just before the trial, Glúm has a dream in which his

dead forebears plead with Frey to permit Glúm to
remain at Thverá, but the god angrily reminds them of
Thorkel's sacrifice. On the following day, Glúm is
banished from the district. He dies, old and blind, in
his new home after failing to lure Gudmund the Mighty
and his brother Einar close enough to kill at least one
of them with a hidden sword. Thus we see the story
developed on two levels, with the warrior-poet and his
patron Ódin succumbing to the farmers of the region
and their guardian Frey.

Glúms saga was probably composed at Munkathverá,
a Benedictine monastery established at the site of
Glúm's home in 1155. Among the author's sources were
skaldic verses by, and local anecdotes about, his hero.
The Skúta-Glúm episode, which this story shares with
Reykdæla, was probably an independent þáttr,
which each author adapted to his own purpose. As
Björn Sigfússon has shown, the Ingólf episode
(chaps. 13-15) combines motifs from an exemplum in the
Disciplina clericalis with thinly veiled allusions to
a murder attributed to Sighvat Sturluson, who was the
preeminent chieftain in the vicinity of Thverá from
1217 to 1238 as Glúm had been in the tenth century
(13).

Ljósvetninga saga. The "story of the people of
Ljósavatn" has such a complicated plot and so many
indifferently portrayed characters that it is difficult
to remember even after repeated readings. Yet the
structure, as Andersson has shown, is clear (14). Like
the author of Færeyinga saga, the author of this
story was fond of intrigue and surprises, and unlike
the author of Reykdæla, he never predicted coming
events except through his slanted character descriptions and other forms of foreshadowing.

The purpose of the first half of the saga is obviously the defamation of Gudmund the Mighty. Thorkel hák,
a son of Thorgeir, the lawspeaker who persuaded the
Icelandic chieftains to accept Christianity in 999,
slanders Gudmund by spreading rumors that he is a
sodomist. In due course, Gudmund and twenty followers
rush into Thorkel's house and kill him. In an effort
to remain out of range of Thorkel's spear thrusts,
Gudmund topples backward into a vat of milk. This
evokes the most scathing of all parting gibes in saga
literature. With a laugh Thorkel calls out: "Now I
declare that your arse has already sought most other
brooks, but I doubt that it has ever drunk milk before.

You may attack me now, Gudmund. My guts are hanging
out" (chap. 11).

Shortly afterward Gudmund, while on a progress
through his district, takes lodging with one of his
liegemen. He is assigned the seat of honor, and a
farmer named Ofeig is seated beside him.

> When the tables were brought, Ofeig laid his
> fist on the table and said, "Don't you think this
> fist is large, Gudmund?"
> He answered, "Large it is."
> Ofeig said, "Do you think it can deliver a hard
> blow?"
> Gudmund said, "Terribly hard."
> Ofeig said, "What kind of damage do you think
> would come of it?"
> Gudmund said, "Broken bones or death."
> Ofeig said, "How do you think death like that
> would be?"
> Gudmund said, "Very bad. I wouldn't want to die
> like that."
> Ofeig said, "Then don't sit in my place."
> Gudmund said, "Just as you say." And he sat down
> on the other side of the table. (chap. 13)

Even Gudmund's death is demeaning. After hearing a
lethal dream directed at him by a seer named Finni,
Gudmund loses his sense of heat, slumps down in his
chair, and expires. To appreciate fully the author's
denigration of Gudmund, we must keep in mind that in
real life Gudmund was a confidant of Saint Olaf and
one of the few Icelandic chieftains to bear the byname
"the Mighty."

The second half of the saga relates the continuation
of the feud between the men of Mödruvellir and those
of Ljósavatn, with Gudmund's son Eyjólf and Thorgeir's grandson Thorvard as the chief antagonists. In
chapter 13, a seeress named Thórhild assures Gudmund
that vengeance for Thorkel will not strike him, but
that one of his sons "will have a narrow escape." In
chapter 16, Gudmund's son Kodrán is fatally wounded in
battle. After Thorvard's brother Thórarin is slain in
counterrevenge, the feuding is brought to an end
through mutual agreement and monetary compensation paid
by Eyjólf.

Valla-Ljóts saga. The "story of Valla-Ljót"
presents a quite different picture of Gudmund (15).

Halli, a man of overweening ambition, leaves Gudmund's
district in the hope of making himself the greatest man
elsewhere. He extorts money from the chieftain Valla-
Ljót by threatening him with the wrath of St. Michael
for having desecrated Michaelmas. Fearing Valla-
Ljót's reprisals, Gudmund urges Halli to return to his
district and even offers to buy land for him there.
Halli disdains his advice. Valla-Ljót is obliged to
kill Halli in order to maintain his prestige. Revenge
and counterrevenge follow, with Gudmund and Valla-Ljót
representing the hostile parties. Gudmund attempts to
kill Valla-Ljót, but in the end the two chieftains are
reconciled in such a way that "Valla-Ljót was regarded
as a very great chieftain," and "Gudmund maintained his
honor until the day of his death." In this short saga
we find a lofty concept of honor, which is represented
by the hóf (self-restraint and fair-mindedness) of
both chieftains. In this respect, Valla-Ljóts saga
is closely akin to several stories relating to north-
eastern Iceland.

Sagas from Western Iceland

About half of the Íslendinga sögur pertain to
the western and northwestern districts of Iceland.
All the transitional sagas and all the major sagas
except Njála are located there. The minor sagas
from these regions, some of which will be treated in
the following chapter, vary greatly in content and
form.

Gísla saga Súrssonar. Few scholars will dis-
agree with Andersson's assessment that "the story of
Gísli, son of Súr" is "easily the most intricately
and self-consciously composed" of the Íslendingasögur (16). Plot interlace is more obtrusive in
Eyrbyggja and more elaborate in Njála, but the
intertexture of Gísla saga is tighter and more
varied than that of any other minor saga. In the
economical introduction in Norway, Gísli preserves the
integrity of the family by killing three suitors for
the hand of his sister Thordís, a woman who is both
attractive to men and vulnerable to their advances.
Thordís was fond of two of them, both of whom were
also friends of Gísli's brother Thorkel, and "there
was never full friendship between the brothers again"
(chap. 2).

In the Dýrafjord of northwestern Iceland, the tense
family relationship is further complicated. Thorkel
learns that his wife Ásgerd is enamored of Véstein,
close friend of Gísli and brother of Gísli's wife
Aud. At Thorkel's instigation, his friend Thorgrím,
the husband of Thordís, kills Véstein secretly by
night, and Gísli avenges Véstein's death by murdering
Thorgrím in a nocturnal attack, the details of which
were borrowed from Droplaugarsona saga. Like Víga-
Glúm, Gísli reveals his guilt in a skaldic stanza,
which Thordís unriddles. Thordís betrays Gísli's
secret to her second husband Börk, Thorgrím's
brother, who thereafter never ceases in his efforts to
kill Gísli. Gísli is outlawed and finally slain
after a heroic last stand. His wife Aud, who has been
his only source of comfort during fourteen years of
outlawry, remains at his side to the very end.

The author forged his story from many sources. The
influence of Eddic poetry is stronger in this saga than
in any other Íslendingasaga except Laxdæla.
After Thordís has betrayed him, Gísli in a skaldic
stanza compares her unfavorably with the Eddic heroine
Gudrún Gjúkadóttir, who, true to the pagan-heroic
code, slew her husband Atli and their two sons to
avenge her brothers. The language of the saga, both
prose and verse, shows influence from the heroic poems
(17).

There are also strong affinities between Gísla
saga and contemporary events. In his Íslendinga
saga, Sturla Thórdarson records the killing of a man
in 1221 "with the spear that they called Grásída
["Greyflank"] and said Gísli Sursson had owned" (chap.
39). At the Battle of Örlyggsstadir (1238), the
historian's cousin and namesake Sturla Sighvatsson
"defended himself with the spear that was called
Grásída, an ancient and not well-tempered damascened spear" (chap. 138). In Gísla saga, the
weapon is also described as damascened (chap. 11).
Several incidents recorded about an outlaw named Aron
in the northwest of Iceland (1222-25) have such
striking parallels with events in the saga that they
can scarcely be fortuitous (18). Peter Foote has also
discerned an emotional kinship between the author of
Gísla saga and writers of contemporary sagas and
between stanzas in Gísla saga and poems and verses
of the twelfth century (19).

The intriguing verse of this saga has been the subject of considerable scholarly debate. Few, if any, of
the thirty-six stanzas attributed to Gísli can be
genuine, both on linguistic grounds and because of
their Christian sentiment. Nor can they all, as
scholars once believed, be the creation of the author,
since he did not always succeed in fitting them into
his narrative. There is now general agreement that the
stanzas are somewhat older than the saga, but whether
the author received them in written form, as Björn K.
Þórólfsson maintained, or in oral form, as Peter
Foote has argued, is too complicated a question to be
discussed here (20). The most remarkable stanzas are
those in which a malevolent and a benevolent dream
woman appear to torment and to console Gísli. The
purpose of these stanzas, several of which were influenced by the semicanonical book Esdras, is to reflect
the conflict between paganism and Christianity in
Gísli's heart.

Thordís is the most intriguing character in the
story. Her ambivalent feelings toward her brother
Gísli and her betrayal of him to Börk are not difficult to understand. Not only had Gísli killed two of
her suitors in Norway; his murder of Thorgrím as he
lay beside her was committed in a very cruel manner.
Yet when Börk's henchman Eyjólf kills Gísli,
Thordís stabs Eyjólf with Gísli's sword and divorces
Börk. Aud is admirable in her steadfast loyalty and
magnificent in a scene in which Eyjólf tries to bribe
her into betraying her husband's place of concealment:
she lets him give her a large purse full of coins and
then hurls it into his face.

Although Gísli is inclined to self-pity at times,
he bears up well under his many trials. His spiritual
conflicts are revealed primarily in his haunting verse.
After fourteen harrowing years of narrow escapes from
his relentless pursuers, Gísli finally yields to his
dream guardian's promises of relief from his suffering
in "another world" (stanzas 23 and 26): as he moves
from his place of concealment onto a cliff for his
final defense, he clearly marks his path for his
enemies. Although emotionally exhausted, Gísli maintains his courage to the end. Before dying of his many
wounds, he kills eight of his twelve assailants and
wounds the rest. Instead of uttering a scornful gibe

at his enemies, Gísli speaks his last verse: "The beautiful woman who gladdens me will learn of the bold achievements of her valiant friend. I am content to fall before swordblades. My father gave his son such a bold heart."

Even though conventional vengeance was not exacted for Gísli, it can hardly be said that he remained completely unavenged. The havoc Gísli wreaked during his last stand and the humiliation he and Aud and Thordís inflicted upon Börk and Eyjólf were certainly substantial requital for his death.

Vatnsdæla saga. Like Laxdæla the "story of the people of Vatnsdal" is a family chronicle covering four generations (21). Superficially, this story resembles Laxdæla--in the description of beautiful objects, for example, and in the subjective commentary on people and events. The characters of Vatnsdæla, however, completely lack the emotional intensity--of friendship, love, jealousy, and hatred--that informs the men and women of Laxdæla and Gísla saga. The characters of Vatnsdæla are either noble heathens who possess the virtues of goodness and moderation and are blessed with good fortune or rascals who are evil, avaricious, and dabble in pagan magic. "Few things," said Grettir's mother, "are more powerful than heathen witchcraft," and this held true for Grettir. The doughty chieftains of Vatnsdæla, however, succeed admirably in cleansing their district of witches and warlocks. Indeed, that appears to have been their chief function.

The structure of the first half of the story is firm, but the episodic second half is held together primarily by its two basic themes: family good fortune and the ideal chieftain. The reason for this difference is to be found in the fact that the first part of the story seems to be largely the author's imaginative creation, whereas the second part is based on various sources including earlier sagas and local oral anecdotes. The style is characterized by antithesis, alliteration, and the abundant use of synonyms. The antithesis results naturally from the conflict between good and evil. Of the ninety examples of alliteration, sixty-four occur in the first half of the story. In addition to pairs of synonyms used for emphasis, the author employed synonyms to avoid monotonous repeti-

tion. Thus he used over two dozen colorful epithets--
few of them more than twice--to label and to berate his
many rogues and rascals.

Ingimund, a friend and supporter of Harald Fairhair,
is destined to leave Norway against his will and to
settle in Iceland, where he establishes himself as godi
at Hof in Vatnsdal. Like Áskel in Ljósvetninga
saga, Ingimund is mortally wounded while performing a
good deed, and he conceals his wound long enough to let
the perpetrator escape. After his four sons have
avenged his slaying, Thorstein, the wisest and wiliest
of them, assumes the chieftaincy. A wise man needs a
warrior by his side, and Thorstein had his in the
person of his brother Jökul. The most exciting events
in this section of the story are clashes between Jökul
and Finnbogi, the champion of a neighboring valley,
which we shall find related from a different perspec-
tive in Finnbogi's biography. Following the death of
Thorstein, his sons Ingólf and Gudmund divide the
inheritance. Ingólf's dalliance with Valgerd, the
sister of the poet Hallfred--the episode was adapted
from Hallfreðar saga--leads to Gudmund's death, and
Ingólf dies shortly afterward from wounds sustained in
a foolhardy attack on a den of robbers. The godord is
assumed by Thorgrím of Kárnsá and after his death
passes to his illegitimate son Thorkel krafla, the last
of the great chieftains of Vatnsdal.

Although the action of Vatnsdæla takes place
before the advent of Christianity, the story abounds in
Christian sentiment. In Norway a mortally wounded highwayman named Ingimund forgives his assailant Thorstein
and urges him to marry his sister. Their son is the
settler Ingimund. On his deathbed, Thorstein declares,
"What pleases me most about my life is that I have not
been an aggressor against men" (chap. 11). As we have
seen, Ingimund tried to save his slayer's life, and on
a previous occasion, he rebuked him for not returning
"good for good" (chap. 21). Ingimund, too, is praised
by the author for being "agreeable with most men and a
nonaggressor" (chap. 17). Although Ingimund is given a
pagan burial, his son Thorstein expects that his father
will be rewarded "by him who has created the sun and
the whole world, whoever he is" (chap. 23). Later
Thorstein cures his brother Thórir of the berserk rage
by rescuing a child abandoned to die--Thorkel krafla--
and by calling upon "him who has created the sun, that
this affliction may fall from you, for I believe him to

be the most powerful. In return I shall do this for his sake: I shall help the child and rear it so that he who has created man may turn him unto himself, for I believe that this will be his fate" (chap. 23). Thorstein's prophecy is fulfilled. With the advent of Christianity, Thorkel--although somewhat reluctantly-- submits to baptism. In his necrology, the author declared that Thorkel was superior to all former chieftains of Vatnsdal because "he was a man of the true faith and loved God and prepared for his death in the proper Christian manner" (chap. 47).

It is generally believed that the author of Vatnsdæla was a native of Vatnsdal and a monk at Thingeyrar. Like the earlier historians of that monastery, he was a royalist, and we may surmise that he hoped that the submission of the Icelanders to the king of Norway would restore peace to his country, devastated by the savagery of the Sturlung Age. He clearly intended his saga to be a glorification of the chieftains of Vatnsdal and a Christian exemplum for the chieftains of his own day. On the basis of internal and external evidence, Vatnsdæla saga has been dated to about 1270.

Bandamanna saga. The "story of the Confederates," which was written at about the same time as Vatnsdæla and relates to the same geographical area, is unique in several respects. It is an antiaristocratic comedy--W. P. Ker characterized it as "the first reasonable and modern comedy in the history of modern Europe"--and it is a Rahmenerzählung, that is, a story within a story. Above all, however, it is a withering satire on the avarice of Icelandic chieftains and on their perversion of the legal system for selfish ends. As we read it, we are reminded of numerous personages and scenes from Sturlunga saga (22). The author of Bandamanna saga drew on various sagas and þættir, one of which, Ölkofra þáttr (The tale of Beer-hood), seems to have inspired his satire. Bandamanna exists in two versions known as B and K; the former is the one discussed here.

For reasons not disclosed Ófeig, a wise but poverty-stricken farmer, and his ambitious son Odd become estranged. Odd soon gains fame and fortune as a seafaring merchant and buys a godord. Upon returning from a voyage abroad, he has difficulty in recovering his chieftaincy from Óspak, to whom he has entrusted it during his absence. Odd prosecutes Óspak for the

theft of forty sheep and for the killing of his friend
Vali but loses his case on a slight technicality.
Ófeig now puts in his appearance and through eloquence
and bribery persuades the jury to reverse its decision.

Enraged at the reversal, eight envious chieftains
who wanted to humiliate Odd now agree to prosecute him
for bribery in the hope of legally confiscating half
his wealth. Ófeig convinces two of the confederates,
Egil and Gellir, that Odd has gone abroad with all his
moveable wealth, and he bribes them to award the prosecutors a mere pittance. The chieftains now blame and
berate one another for losing the case. Odd handsomely rewards Egil and marries Gellir's daughter.
Óspak is found dead in a cave. "The friendship between father and son lasted ever afterwards with good
fellowship."

It is generally believed that the author of this
social satire was a monk at Thingeyrar. There are more
persuasive reasons, however, for assigning Bandamanna
to a "priestling," that is, a poor priest whose education had been paid for by a wealthy farmer in whose
service he was therefore obliged to remain until he had
found and trained a replacement. Such a man would have
a better opportunity to observe the follies and vices
of the rich as well as greater reason to satirize them
than would a sequestered monk. Whoever he was, the
author was a master of scintillating repartee and of
devastating sarcasm.

Hænsa-Þóris saga. In the "story of Hen-
Thórir," we can observe more readily than in any other
Íslendingasaga the manner in which sober history
could be transformed into imaginative literature under
the impact of contemporary events (23). The author
found the nucleus of a plot for his story in
Íslendingabók (chap. 5), where Ari recorded a
conflict between two prominent chieftains, Thórd
Yeller and Tungu-Odd, resulting from litigation for
homicide. The purpose of this account was to explain
the reason for the establishment of quarter assemblies.
According to the Icelandic annals, the killing
occurred in 962 (24). Although there is a discrepancy
in names between Íslendingabók and the saga, the
names and genealogies of chapter 1 agree with those in
Sturla Thórdarson's redaction of Landnámabók
(chaps. 36 and 45-46). Jónas Kristjánsson's suggestion that the author here extracted material from

Sturlubók   or   from   a   closely   related   text   seems
reasonable.

The impetus for the creation of this saga came from
the imposition of a Norwegian law code upon the Icelanders in 1281. One regulation in that law empowered
farmers in need of fodder to appropriate hay from those
who had a surplus of it with the stipulation that they
provide reliable sureties for its payment. This regulation, regarded as an infringement of the inviolability
of private property, was long and vigorously opposed by
large landowners including the church. Since Hænsa-
Þóris saga reflects the ideas and occasionally even
the phraseology of the new law code, we may assume that
the story was written some time after 1281, possibly at
the monastery Hítardal.

The initial adversaries of the story are Blund-
Ketil, a prosperous farmer who is the embodiment of
forebearance and generosity, and Hen-Thórir, a surly
and miserly landholder who has acquired wealth through
peddling merchandise including chickens, whence his
nickname. When Thórir refuses to sell Ketil surplus
hay for his hard-pressed tenants, he appropriates as
much as they need and leaves ample payment for it.
Thereupon Thórir demands that the chieftains Arngrím
and Tungu-Odd prosecute Ketil for theft, but they
refuse upon hearing the truth from Helgi, Arngrím's
son, whom Arngrím has given to Thórir in fosterage in
return for a promise of half his wealth.

Thórir now persuades Odd's son Thorvald--again with
a promise of half his wealth--to summon Ketil for
theft, and Arngrím and his men accompany them to
Ketil's estate. Ketil's house guest, a Norwegian
merchant, is so outraged at their behavior that he
shoots an arrow at them. Helgi is killed. During the
night, the summoners burn down Ketil's house, killing
him and his entire household. Odd now attempts to
seize Ketil's property, but his son Herstein rescues
the livestock and moveable goods. Thord Yeller is
tricked into assuming responsibility for the prosecution, and eventually all the burners are sentenced to
banishment and forfeiture of all their property except
Thorvald, who is exiled for three years. While in
exile Thorvald is enslaved in Scotland. His brother
Thórhadd goes in search of him. Neither one is heard
of again.

Ari concluded his account with the statement that

"Hen-Thórir was outlawed and later killed, as well as others who were at the burning." Through the use of plot stranding, however, the author of the saga has Thórir try to lure Herstein into an ambush while the haggling over the lawsuit is in progress. But Herstein catches sight of a shield, calls his followers, and they kill Thórir and his henchmen. Herstein rides onto the assembly grounds with Thórir's head before the verdict has been announced. "Herstein gained much fame and great honor for this deed, as was to be expected" (chap. 15). The author of the saga, of course, makes no mention of the historical significance of this court action, since that is irrelevant to his narrative purpose.

Hænsa-Þóris saga is one of the most obviously moralistic of the Íslendingasögur. Blund-Ketil is a paragon of Christian virtues and the most innocent of all innocent victims in the sagas, whereas Hen-Thórir is the blackest of blackguards, with no redeeming virtues. The chieftains Arngrím and Odd are motivated by cupiditas and ambitio. Arngrím is impoverished and banished; Odd dies as a thoroughly frustrated, lonely old man. Hænsa-Þóris saga is also one of the most obviously contrived works of its genre. Structure, style, dialogue, and comic relief are well handled, but the author rather overworked his favorite rhetorical device: the combination of parallelism with the irony of ignorance for the purpose of simultaneously enlisting support for the good side and amusing his readers.

Eiríks saga rauða. Composed about 1270, the "story of Eirík the Red" is an augmented, tendentious reworking of Grænlendinga saga (25). By reducing the number of Vínland voyages from six to three, the author tightened the structure of the story. The style is more flexible and, especially in the Hauksbók redaction, more polished and pleasing. In general Grænlendinga is historically more reliable, but the author of this story corrected his source in several places. Whereas Grælendinga shows no trace of influence from known written works, the author of Eiríks saga drew on a variety of sources. In both sagas, for example, Thorstein Eiriksson is killed--in Grænlendinga by a Skræling (Indian), in this story by a uniped. The presence of such creatures in Vínland is not surprising, since this land was believed to extend southward to Africa, the home of the unipeds,

according to an Icelandic medieval geographical treatise based on Isidore of Seville.

Eiríks saga is a misnomer, for the central characters are Thorfinn karlsefni and his wife Gudríd.
Gudríd is given greater prominence through a detailed
genealogy derived from Landnámabók. Leif
Eiríksson's stature is also enhanced. He replaces
Bjarni Herjólfsson as the discoverer of Vínland,
brings Christianity to Greenland (a loan from
Gunnlaug's biography of Ólaf Tryggvason), and rescues
the crew of a sinking ship. Because of these good
deeds, the author tells us, Leif received the byname
"the Lucky." The most remarkable character transformation is that of his sister Freydís, who is changed
from a greedy murderess into a fearless heroine who
puts attacking Skrælings to flight after all the men
have run away in fright.

Eirík, however, did not fare so well. His closest
associate is Thorhall the Hunter, an abusive troublemaker and worshiper of Thór. In both Vínland sagas,
Eirík is prevented from participating in an expedition
because of a fall from a horse. Only in this story,
however, does he interpret his mishap as punishment for
his greed in burying a chest of gold and silver. His
most severe punishment, however, comes from refusing to
submit to baptism: his wife Thjódhild denies him his
conjugal rights. Christian sentiment is quite as
obtrusive in this story as in Grænlendinga saga.

Gunnlaugs saga ormstungu. The "biography" of
Gunnlaug Serpent-tongue" has been edited more often and
translated into more languages than any other saga
(26). The reasons for its popularity are obvious. It
is a sentimental story of romantic love, it is skillfully constructed, the style is lucid, and the terse
dialogue clearly reveals the moods of the characters
and effectively advances the story. But as we read
this saga, we repeatedly have the feeling that we are
renewing old acquaintances. The basic plot is that of
Bjarnar saga. The introductory description of
Gunnlaug (chap. 4) is almost identical with that of
Hallfred in his saga (chap. 2), and stanza 20 in
Gunnlaugs saga (chap. 11) was taken verbatim from
Kormáks saga (stanza 3, chap. 3).

Gunnlaugs saga is unique in that Thorstein's dream
(chap. 2) foreshadows the entire course of events. But
the framework is modeled on the dream of Hecuba in
Trójumanna saga, as Sigurður Nordal has shown, and

the content, which is similar to that of Kriemhilde's dream in the Nibelungenlied, was derived from a lost Eddic poem (27). There are many other affinities between Gunnlaug's story and older sagas, including riddarasögur. For these and other reasons Peter G. Foote concludes that Gunnlaugs saga was written between about 1260 and 1300. Internal evidence suggests Borg as the place of composition.

The skaldic stanzas attributed to Gunnlaug have been the subject of much scholarly controversy. Finnur Jónsson regarded most of them as genuine, whereas Björn Magnússon Ølsen attributed them to the author of the original Gunnlaugs saga, the extant story being, in his opinion, a reworking of the older one, now lost. However that may be, eleven of the stanzas, as Foote has pointed out, could have provided the author with material for much of his narrative, and several of these appear to be genuine.

The poets Gunnlaug and Hrafn become enemies at the court of the Swedish king after criticizing each other's poems at the king's request. Hrafn finds Gunnlaug's drápa in honor of the king pompous, harsh, and inelegant, like the poet himself, and Gunnlaug describes Hrafn and his flokkr as pretty but puny. When Gunnlaug snidely rebukes Hrafn for not deeming the king worthy of a drápa, Hrafn threatens to avenge this slight to his honor.

Like Björn Hítdælakappi, but for less compelling reasons, Gunnlaug overstays his leave and returns to Iceland to find his sweetheart, Helga the Fair, married to his rival. Helga harshly berates Hrafn for deceiving her into believing that Gunnlaug would never return, and thereafter Hrafn "had little pleasure from his marriage to her" (chap. 11). Helga and Gunnlaug meet at a wedding feast, and in parting, Gunnlaug gives her a precious cloak, a gift from King Ethelred. "Hrafn never again enjoyed intimacy with Helga after she and Gunnlaug had met."

Gunnlaug and Hrafn fight a duel, but their kinsmen part them when Gunnlaug receives a scratch on the cheek. The following day dueling is abolished by the General Assembly. The two poets plan to fight a second duel in Norway, but Earl Eirík of Hladir forbids them to duel in his realm. Gunnlaug now follows Hrafn to Sweden and repeatedly arrives in the evening at the place where Hrafn has spent the previous night. The actual distance traveled by the two rivals is only

twenty-five miles, but retardation before the climax
for the purpose of suspense is an important element of
saga structure. Finally they meet at a place called
Dinganes. After a brief skirmish in which all their
men are killed, the two poets face each other.
Gunnlaug strikes off Hrafn's leg, and Hrafn deals
Gunnlaug a mortal blow on the head as Gunnlaug is hand-
ing him a drink of water in his helmet. Reproached by
Gunnlaug for his treachery, Hrafn says: "My reason for
doing this is that I begrudge you the embrace of Helga
the Fair" (chap. 12). Helga is married to a man named
Thorkel, but she continues to pine for her dead sweetheart. During an epidemic, Helga falls ill and dies
while gazing at the cloak, Gunnlaug's gift.

Critics have tended to be harsh in their judgment of
this story, but usually for the wrong reasons. Several
episodes, some say, could have been omitted since they
do not contribute to the main line of the story. But
the essence of saga art is not plot but character
portrayal, and the "irrelevant" episodes effectively
illuminate Gunnlaug's character from various perspectives. Some are unhappy with the poet because he is
neither a great lover nor a great viking. True, but
the author clearly never intended his hero to be either
one. From beginning to end Gunnlaug is irascible and
abusive--he deserves his byname--but at the same time
he is irresolute and indecisive, especially when
confronted by his father or any other father figure.
His inconsistency is consistently and deliberately
underscored by the author at every opportunity. The
prophetic dream, some say, weakens the story by making
the characters the pawns of fate. But Gunnlaug, like
every other saga hero, fashions his own fate. The
author, some think, went too far in plagiarizing earlier prose and poetry. But sagas can be quite as allu-
sive as skaldic poetry: the obvious plagiarisms invite
comparison and contrast with other sagas, characters,
and skaldic poems. The author was, after all, writing
for a sophisticated, well-read audience (28).

In criticizing <u>Gunnlaugs saga</u>, or any other saga,
we must ask two questions: what did the author set out
to do, and to what extent did he succeed? The author
of this saga clearly wanted to create a pleasing and
appealing story, and the large number of modern
editions and translations suggests that in this he was
successful. Second, he wanted to create a complex
character, a man who was quick to make plans but consti-

tutionally unwilling or unable to carry them out.
Here, too, he succeeded. Gunnlaugs saga is, as
Robert F. Cook has persuasively argued, "the story of a
disappointing man, whose circumstances and physical
strength allow the potential for passionate and heroic
action but who fails to fill this potential because of
inner weakness and irresolution. The story of a weak
man is not the same as a weak story" (29).

Conclusion

Even this brief survey of seventeen so-called lesser
or minor sagas reveals how difficult it is to make
valid general statements about The Saga. In style and
literary merit, these stories range from the clumsy
formlessness of Reykdæla to the consummate artistry
of Gísla saga and Hrafnkatla. Among them, we find
sentimental tragic romance (Gunnlaugs saga), shrewd
political propaganda (Hænsa-Þóris saga), devastating social satire (Bandamanna saga), and pene-
trating psychological analysis (Gísla saga). There
are several exampla for contemporary times, of which
Vatnsdæla saga is the most obvious, but there is
also a cynical reminder that in the Sturlung Age the
ruthless exercise of might made right (Hrafnkels
saga). In the Íslendinga sögur, we read much about
honor and blood vengeance, yet the concept of honor in
Hrafnkatla is diametrically opposed to that in Valla-
Ljóts saga, and in several of these stories conflicts
arising from killings are resolved in a peaceful and
reasonable manner. Christian sentiment and Christian
ethics are no less patent than pagan heroism.

Chapter Seven
Late Sagas about Icelanders

Introduction

Although sagas about Icelanders continued to be written until the mid-nineteenth century, the canon ends with Fljótsdæla saga, the "story of the people of Fljótsdal," believed to have been composed about 1500 in northern Iceland (1). The sagas written after about 1300 fall into two general categories, which cannot, however, be neatly distinguished since the authors of most of these stories borrowed copiously from earlier works: stories that are more or less original and reworkings or conflations of earlier sagas. Most of the late sagas reveal motival and stylistic influence from the riddarasögur or the fornaldarsögur or both. Although most of the late sagas seem to have little relevance for contemporary times, several of them rank stylistically among the best of the Íslendingasögur.

Original Works

Finnboga saga ramma. The "story of Finnbogi the Strong" begins with the motif of child exposure borrowed from Gunnlaugs saga. The first part of the story reads like a fornaldarsaga. Finnbogi travels from Norway to Constantinople, amazing people with his feats of strength, many of which he performs twice. For the most part they are fanciful exaggerations of superhuman exploits known from earlier sagas. The second part, which is in a more realistic vein, deals with the hero's protracted feud with the people of Vatnsdal. In this story, as in Vatnsdæla, Thorstein is depicted as an ideal chieftain. The roles of Finnbogi and Jökul, however, are reversed. In Vatnsdæla, Finnbogi is consistently overcome by Jökul, whereas in this story, Jökul is portrayed as a bellicose but bungling aggressor who has to be rescued repeatedly by his brother Thorstein from the invincible

warrior Finnbogi. Eventually Finnbogi and the men of
Vatnsdal are fully reconciled, exchange gifts, and
become good friends. "Finnbogi lived to be an old man,
and he was regarded as most outstanding in strength,
size, and chivalry" (chap. 43). The style of this saga
is lucid but more colloquial than that of most
Íslendingasögur. The aims of the author were clearly entertainment and the literary rehabilitation of
Finnbogi.

Króka-Refs saga. Banished from Iceland for
justified manslaughter, "Tricky Ref" sails to Greenland, where he marries and earns his living as a carpenter and shipbuilder. After taking bloody vengeance for
gross insults, Ref moves his family into the wilderness. Here he builds a stronghold so skillfully that
it looks "like a single board" (chaps. 10 and 14). His
enemies, led by a royal retainer named Bárd, discover
the fortress but are unable to burn it down because of
an ingenious sprinkling system supplied with water
through a hidden conduit. King Harald the Harsh, known
from his biography as an expert in such matters,
advises Bárd how to destroy the conduit (2). Bárd
now succeeds, but Ref kills him and sails to Norway.

In Norway Ref is obliged to kill Harald's favorite
retainer, Grani, for trying to assault his wife. Ref
boldly proclaims the killing to King Harald but in such
kenning-like puns that he is able to escape before the
king can unriddle the message (3). King Harald now
lengthens his name to Króka-Ref because of his cleverness, but King Svein of Denmark changes it to Sigtrygg
("victory-faithful") because of his martial exploits.
Sigtrygg dies while returning from a pilgrimage to Rome
and is buried in a monastery in France.

The author was an excellent stylist and a master of
the stranded plot. He was not well versed in history,
however, as we can see from his confusion about Norwegian kings in chapter 1 and the chronology of his saga.
His most glaring anachronism was the request he
attributed to the sage Gest (best known from
Laxdæla) that Ref have a report (frásögn)
written about his voyage to Greenland (chap. 6). But
his purpose was, after all, not to write history but to
create an entertaining story about a clever character.

Þórðar saga hreðu. Another famous carpenter
and shipbuilder in saga literature was Thórd "Strife,"
whose story was composed about 1350 in northern Ice-

land. Although not overly aggressive, Thórd does not
hesitate to use his sword when necessity demands, as it
does with rather monotonous frequency because of
Thórd's complex relationship with the chieftain
Skeggi. From the outset, Skeggi resents Thórd, a
Norwegian newcomer to the Midfjord district, because of
the popularity he gains through building houses and
boats for people. Thórd saves Skeggi's son Eid from
drowning, after which Eid remains with Thórd as his
foster son. The strained relationship betweeen the two
men erupts into open hostility when Thórd slays
Skeggi's nephew Orm for attempting to seduce Thórd's
sister Sigríd, who is betrothed to Orm's brother
Ásbjörn. Eid repeatedly intervenes to prevent or to
stop serious fighting between his father and his foster
father and eventually brings about a reconciliation.
Ásbjörn and Sigríd are married and move to Norway,
Thórd and Eid remain good friends, and Skeggi spends
his old age at the home of his son.

The most realistic of the late sagas, Dórðar saga
is singularly free of influence from the riddarasögur and the fornaldarsögur. The generation-gap
theme is central to the story, but it seems to lack the
symbolic significance it has in Eyrbyggja and
Dorsteins saga stangarhöggs. Although individual
scenes are effectively related, the structure of the
story is strained by the plethora of fights between
Thórd and his many adversaries. The author's main
purpose seems to have been to create a story in the
style and spirit of the older sagas, possibly in opposition to the more fanciful popular fiction of his day.

Víglundar saga. By contrast, the sentimental
love story of Víglund and Ketilríd was concocted of
fanciful motifs from many sources and modeled on
Friðþjófs saga, a viking romance widely known from
Esaias Tegnér's oft translated Swedish verse rendition. The spirit of the saga is suggested by several
names: Víglundr ("battle tree") is a kenning for
"warrior," the hero's mother had the byname geisli
("sunbeam"), and his brother is named Trausti
(traust means "help, support, firmness"). Víglund
and Ketilríd are mentioned nowhere else in the
Íslendingasögur except in a late paper transcript of
Bárðar saga.

In the prelude, which adumbrates the main story,
Thorgrím abducts his sweetheart Ólof from her wedding

feast, and the two escape to Iceland. Their sons are
Víglund and Trausti. Thorgrím's friend Hólmkel and
his wife Thorbjörg have a daughter named Ketilríd and
two sons. Víglund and Ketilríd wish to marry, but
her mother insists that she marry a Norwegian named
Hákon. Víglund and Trausti are ambushed by a band of
men led by Hákon and the two brothers. Hákon and the
brothers are killed and Víglund and Trausti severely
wounded. They go abroad and on their return take
lodging with an old farmer named Ketil. To their great
surprise they discover that the farmer's wife is
Ketilríd. As in Friðþjófs saga, the hero resists
the temptation of killing his host while he is asleep.
Ketil now reveals that he is Víglund's uncle Helgi and
that he and Ketilríd are not really man and wife.
Víglund offers Hólmkel redress for the killing of his
sons, and the two lovers are married.

Characterization and motivation in this romance are
equally inane. Thorbjörg, for example, hates her
daughter and incites her scoundrelly sons to evil for
no apparent reason. Ketilríd is apathetic or at best
passive. The reconciliation between Hólmkel and
Víglund is too casual even for a fairy tale. The only
characters who are memorable are Víglund, who gives
vent to his rage, jealousy, and frustration in numerous
verses that Heusler rather overrated, and Trausti, who,
true to his name, staunchly supports his brother in
word and deed. Víglundar saga was probably composed
about 1400. Topographical descriptions and terms of
direction in the story indicate Snæfellsnes as the
place of composition.

Kjalnesinga saga. The so-called "story of the
people of Kjalarnes" is primarily the biography of Búi
Andríðsson. Outlawed for refusing to sacrifice to the
pagan gods, Búi retaliates by burning down the temple
before going abroad. In Norway Harald Fairhair punish-
es him for this deed by sending him to fetch a chess-
board that Harald's foster father, the giant king
Dofri, is withholding from him. Búi succeeds, only to
be confronted with another demand: he must wrestle a
black giant. Búi kills the giant by causing him to
fall on a pointed rock. Upon returning to Iceland,
Búi marries the daughter of the chieftain who outlawed
him and inherits his property and godord. Twelve years
later, Búi is confronted by his son, whom he has engen-
dered with Dofri's daughter. The two wrestle, and the

son kills Búi exactly as he killed the black giant (4).

The author of this fanciful fabrication garnered his material from several older sagas. Búi resembles "Arrow-Odd," the hero of Örvar-Odds saga, except that he carries a sling instead of a bow as a weapon. The description of the temple was taken from Eyrbyggja, whose author, we recall, borrowed it from Heimskringla. The popularity of this story is attested by the fact that five sets of rímur were derived from it. Kjalnesinga saga is thought to have been composed about 1320, possibly, as Finnur Jónsson believed, in the monastery at Videy (5).

Flóamanna saga. Even more incongruous is the "story of the people of Flói," which was composed about 1300. The first part is a hodgepodge of loans from Landnámabók and motifs from various fornaldar- sögur. It relates the quarrels of Earl Atli and his sons with Ingólf Arnarson, the first settler in Ice- land, and his sworn brother Hjörleif. The second part is of interest especially because of its dreams from disparate sources (6). The central figure of the story is Atli's grandson Thorgils, who returns to Iceland after gaining fame and fortune abroad by killing vikings.

"Now Christianity came to Iceland, and Thorgils was among the first to accept the faith" (chap. 20). Immediately after his conversion, Thorgils is harassed by his former patron Thór, who threatens him in dreams, kills his domestic animals, and once attacks him physically. In the most remarkable of these dreams, Thór tries to dissuade Thorgils from accepting Eirík the Red's invitation to migrate to Greenland. "Then it seemed to him that Thór led him unto some cliffs, where the raging sea broke against the crags. 'You will be in such heavy seas and never escape unless you turn to me.' 'No,' said Thorgils. 'Depart from me, you foul fiend! He who redeemed all with his blood will save me'" (chap. 21). The dream is, of course, an adaptation of Matthew 4:8-10. The denigration and demonization of pagan deities is a commonplace in the hagiographic konungasögur, but not in the Íslendingasögur.

Despite Thór's warning, Thorgils leads an expedi- tion to Greenland. After months of being tossed about at sea, Thorgils's ship is wrecked on the barren coast

of Greenland, where the crew are forced to remain for
two years. Near the end of this time, Thorgils's wife
Thórey has a dream in which she seems to see "a fair
countryside and beautiful and radiant people--'and I
anticipate that we shall be delivered from these
troubles.'" Thorgils agrees with Thórey that this is
a good dream but interprets it as an intimation of the
world to come, where "holy men will help you because of
your pure life and your tribulations" (chap. 23).
Several days later, Thórey is stabbed to death by a
slave.

Not long afterwards, Thorgils experiences a version
of the tree dream. "'Again I dreamed,' said Thorgils,
'that I was at home in Tradarholt. I saw that on my
right knee there were five angelica stalks [hjálmlau-
kar] growing together, and from them branched off many
flowers [laukar], one of which towered high above my
head, and it was as beautiful as though it had the
color of gold'" (7). The dream is interpreted as
prophetic of Thorgils's many descendants, one of whom
will become famous. "And that," the author assures us,
"later proved to be true, for from Thorgils is
descended Bishop Thorlák the Holy" (chap. 24).

From the standpoint of style and structure Flóamanna is one of the weakest of the late sagas. The
sentences are short and monotonous, and the dialogue is
dull. The action is largely unmotivated, consisting of
a string of loosely connected incidents. There are few
memorable scenes in the story, and one incident is
repeated almost verbatim (chaps. 19 and 32). The
delineation of Thorgils's character is not convincing.
He is pious and firm in the faith, yet at the same time
a fierce killer. He callously gives his first wife to
a friend as a gift but is kind and considerate to his
second wife. After Thórey's death, he breast-feeds
their son Thorfinn, later orders him to be killed, and
then is grateful that the order is not carried out.
After many adventures in Greenland, Iceland, and Norway, Thorgils returns home, where he marries once more
and continues to live an active life until he dies at
the age of eighty-five. The author of Flóamanna was
obviously a well-read scholar who was clever at using
words in a double sense (especially in the dreams) but
inept at putting them together to form pleasing sentences and coherent narrative.

Gunnars saga Keldugnúpsfílfs. The "story of

Gunnar, the fool of Keldugnúp" is unique among the Íslendingasögur in that Earl Hákon is the only person in the story known from other sources. The plot closely follows that of Kjalnesinga saga, with loans from various other tales and stories (8). Gunnar, a typical "coal-biter," that is, an idler who loafs by the fire, suddenly casts off his lethargy and in a wrestling match kills an aggressive thrall belonging to the local chieftain. To escape the wrath of the chieftain and his sons, Gunnar and his brother Helgi spend the winter in a cave. Subsequently, they extend hospitality to a Norwegian merchant named Bárd whom the chieftain has forbidden to trade in the district. After killing the chieftain's two sons, who with a dozen henchmen ambushed him, Gunnar sails with Helgi and Bárd for Norway. Before reaching that country, however, they drift to a land covered with glaciers, where Gunnar kills a bear and some trolls. Earl Hákon insists that Gunnar wrestle a black troll, which he kills by pushing it onto a sharp rock. Both the earl's dislike of Gunnar and their subsequent reconciliation are unmotivated. Eventually Gunnar returns to Iceland, marries his sweetheart Helga, and pays compensation to a woman whose brother he has killed.

Gunnars saga has little substance and no apparent purpose except entertainment. Probably readers found it interesting--it is preserved in two versions in numerous transcripts from the seventeenth to the nineteenth centuries--because of the motifs and situations it has in common with other tales and stories.

Þorsteins saga uxafóts. The first chapter of the "story of Thorstein Oxleg" contains a version of the so-called "beginning of Úlfljót's law" similar to the one found in the older redaction of Þórðar saga hreðu. Although these passages have no relevance for either story, they shed light on the manuscript history of Landnámabók (9).

Thorstein is the son of Oddný and a Norwegian warlord, Ívar, who refuses to acknowledge his paternity of the child. Oddný's brother Thorkel has the child exposed, but as in Finnboga saga, it is saved by a poor married couple and eventually returned to its mother. In a dream Thorstein participates in a battle between twelve red-clad and twelve blue-clad mound dwellers, whereby he gains a metal object that enables his mother to speak. (Previously she has communicated by scratching runes on a runestick.) One of the mound dwellers named Brynjar urges Thorstein to embrace the new faith when it comes to the North and to name one of his sons for him.

In Norway Thorstein has a series of encounters with trolls, and when one of them is on the point of overcoming him, he vows to accept the faith that Ólaf Tryggvason is preaching. Immediately, a bright light shines into the troll's eyes and renders him helpless. Shortly afterward, Thorstein's companion Strykár, fearing for Thorstein's safety, "promises the creator of heaven and earth to adopt the faith that King Ólaf is proclaiming if he finds . . . his companion alive and well" (chap. 11). He soon finds him pinned to the ground (like the poet Kormák) by the body of a huge troll he has killed. Thorstein submits to baptism, forces Ívar at swordpoint to recognize him as his son, and tears a hind leg from an ox intended for pagan sacrifice. After dispatching some more trolls, he marries, names his son Brynjar, joins King Ólaf, and is killed on the Long Serpent in the king's final battle.

The author of Þorsteins saga firmly anchored his story in time and place through loans from Landnáma at the beginning and through historical references at the end of his work. The main action of the story, however, belongs to the never-never land of popular tales and fornaldarsögur.

Late Versions of Older Sagas

Svarfdæla saga. The "story of the people of Svarfadardal" is remarkable for its conglomeration and exaggeration of literary motifs. Because of a lengthy lacuna beginning in chapter 10 and numerous shorter gaps, the story is sometimes difficult to follow.

Thorstein, the hero of the first part of the saga, begins as a kolbítr ("coal-biter"), wins fame and fortune as a viking, and marries the daughter of a Swedish earl (10). His grandson (?) and namesake settles in a valley in the Eyjafjord district that takes its name from his sobriquet svörfuðr ("unruly"?). The son of this Thorstein, Karl the Red, becomes embroiled in a feud with the chieftain Ljótólf largely because of the unmotivated mischief of Karl's cousin Klaufi, the detailed description of whose hideous appearance ends with this sentence: "He was open-mouthed, and two tusks projected from his head, and he looked as though he were all crippled and knotted" (chap. 15). Karl tricks a man named Ásgeir into pledging his daughter Yngvild, the mistress of Ljótólf, to Klaufi in marriage. Yngvild contrives Klaufi's death, after which he haunts the district, using his severed head as a weapon. We are reminded of Sigmund in Færeyinga saga. Karl tortures Ljótólf's bondsman Skídi for concealing two enemies. He breaks Skídi's jaw and splits his lip. Skídi is rewarded by Ljótólf with the hand of Yngvild, who thwarts efforts to arbitrate between Ljótólf and Karl with the comment that such a settlement would not heal the cleft in Skídi's lip. The feud continues until Karl is ambushed and killed.

Karl's posthumous son, also named Karl in accordance with ancient custom, pretends to be a mute fool until age twelve. Then he suddenly comes to life, rides an untamed horse, and devises a scheme to avenge the death of his father. This he does by decapitating Yngvild's three sons before her eyes, wiping his bloody sword on her dress (a loan from Laxdæla), and banishing Skídi from Iceland. To the Hamlet motif the author adds that of the taming of the shrew. Since Yngvild still insists that the cleft in Skídi's lip is completely healed (through the killing of Karl the Red), Karl twice sells her into slavery abroad. After her second harrowing humiliation--she is beaten bloody and led around naked by her owner--Yngvild weepingly admits that nothing will ever heal Skídi's wound. Karl now attempts to return Yngvild first to Skídi and then to Ljótólf, but both reject her, declaring that she persuaded them to commit their most evil crime, namely, the killing of Karl the Red.

The turbulence in Svarfadardal subsides. Ljótólf becomes reconciled with Karl, relents in his treatment of Yngvild, and is found dead--the victim of Klaufi. Karl brings Klaufi's depredations to an end by burning his corpse and sinking the ashes, enclosed in a leaden container, into a spring. Karl then moves out of the district in order to avoid strife with Ljótólf's son, the titular hero of Valla-Ljóts saga.

There is general agreement that Svarfdæla is a late version of an earlier saga but wide disagreement concerning the relationship of the older work to the younger one and to Landnámabók (11). The present

story deviates markedly from most other Íslendingasögur in the violent torture of Skídi and especially
in the protracted physical and emotional torment and
repeated degradations of Yngvild. Torture, to be sure,
does occur elsewhere--in Hrafnkatla, for example--and
women are treated callously in several stories including Heiðarvíga, Vápnfirðinga, and Kjalnesinga
saga. But Svarfdæla is almost completely lacking
in the idealization of women that distinguishes the
Íslendingasögur from the more realistic konungasögur, byskupasögur, and Sturlunga saga (12).

Harðar saga ok Hólmverja. Like Svarfdæla,
the "story of Hörd and the island-dwellers" is characterized by breathless action, but it contains more
dialogue and fully developed scenes. At the age of
fifteen, Hörd goes abroad to earn fame and fortune and
returns fifteen years later to settle in southwestern
Iceland. As so often in the Íslendingasögur, the
hero becomes involved in a bloody feud through the
impetuous action of an irresponsible henchman. Banished for the killing of a neighbor, Hörd builds a
stronghold on the island of Geirshólm, to which many
other outlaws are attracted. From the island they
undertake frequent sallies to the mainland for food and
other supplies. After three years of this precarious
existence, the outlaws succumb to an offer of a truce
and safe conduct from the district. All of them are
taken to the mainland and slaughtered by the plundered
farmers. Hörd suspects treachery but cannot remain
behind when accused of cowardice. He too is killed
after a superhuman defense. During the night, his wife
Helga swims ashore with their two children, and they
are given shelter by Hörd's sister Thorbjörg.

By far the most interesting character in the story,
Thorbjörg is married to Indridi, one of Hörd's most
formidable adversaries. She thwarts Hörd's attempt to
burn down their house by means of a concealed water
conduit--we are reminded of Króka-Ref's sprinkler
system--but after Hörd's death she tries to kill
Indridi for his participation in Hörd's capture. She
inveigles her husband into slaying Hörd's killer
Thorstein and tricks him into promising to protect
Helga and her children. Twenty-four men are killed
without atonement in vengeance for Hörd, most of them
"at the instigation of Thorbjörg. . . . She is regarded as having been a very notable woman" (chap. 41).

The author made frequent use of various forms of foreshadowing. Two tree dreams foretell the birth of Hörd and his sister Thorbjörg (chaps. 6-7). Thorbjörg's more conventional wolf dream foreshadows Hörd's attempt to burn their house. When Hörd breaks into the viking Sóti's grave mound and seizes his gold ring, Sóti predicts that Hörd and all other future owners of the ring will be killed. The prediction proves to be true.

The end of Harðar saga is so similar to that of Grettis saga that there must be some connection between them, but it is not clear which story is the source and which the borrower. The author of Grettla cited Sturla Thórdarson as his authority for Grettir's exceptional fate as an outlaw; in like manner the author of Harðar saga cites Priest Styrmir the Learned to prove that his hero was among the most noteworthy of Icelandic outlaws. Both heroes spent their last three years on an island, and both Sturla and Styrmir advanced three reasons in support of their assertions about Grettir and Hörd, respectively.

Gull-Þóris saga. The "story of Gold-Thórir," composed about 1310, is a reworking of an older saga, portions of which are found in Sturlubók. Influence from the fornaldarsögur is strong. In its present form, the saga has a lacuna between chapters 10 and 13. The story reads well for the most part, and the composition is cohesive.

Thórir Oddsson sails to Norway with nine foster brothers to win fame and fortune during the days of Harald Fairhair. His uncle Agnar, a troll, gives him certain magic gifts with which to break open a viking cave guarded by dragons. Agnar warns Thórir, however, that his avarice will eventually cause his downfall. Thórir enters the cave and overcomes the viking, but only after calling on Agnar for help. Thórir keeps almost all of the treasure for himself. His companions "found that Thórir was a completely different man than he had been" (chap. 4).

After many adventures abroad, Thórir and his foster brothers return to Iceland. A chieftain named Hall, the father of one of Thórir's foster brothers, claims a share of the treasure since his son helped Thórir acquire it, but Thórir rejects his demands. The quarrel between Thórir and Hall develops into a feud that leads to much bloody fighting in the Thorskafjord

district.   Finally Thórir succeeds in overcoming all
his adversaries.   After his final battle, "Thórir's
disposition changed.   He became very difficult to deal
with" (chap. 19).   The false report of the death of his
son Gudmund is so unsettling to Thórir that he disap-
pears with his treasure and is never seen again.
"People believed that he had become a dragon and had
lain down on his chests of gold.   For a long time
afterward they continued to see a dragon on the far
side of the fjord flying down from Thórisstadir, which
is called Gullfors ("golden waterfall") (chap. 20).

The author's purpose in composing this story was
obviously to show the disintegration of human personality and the disruption of community life through
avarice.   The theme of the curse of gold was timely in
the thirteenth century, when the original version of
the story was presumably composed, and the approach was
imaginative, but the execution--to judge from the
present state of the text--did not quite match the bold
conception.   The character of Thórir remains shadowy
and indistinct.   The author's inspiration, of course,
came from stories about the dragon Fáfnir such as that
in the Eddic lay Reginsmál.

Hávarðar saga Ísfirðings.   The "story of
Hávard from the Ísafjord" (ca. 1330) is another
reworking of an older saga of which excerpts have been
preserved in Landnámabók.   Hávard's son Ólaf, who
finds lost sheep for farmers and rids the district of a
revenant, is slain by the chieftain Thorbjörn, an
ójafnaðarmaðr who violates the daughters of his
liegemen.   Ólaf's aging father Hávard three times
seeks redress from Thorbjörn, and each time is
rebuffed and insulted, whereupon he takes to his bed
for a year.   Hávard's wife Bjargey enlists support
from her kinsmen and devises a plan to ambush
Thorbjörn.   Hávard's former viking nature reawakens,
and he boldly executes his wife's plan.   He swims
across a sound in full armor in pursuit of his enemy.
Thorbjörn is on the point of crushing Hávard with a
rock when Hávard recalls having heard about the new
religion being preached by Ólaf Tryggvason.   He vows
to submit to baptism, Thorbjörn slips and falls, and
Hávard kills him.   In due course Hávard and Bjargey
sail to Norway and are baptized by King Ólaf.

Despite its burlesque heroics, Hávarðar saga is a
most enjoyable story, especially if read as generic

farce. Several of the characters, such as the miser Atli and his clever and lovely wife Thórdís, are well portrayed, the style is excellent, and several scenes are cleverly set and effectively executed. The humor, of which there is much in this saga, is sometimes subtle, sometimes cruel, but mostly boisterous.

Bárðar saga Snæfellsáss. The "story of Bárd, the god of Snæfellsnes," which seems to be an augmented version of an earlier Gests saga, consists of freely treated borrowings from Landnámabók and from various konungasögur and fornaldarsögur. Bárd, the son of a giant, grows up in the cave of his foster father Dofri, where he experiences a version of the tree dream (13). This dream signifies the imminent reign of Harald Fairhair and the future conversion of Norway by Ólaf Tryggvason. To escape the tyranny of King Harald, Bárd migrates to Iceland, where he soon becomes the patron deity of the people of Snæfellsnes. He protects all who call upon him against attacks from trolls and witches and even against Thór and Ódin. On a smaller scale, his son Gest does likewise.

Curious about King Ólaf, Gest accompanies two half-brothers and a sister-in-law to Norway. All submit to baptism except Gest, who has a premonition that forsaking the faith of his ancestors will bring sudden death. At the request of King Ólaf, Gest sets out to plunder the grave mound of King Raknar in Helluland. With the help of a priest, Gest finds the mound at the end of a narrow tongue of land and breaks into it, but when his candle burns out, Raknar overcomes him with heathen sorcery. In this extremity Gest calls on his father Bárd to protect him, but Bárd's strength is insufficient. Then Gest vows to accept the faith proclaimed by Ólaf and appeals directly to the king for help. As so frequently in saga literature, Ólaf Tryggvason (or Saint Ólaf, as the case may be) intervenes, and the hero accomplishes his mission. Raknar's pagan magic, however, has not been completely destroyed. Surging waves cover the peninsula, but the priest moves forward with cross and holy water. "Then the waters parted so that they went ashore with dry feet" (chap. 21).

Upon his return Gest submits to baptism. During the night, however, his father appears to him in a dream. "You have done an evil thing to forsake your faith, that of your forefathers, and to let yourself be cowed into a change of faith out of paltriness, and for that

you will lose both your eyes" (chap. 21). Bárd
strikes Gest's eyes, and when he awakens, they hurt so
terribly that they burst. Shortly afterwards he dies
and is buried in his baptismal robes.

Like many sagas, this one can be interpreted in
several ways--as serious fiction by a superstitious
author, as generic farce by a sophisticated one, as a
warning to contemporary readers not to dabble in witchcraft or other forms of paganism, or simply as an exciting troll story. However we interpret it, Bárðar
saga is further evidence of the persistent fascination
of saga writers and readers with the person and the
theme of the reluctant Christian. Although the author
employs threadbare materials, he treats them imaginatively. The details of the tree dream are cleverly
adapted to the scene. Two motifs connected with the
theme of the reluctant Christian--fear of reprisals
from kinsmen and fear of punishment by the gods--are
combined. And in the mysterious Bárd, the author and
the redactor have created a supernatural being that is
both antipagan and anti-Christian.

Fljótsdæla saga. The "story of the people of
Fljótsdal" was compiled by a man who was thoroughly
acquainted with the sagas contained in the codex
Möðruvallabók. He began his compilation with what
seems to be a continuation of Hrafnkatla. The main
body of the story is an augmented, fanciful adaptation
of Droplaugarsona saga, in which he embedded Gunnars
saga Þiðrandabana. Structurally, this "longer saga of
Droplaug," as it is sometimes called, lacks symmetry,
but it reads well since the compiler modeled his style
on that of Hrafnkels saga.

Two episodes will suffice to illustrate the difference between the original saga and its later reworking.
In the former, the marriage of Droplaug to Thorvald,
the father of Helgi and Grím, is briefly mentioned:
"Thorvald asked for Droplaug in marriage, the marriage
took place, and they had two sons" (chap. 2). In
Fljótsdæla, Droplaug is the daughter of a Norwegian
earl, whom Thorvald wins as his wife by rescuing her
from a giant. The actual rescue is foreshadowed in
detail in a dream. The episode, which is vividly
related, is ten pages in length.

In Droplaugarsona saga, Helgi and Grím during a
snowstorm happen upon a pagan temple belonging to their
foster father Bersi. In the derived saga this

fourteen-line incident is expanded into a detailed description of the temple and of Helgi's thorough destruction of the building and its pagan gods. The five-page episode is preceded by a confrontation between Bersi and Helgi, in which Helgi expounds on the futility of worshiping gods "that men make with their hands and are blind and deaf and speechless" (chap. 25).

Unfortunately, Fljótsdæla has been poorly preserved, and some scholars have even questioned its existence as an independent work. Even in its present dilapidated state, however, it affords valuable insights into the treatment of sources in saga composition and into changing literary tastes in Iceland.

Conclusion

In the Íslendingasögur composed or compiled between 1300 and 1500 we find striking diversity in spirit, form, and content. In general the language of the late sagas is more lucid than that of the earliest ones, and the punning is more sophisticated. Almost all these stories contain well-developed scenes, but far too often the action of a story is simply reported instead of being turned into vivid narrative and pithy dialogue.

Authors of late sagas introduced several new themes and motifs into the genre. Here we find for the first time the Hamlet theme and that of the taming of the shrew, and (in Flóamanna) the popular medieval parable of the refractory wife whose husband learns how to deal with her by watching a rooster chastise a rebellious hen (chap. 31). The prophetic tree dream, which we associate primarily with legendary tales, occurs four times in the late stories but nowhere else in the Íslendingasögur.

Biblical influence is found in several of these stories. The most obvious example is the episode in Flóamanna discussed above. We are reminded of Helgi the Lean in Landnámabók, who was nominally a Christian but "invoked the aid of Thór before sea voyages and in difficult situations" (14). The motif of the blood-drenched cloak of Joseph (Genesis 37:31-32) is found in Svarfdæla. We noted above that Karl Karlsson's cruel treatment of Yngvild is unique in the Íslendingasögur. The closest parallel and possible ultimate source is found in 2 Maccabees, chapter 7, where Antiochus has seven brothers roasted to death in the presence of their mother after first having their tongues torn out and their extremities cut off. The crossing of the Red Sea by the Israelites (Exodus 14: 21-22) is reflected in Bárðar saga (chap. 21) (15).

Since the authors of late Íslendingasögur were competing with the adventurous fornaldarsögur and the fantastic native imitations of riddarasögur (dozens of which remain unedited), they strove for dramatic effect by using popular old motifs in new ways. Thus the killing of Búi by his son and of Gest by his father Bárd represent new twists to the old father-son conflict in the Íslendingasögur. This incident also illustrates another way of using old themes, for it combines the father-son conflict with the theme of the reluctant Christian.

Influence from contemporary popular tales can be seen especially in the gross exaggeration of adventures abroad and in the bizarre treatment of supernatural events, usually in scenes set in Iceland. An excellent example of the former is the rescue of Droplaug from a giant in Fljótsdæla. In the older sagas-- Eyrbyggja provides a good basis for comparison-- supernatural events are portrayed soberly (16). By contrast, the antics of Bárd and Klaufi are grotesque. Both Grettir and Skalla-Grím convincingly demonstrate their superhuman strength by lifting huge stones. Finnbogi outdoes them. Just before returning to Iceland, he pays a visit to the king of Greece. The king and twelve of his courtiers are seated on a throne. Finnbogi raises the throne to his shoulder, carries it some distance, and sets it down.

Although the late sagas, with few exceptions, seem to be a form of escape literature--like most of the riddarasögur and fornaldarsögur--we are occasionally surprised to find passages that reflect Icelandic life during the commonwealth period. The most intriguing example is found in Svarfdæla. After Ásgeir has been duped into pledging his daughter Yngvild to Klaufi in marriage, "Karl and his companions ride down to Brekka and bring Klaufi and Yngvild into one bed" (chap. 21). This is in accordance with the Icelandic law book known as Grágás (Gray goose), which stipulates that at least six witnesses were to observe the bride and groom go to bed during daylight (17). In many respects, the latest sagas resemble the earlier <u>konungasögur</u> and transitional <u>Íslendinga-sögur</u> more closely than they do the major and minor Sagas of Icelanders composed during the thirteenth century.

Chapter Eight
Summary and Conclusions

One obvious conclusion to be drawn from this brief survey of saga literature is that we must be cautious about making sweeping generalizations. What, for instance, is meant by "saga style"? (1). As we have seen, narrative style in the sagas is usually straightforward and paratactic, whereas expository style tends to be rather complex. Dialogue is often terse and finely honed, but sometimes it is long-winded, with sentences up to ten lines in length. Indeed, in a few sagas, we find instead of dialogue long passages of indirect discourse, interspersed with occasional brief direct quotations. Furthermore, scribes unfortunately took liberties with the manuscripts they copied, usually by shortening and simplifying sentences and by omitting the authorial first person. Despite this, however, marked individual differences remain, so that the ample, leisurely style of Laxdæla, for example, contrasts sharply with the pithy, rhythmical language of Njáls saga. A history of saga style cannot be written until we have much more information about the language of the sagas in their manuscript variants. At present, we can merely observe that the style of the earliest sagas is often clumsy or verbose, whereas the language of later sagas tends to be limpid, terse, and fluent.

Rhetorical and structural development is less difficult to follow. For the sake of brevity, we must limit ourselves here to one rhetorical and two structural techniques. Foreshadowing, which was known from Eddic poetry, the Bible, and saints' lives and occurs in patent forms in the earliest sagas, undergoes a process of refinement that culminates in Gísla saga and Njála, where we find it employed in a highly subtle and diversified manner (2). In most of the transitional Íslendingasögur as well as in Egils saga, the protagonist's death does not result from a major conflict, and for this reason, these stories lack both the revenge and reconciliation sections that are characteristic of many later sagas. Digression occurs in older sagas, but plot stranding is first introduced in Sverris saga, is highly developed in Heimskringla, and reaches its maximal complexity in Njála.

Parallel to, and partly because of, this rhetorical and structural development, we can observe a progressive refinement in character delineation. In the earliest royal biographies, the missionary king and Saint Ólaf, despite their imperfections, were heroes, and their pagan adversaries were villains. In Sverris saga, however, Karl Jónsson was able to maintain a stance of neutrality and to portray Sverrir and his enemies with greater detachment by telling his story alternately from opposite points of view. This technique was improved by Snorri and by later authors of Íslendingasögur, with the result that character portrayal truly became the alpha and omega of saga art. The Íslendingasögur contain more memorable portraits of complex men and women than any other medieval literary genre.

The Íslendingasögur were once believed to be the heirs and prose continuators of the heroic poetry of the North. Like so many of our former beliefs, this one has to be abandoned on the basis of recent research. In saga literature, the berserker and the viking are nearly always villains--the poet Egil is a notable exception, and he dies of old age. Not Killer-Styr and the superannuated viking Thórólf win praise in Eyrbyggja saga, but Arnkel and Snorri, who are embodiments of hóf, the highest ideal for many, if not most, saga writers. For this reason, Eyrbyggja can be interpreted as an exemplum of moderation for the Sturlung Age of excess, although it is, of course, more than that, just as Njála is more than a Christian homily. The individual warrior may be admired (Gunnar, Gísli), but the individualistic warrior ethos is rejected in favor of a more social ideal. In Eyrbyggja, as in several other sagas, the contrast between the heroic and the social codes is made vivid through the use of the generation-gap theme.

If, as has often been maintained, the pagan mode of thought is dominant in the Íslendingasögur, we must ask ourselves why antipagan sentiment permeates the corpus from the beginning to the very end. The chieftains in Vatnsdæla devoted much time and energy to cleansing their district of witches and warlocks.

Grettir was immune to all hostile forces except heathen
sorcery, and in the cathedral in Trondheim, the imp
that baited him was equated with the evil spirit.
There are numerous instances of saga characters being
punished for rejecting baptism or for refusing to abandon paganism, and several saga heroes who were injured
or killed by pagan spirits for forsaking the ancient
faith. No less than cupiditas and ambitio, pagan
practices were an ever-present pernicious force in saga
literature.

As we have seen, however, the noble pagan is a
frequent and laudable hero in the sagas. Despite his
paganism, he scorns pagan sacrifice, overcomes vikings,
embodies Christian virtues, and sometimes anticipates
baptism. The virtuous heathen has been interpreted as
signifying the exculpation and justification of pagan
forebears from the standpoint of medieval theology, and
that interpretation is probably correct as far as it
goes. The reluctant Christian can be seen as a counterpart of the noble heathen. Through his spiritual struggles and his confrontations with Christian missionaries, he dramatizes the importance of baptism. Like
the chieftains of the Icelandic General Assembly in
999, he accepts Christianity reluctantly but--and this
is extremely important--of his own free will. Some
noble heathens are also reluctant Christians. After
three generations of virtuous pagans in Vatnsdæla,
the last of the great chieftains of the district,
Thorkel, becomes first a reluctant, then a devout,
Christian. Thus Vatnsdæla, like Eyrbyggja, can be
read as an exemplum for the Sturlung Age; but whereas
Eyrbyggja is secular in tone, Vatnsdæla abounds in
Christian sentiment.

Hóf, of course, is not an exclusively Christian
virtue (3). The restraint and moderation of Snorri the
Chieftain, for example, were motivated by secular, pragmatic considerations. Unlike Grettir, he realized that
heroic deeds and good fortune were incompatible in the
restrictive, postviking Icelandic commonwealth. The
survival of both the individual and society demands
compromise and accommodation. But when hóf occurs
in combination with humility and magnanimity, and even
with the readiness to forego blood vengeance--a virtue
that even the Christian Njál could not attain--then we
are dealing with true Christian sentiment. Admittedly
there are few such forgiving pagans, or even Chris-

tians, in saga literature--Eid in <u>Heiðarvíga saga</u>, Thorstein and Björn in <u>Bjarnar saga</u>, Áskel in <u>Reykdæla</u>, Thorstein hvíti in his story, the Norwegian highwayman and Ingimund in <u>Vatnsdæla</u>, and Hall of Síða and the saintly Höskuld in <u>Njála</u> come to mind.

It might be argued that antipagan sentiments are not necessarily pro-Christian attitudes and that the virtuous heathens and reluctant Christians in the sagas are the exception that proves the rule: the prevailing temper of the Sagas of Icelanders is pagan. This, of course, is true: the cultural reference is pagan. But the cultural milieu is Christian, and the functions of the virtuous heathen and the significance of antipagan predilections were certainly clear to the medieval reader. Few scholars would deny that saga authors present an idealized picture of the world of their pagan forebears, especially as far as fighting and killing are concerned. We find in the <u>Íslendingasögur</u> almost no examples of the revolting torture--blinding, castration, the hacking off of arms and legs--that characterize the historical sagas, including <u>Sturlunga saga</u>. But most amazing of all in the Sagas of Icelanders is the attitude toward women and sexual morality: rape, concubinage, and extramarital dalliance--again in contrast to the more realistic sagas--are as uncommon as torture. We find in this pagan society the realization of many of the ideals of sexual morality taught by the church, but not generally respected by the people, in Christian Iceland. Again the only reasonable explanation is that the Sagas of Icelanders were intended as moral exempla for the thirteenth century.

As we have seen, Ari's <u>Íslendingabók</u> is tendentious and nationalistic. <u>Íslendingabók</u> and <u>Landnámabók</u> mark the beginning of Iceland as a free, proud, and independent country. The earliest þættir, written during a time of worsening political relations with Norway, asserted the importance of Icelanders at the Norwegian court. The royal biographies of Thingeyrar glorified three kings who were both the secular and religious leaders of their people and thus, in a sense, the symbolic allies of the Icelandic church proprietors in their struggle to preserve their independence of the Norwegian archiepiscopal see. Both <u>Egils saga</u> and portions of <u>Heimskringla</u> reflect the Icelanders' endeavor to maintain their political independence of Norway. Their worst enemy was the lack of hóf on the part of chieftains striving for self-assertion, for self-aggrandizement through disdain for, and manipulation of, the law. And thus, as we can see best in Njála, the unwillingness or inability of the Icelandic chieftains to discipline themselves led eventually to the collapse of the commonwealth and the loss of political freedom. To be sure, Njála ends in a spirit of Christian reconciliation, but at the time when the author created this literary monument, Iceland had been tributary to Norway for at least two decades. Lawlessness had indeed laid waste his land.

Since, as Lönnroth and others have convincingly argued, the concept of the virtuous pagan is based on the writings of Saint Paul and of the Church Fathers, the question arises to what extent the Icelanders' claim to political independence from Norway might also be founded on the same religious-philosophical concepts. This exceedingly complex problem, which has been thoroughly studied by Gerd Wolfgang Weber, needs to be touched on briefly here (4). According to Icelandic traditions, many settlers fled Norway in order to maintain the personal freedom that they felt was threatened by Harald Fairhair. Part of Iceland had been occupied before the Norse settlement by Christian anchorites and thus remained, according to church doctrine, Christian territory. Some settlers, we recall, had no other faith than their reliance in their own "might and main," and since such men did not engage in pagan sacrifice, they may be regarded as virtuous heathens. A rather large number of settlers were Christians, and even though their descendants drifted away from the true faith, it was because of ignorance, not because of deliberate defection. For these reasons, the Icelanders, unlike the other Scandinavians, did not have to be converted by force of arms. And for these same theological reasons, as Weber has cogently argued, the Icelanders could claim a right to personal freedom and political independence despite the declaration of Cardinal William of Sabina in 1247 that they, like all other peoples, should be subject to a king (5).

According to Schier, a major impulse for the writing of sagas came from an awareness of creating a new nation (6). This awareness is manifest in Íslendinga-bók and Egils saga and apparent in several other sagas. The uniqueness of this new nation, however, consisted largely in its endeavor to preserve something old. In this sense, the Íslendingasögur can be interpreted as the Icelanders' declaration of their rights to be free and independent, and this freedom mythos derived its legitimation from Christianity (7).

The Icelandic sagas are indeed Scandinavia's unique contribution to world literature and the most extraordinary literary creation of medieval Europe. Even if we choose to ignore, or perhaps to deny, their social, religious, and political significance, we can aesthetically enjoy their "strange and characteristic charm," their "unerring portrayal of the human heart," their "concentration on inner conflicts, on the clash of wills, on that which is seething within human beings." This, according to Otto Springer, is the essence of the art of the stories that continue to intrigue and to delight laymen and scholars alike (8).

Notes and References

Preface

1. Theodore M. Andersson, The Legend of Brynhild (Ithaca and London: Cornell University Press, 1980), p. 16.

2. On this genre, see Joseph Harris, "Genre and Narrative Structure in Some Íslendinga þættir," Scandinavian Studies 44 (1972):1-27; "Theme and Genre in Some Íslendinga þættir," Scandinavian Studies 48 (1976):1-28; and "Christian Form and Christian Meaning in Halldórs þáttr I," Harvard English Studies 5 (1974):249-64.

3. Peter Hallberg, The Icelandic Saga, trans. Paul Schach (Lincoln, 1962), p. 1.

4. See Hallberg, The Icelandic Saga, pp. 49-68, and Andersson, The Problem of Icelandic Saga Origins (New Haven and London: Yale University Press, 1964).

5. See Walter Baetke, Uber die Entstehung der Isländersagas, in Berichte über die Verhandlungen der Sächsischen Akademie der Wissenschaften zu Leipzig, Philosophisch-historische Klasse, 102, part 5 (Berlin, 1956), pp. 1-108. A significant contribution to saga research from this school is Die Laxdælasaga by Rolf Heller (Berlin, 1976).

6. Leading representatives of this school are Sigurður Nordal, Einar Ólafur Sveinsson, and Jónas Kristjánsson.

Chapter One

1. Íslendingabók. Landnámabók, ed. Jakob Benediktsson, Íslenzk fornrit, vol. 1 (Reykjavík: Hið íslenzka fornritafélag, 1968), p. 34; The Book of Settlements: Landnámabók, trans. Hermann Pálsson and Paul Edwards, University of Manitoba Icelandic Studies, vol. 1 (Winnipeg: University of Manitoba Press, 1972), pp. 16-17.

2. See Annálar og nafnaskrá, ed. Guðni

Jónsson (Akureyri, 1953), pp. 25, 30, 131-32, 142-43.

3. On this, see W. Lehn, H. Sawatzky, and I. Schroeder, "Lore, Logic, and the Arctic Mirage," Scandinavian Review 66 (1978):36-41 and the literature cited there.

4. See Eiríks saga rauða, chap. 8, and The Vinland Sagas: The Norse Discovery of America, trans. M. Magnusson and H. Pálsson (New York, 1966), p. 94.

5. See The Book of the Icelanders (Íslendingabók) by Ari Thorgilsson, ed. and trans. Halldór Hermannsson (Islandica, vol. 20, Ithaca, N.Y., 1930), p. 6, and The Vinland Sagas, p. 13.

6. See Jón Jóhannesson, A History of the Old Icelandic Commonwealth. Íslendinga saga, trans. Haraldur Bessason (Winnipeg, Canada, 1974), pp. 24-28, and Peter G. Foote and David M. Wilson, The Viking Achievement: A Survey of the Society and Culture of Early Medieval Scandinavia (London, 1970), pp. 52-56.

7. In this paragraph, I have generally followed Jón Jóhannesson, Íslendinga saga, pp. 1-34. A slightly different interpretation, which is closer to saga tradition, is given by Peter Hallberg, The Icelandic Saga (Lincoln, Nebr., 1962), pp. 1-17. See also G. Turville-Petre, Origins of Icelandic Literature (Oxford, 1953), pp. 1-7, and The Book of the Icelanders, pp. 6-11.

8. On the origin, duties, and powers of the goðar, see Olaf Olsen, Hørg, hov og kirke (Copenhagen, 1966), pp. 42-43.

9. Hallberg, The Icelandic Saga, pp. 8-9.

10. Njáls Saga, trans. Magnus Magnusson and Hermann Pálsson (Baltimore, 1960), p. 16.

11. See Hallberg, The Icelandic Saga, pp. 97-113.

12. See Gunnar Karlsson, "Goðar and Höfðingjar in Medieval Iceland," Saga-Book of the Viking Society 19 (1977):358-70.

13. See Olsen, Hørg, pp. 55-66 and the literature cited there.

14. On Eddic and skaldic poetry, see Turville-Petre, Origins, pp. 7-47; Peter Hallberg, Old Icelandic Poetry: Eddic Lay and Skaldic Verse (Lincoln and London, 1975); and Jón Helgason, "Noregs og Islands digtning," in Litteraturhistorie B. Norge og Island, ed. Sigurður Nordal (Oslo, Stockholm, and Copenhagen, 1953), pp. 3-110.

15. The best treatments in English are Turville-

Petre, <u>Origins</u>, pp. 1-69, and Dag Strömbäck, <u>The</u> <u>Conversion of Iceland</u>, trans. Peter Foote (London, 1975). For information on pagan beliefs, see Turville-Petre, <u>Myth and Religion of the North: The Religion</u> <u>of Ancient Scandinavia</u> (New York, 1964); Jon Steffensen, "Aspects of Life in Iceland in the Heathen Period," <u>Saga-Book</u> 17 (1967-68):177-205; and Olsen, <u>Hørg</u>.

16. The translation is from Jón Jóhannesson, <u>Íslendinga saga</u>, p. 70.

17. Ibid., p. 71.

18. <u>History of the Archbishops of Hamburg-Bremen</u>, trans. Francis J. Tschan (New York: Columbia University Press, 1959), p. 218.

19. See <u>Íslendinga sögur</u>, ed. Guðni Jónsson (Akureyri, 1953), 1:235.

20. See Jón Jóhannesson, <u>Íslendinga saga</u>, pp. 149, 173.

21. <u>Íslendingabók</u>, chap. 10.

22. See <u>Íslendinga sögur</u>, ed. Guðni Jónsson, 1:275; Jón Jóhannesson, <u>Íslendinga saga</u>, pp. 160-62.

23. <u>Jóns saga helga</u> (later redaction) in <u>Byskupa sögur</u>, ed. Guðni Jónsson, 2d ed. (Akureyri, 1953), chap. 3 and Jón Jóhannesson, <u>Íslendinga saga</u>, pp. 153-54.

24. See <u>Byskupa sögur</u>, ed. Guðni Jónsson, 2d ed. (Akureyri, 1953), 2:44. Klæng Thorsteinsson taught at Hólar from ca. 1130 until 1152, when he became bishop of Skálholt. The quotation is from the older of the two vernacular renderings.

25. On this, see Paul Schach, "Antipagan Sentiment in the Sagas of Icelanders," in <u>Gripla</u> I, ed. Jónas Kristjánsson (Reykjavík: Stofnun Árna Magnússonar, 1975), pp. 105-34.

26. For a discussion of one example, see <u>The First</u> <u>Grammatical Treatise</u>, ed. Einar Haugen, 2d ed. (London, 1972), pp. 73-77.

27. On this, see Otto Springer, "Medieval Pilgrim Routes from Scandinavia to Rome," <u>Medieval Studies</u> 12 (1950):99-122; reprinted in revised form as "Mittelalterliche Pilgerwege von Skandinavien nach Rom," in his <u>Arbeiten zur germanischen Philologie und zur</u> <u>Literatur des Mittelalters</u> (Munich: Wilhelm Fink Verlag, 1975), pp. 338-72.

28. <u>Oddverja þáttr</u>, chap. 2, in <u>Byskupa</u>

sögur, ed. Guðni Jónsson, 1:137. The translation is from Jón Jóhannesson, Íslendinga saga, p. 185.

29. Jón Jóhannesson, Íslendinga saga, p. 218.

30. Guðmundar saga Arasonar, chap. 35, in Byskupa sögur, ed. Guðni Jónsson, 2:362-63. On this, see Lars Lönnroth, "Studier i Olaf Tryggvasons saga," Samlaren 84 (1963):54-94 and Dietrich Hofmann, "Die Yngvars saga víðförla und Oddr munkr inn Fróði," in Speculum Norroenum, ed. Ursula Dronke et al. (Odense University Press, 1981), pp. 188-222.

31. Íslendingabók. Landnámabók, 2:337. See Jón Jóhannesson, Íslendinga saga, pp. 29-31.

32. On this, see Paul Schach, "Character Creation and Transformation in the Icelandic Sagas," in Germanic Studies in Honor of Otto Springer, ed. Stephen J. Kaplowitt (Pittsburgh: K & S Enterprises, 1978), pp. 237-79.

33. Morkinskinna, ed. Finnur Jónsson (Copenhagen: Jørgensen, 1932), p. 170. The translation is from Jón Jóhannesson, Íslendinga saga, p. 115.

34. Haralds saga Sigurðarsonar (chap. 36), in Heimskringla, vol. 3, ed. Bjarni Aðalbjarnarson, Íslenzk fornrit, vol. 28 (Reykjavík: Hið Íslenzka fornritafélag, 1951).

35. On this, see Paul Schach, "Symbolic Dreams of Future Renown in Old Icelandic Literature," Mosaic 4 (1972):51-73 and the literature cited there.

36. Óláfs saga helga, chap. 125. Quoted from Einar Ól. Sveinsson, The Age of the Sturlungs, Icelandic Civilization in the Thirteenth Century, trans. Jóhann S. Hannesson (Ithaca, N.Y., 1953), pp. 159-60.

37. See Jón Jóhannesson, Íslendinga saga, p. 225.

38. Þorgils saga ok Hafliða, ed. Ursula Brown (London: Oxford University Press, 1952), p. x.

39. On this, see Gunnar Karlsson, "Goðar og bændur," Saga 10 (1972):5-57; the conclusions and some of the argumentation are summarized in his "Goðar and Höfðingjar in Medieval Iceland."

40. See "Goðar and Höfðingjar," p. 363.

41. See The Saga of the Icelanders, in Sturlunga Saga, vol. 1, trans. Julia H. McGrew (New York: Twayne Publishers and ASF, 1970), chaps. 35, 38.

42. Jón Jóhannesson, Íslendinga saga, p. 243.

43. See Einar Ól. Sveinsson, "The Icelandic Sagas and the Period in which Their Authors Lived," Acta

Philologica Scandinavica 12 (1937):71-90; G. Turville-Petre, "Notes on the Intellectual History of the Icelanders," History 27 (1942):111-23; and R. George Thomas, "The Sturlung Age as an Age of Saga Writing," Germanic Review 25 (1950):50-66.

44. Jón Jóhannesson, Íslendinga saga, p. 227. Cf. also Sigurður A. Magnússon, Northern Sphinx (McGill: Queen's University Press, 1977), p. 102: "Many of the chieftains of the thirteenth century . . . were much closer in behaviour and mentality to savage Vikings on the run . . . than to responsible rulers."

45. For a carefully considered discussion of the role of hóf in the sagas, see Theodore M. Andersson, "The Displacement of the Heroic Ideal in the Family Sagas," Speculum 45 (1970):575-93.

46. For examples of the thematic approach to saga research, see L. Lönnroth, "The Noble Heathen: A Theme in the Sagas," Scandinavian Studies 41 (1969): 1-29; K. Hume, "The Thematic Design of Grettis saga," Journal of English and Germanic Philology 73 (1974): 469-86; P. Schach, "Some Observations on the Generation-Gap Theme in the Icelandic Sagas," in The Epic in Medieval Society, ed. H. Scholler (Tübingen: Max Niemeyer Verlag, 1977), pp. 361-81, and "The Theme of the Reluctant Christian in the Icelandic Sagas," JEGP 81 (1982):186-204. On the development of the structure of the sagas, see C. Clover, The Medieval Saga (Ithaca, N.Y.: Cornell University Press, 1982).

Chapter Two

1. For discussions of this literature, see Turville-Petre, Origins, pp. 109-42; Hallberg, The Icelandic Saga, pp. 35-48; Hans Bekker-Nielsen, "Den ældste tid," in Norrøn Fortællekunst (Copenhagen, 1965), pp. 9-26; and Dag Strömbäck, "The Dawn of West Norse Literature," trans. Peter Foote, in Bibliography of Old Norse-Icelandic Studies 1963 (Copenhagen, 1964), pp. 7-24.

2. For the Icelandic text see Einar Haugen, First Grammatical Treatise, 2d rev. ed. (London, 1972), p. 12 and Hreinn Benediktsson, The First Grammatical Treatise (Reykjavík, 1972), p. 208.

3. On the meaning of þýðingar helgar, "interpretations of sacred writings," see Benediktsson, The First Grammatical Treatise, pp. 182-84.

4. See Turville-Petre, Origins, pp. 134-42.

5. Ibid., pp. 86-87.

6. See Svend Ellehøj, Studier over den ældste norrøne historieskrivning (Copenhagen, 1965), pp. 15-24, 258-76, and 301-2.

7. See Annálar og nafnaskrá, ed. Guðni Jónsson, pp. 13 and 83.

8. A translation of this tale is found in Gwyn Jones, The Norse Atlantic Saga. Being the Norse Voyages of Discovery and Settlement of Iceland, Greenland, America (London: Oxford University Press, 1964), pp. 191-203.

9. Thus Ellehøj, Studier, p. 84. But see also Íslendingabók. Landnámabók, ed. Hreinn Benediktsson, Íslenzk fornrit, vol. 1 (Reykjavík: Hið íslenzka fornritafélag, 1968), pp. xviii-xx.

10. See Íslendingabók. Landnámabók, 1:ciii.

11. The stemma is adapted from Jón Jóhannesson, Gerðir Landnámabókar (Reykjavík: Félagsprentsmiðjan, 1941), p. 226.

12. Íslendingabók. Landnámabók, 1:cii and The Book of Settlements, trans. Hermann Pálsson and Paul Edwards (Winnipeg, 1972), p. 6.

13. See Íslendingabók. Landnámabók, 1:cii. For an alternative interpretation see The Book of Settlements, pp. 6-7.

14. Heimskringla, vol. 3, ed. Bjarni Aðalbjarnarson, Íslenzk fornrit, vol. 28 (Reykjavík: Hið íslenzka fornritafélag, 1951), chap. 12.

15. Ibid.

16. Turville-Petre, Origins, pp. 167-68.

17. See Nordal, "Sagalitteraturen" (Stockholm, Oslo, Copenhagen, 1934), pp. 196-97.

18. See Turville-Petre, Origins, pp. 204-5.

19. See Veraldar saga, ed. Jakob Benediktsson (Copenhagen: Samfund til udgivelse af gammel nordisk litteratur, 1944), pp. liii-liv.

20. See Paasche, Noregs og Islands litteratur, 2d ed. (Oslo, 1957), pp. 318-19. But see also Veraldar saga, pp. liv-lv and the literature cited there.

21. See Jón Helgason, Norrøn Litteraturhistorie (Copenhagen: Levin & Munksgaard, 1934), p. 104. See also The First Grammatical Treatise, ed. Haugen, pp. 78-79.

22. See Ellehøj, Studier, pp. 255-58.

23. For a discussion of this question, see Jón

Jóhannesson, Gerðir Landnámabókar (Reykjavík, 1941), pp. 73-75.
24. See Ellehøj, Studier, pp. 240-55 and 258-66.
25. See Ágrip af Nóregs konunga sögum, ed. Finnur Jónsson, Altnordische Saga-Bibliothek, vol. 18 (Halle [Saale]: Max Niemeyer, 1921), note to page 3, line 10.
26. See Ellehøj, Studier, pp. 262-66.
27. See Einar Ól. Sveinsson, Sagnaritun Oddaverja, Studia Islandica, 1 (Reykjavík: Leiftur, 1937), pp. 16-39. For a different attribution, see Finnbogi Guðmundsson, ed., Orkneyinga saga, Íslenzk fornrit, vol. 34 (Reykjavík: Hið Íslenzka fornritafélag, 1965), pp. xc-cviii.
28. On this, see Paul Schach, "The Dollzhellir Episode in the Orkneyinga saga," Scandinavian Studies 21 (1949):181-83.
29. On this form of foreshadowing, see Paul Schach, "The Anticipatory Literary Setting in the Old Icelandic Sagas," Scandinavian Studies 27 (1955):1-13.
30. On this, see Orkneyinga saga, ed. Finnbogi Guðmundsson, pp. xxv-xxvii and p. 25, n.2.
31. The closest analogue is found near the end of the Middle High German epic Oswald.
32. See Um Skjöldungasögu, ed. Bjarni Guðnason (Reykjavík: Bókaútgáfa Menningarsjóðs, 1963), pp. 152-56.
33. See The Saga of the Icelanders, chap. 35, in Sturlunga Saga, vol. 1, trans. Julia H. McGrew (Twayne Publishers & ASF, 1970).
34. See Um Skjöldungasögu, p. 265.
35. This and similar genealogies are found in Fornaldarsögur norðurlanda, ed. Guðni Jónsson (Akureyri, 1954), 2:75-86.
36. See Beowulf, ed. Fr. Klaeber, 3rd ed. (New York: D. C. Heath & Co., 1936), pp. xxx-xxxvii and the literature cited there.
37. See Um Skjöldungasögu, pp. 16-17.
38. On the manuscript tradition, see N. F. Blake, trans., The Saga of the Jomsvikings (London: Thomas Nelson & Sons, 1962), pp. xv-xxi.
39. On this, see Paul Schach, "Some Parallels to the Tree Dream in Ruodlieb," Monatshefte 46 (1954): 45-54.
40. The Saga of the Jómsvikings, trans. Lee M. Hollander (Austin, 1955), p. 21. Hollander's literary analysis of this "historical novel" is very perceptive.

41. On this technique, see Peter G. Foote, "On the Saga of the Faroe Islanders." An Inaugural Lecture Delivered at University College London, 12 November 1964. Published for the College by H. K. Lewis & Co Ltd London, 1965, pp. 12-24.

42. On the location of Vínland, see Jones, The Norse Atlantic Saga, pp. 81-97 and Magnusson and Pálsson, The Vinland Sagas, pp. 7-10.

43. See Annálar og nafnaskrá, ed. Guðni Jónsson, pp. 13 and 83. This bishop, named Eirík upsi ("coal-fish") in one of the two short entries, must have been a missionary bishop, since Arnald, the first bishop of Iceland, was not appointed until 1126.

44. On these two sagas, see Turville-Petre, Origins, pp. 167-68 and 217-19, and Thorkill Damsgaard Olsen, "Kongekrøniker og Kongesagaer," in Norrøn Fortællekunst (Copenhagen, 1965), pp. 65-66.

45. See Hallberg, The Icelandic Saga, p. 75.

Chapter Three

1. See Jónas Kristjánsson, Um Fóstbræðrasögu (Reykjavík: Stofnun Árna Magnússonar, 1972), p. 144.

2. In his monumental study of Fóstbræðra, Jónas Kristjánsson has challenged Sigurður Nordal's early dating of this work, of the oldest synoptics, and of the earliest biographies of Saint Ólaf. If his views are correct, Fóstbræðra is one of the latest rather than one of the earliest of the Íslendinga-sögur, and the relative dates of the oldest konunga-sögur have to be revised.

3. First published by Gustav Storm in 1893, these fragments can be read conveniently in Guðni Jónsson's Konunga sögur (Akureyri, 1957), 1:403-20. The seventh and eighth fragments are not part of the Eltza saga, as Jonna Louis-Jensen has shown in "'Syvende og ottende brudstykke': Fragmentet Am 325 IC a 4to," in Opuscula, vol. 4, ed. Jón Helgason, Bibliotheca Arnamagnæana 30 (Copenhagen: Munksgaard, 1970), pp. 31-60.

4. On Sighvat Thórdarson, chief of Saint Ólaf's court poets, see Lee M. Hollander, The Skalds (Princeton, 1945), pp. 147-70 and Peter Hallberg, Old Icelandic Poetry: Eddic Lay and Skaldic Verse (Lincoln, Neb., and London, 1975), pp. 162-67.

5. For more detailed information on the prolifera-

tion of the cult of Saint Olaf, see Marlene Ciklamini, *Snorri Sturluson* (Boston: Twayne Publishers, 1978), p. 92.

6. See Ellehøj, *Studier*, pp. 179-82.

7. On the legend, see Olsen, "Kongekrøniker og kongesagaer," pp. 50-51.

8. See Ciklamini, *Snorri Sturluson*, pp. 93-94.

9. For an explanation of the manner in which the compiler used and misused these stanzas, see Turville-Petre, *Origins*, pp. 183-89.

10. See Jan de Vries, "Normannisches Lehngut in den isländischen Königssagas," in *Kleine Schriften*, ed. Klaas Heeroma and Andries Kylstra (Berlin: Walter de Gruyter & Co., 1965), p. 349; see also *Sverris saga*, in *Konunga sögur*, ed. Guðni Jónsson, 2:63.

11. See Jónas Kristjánsson, *Um Fóstbræðra-sögu*, pp. 192-93.

12. See *Saga Olafs Tryggvasonar, af Oddr Snorrason, munk*, ed. Finnur Jonsson (Copenhagen: G.E.C. Gads, 1932).

13. See Bjarni Aðalbjarnarson, *Om de norske kongers sagaer*, Skrifter utg. av Det Norske Vitenskaps-Akademi i Oslo. II. Hist.-filos. klasse. 1936. No. 4 (Oslo, 1937), p. 80.

14. See his "Studier i Olaf Tryggvasons saga," *Samlaren* 84 (1963):54-94.

15. See Olsen, "Kongekrøniker og kongesagaer," p. 51.

16. See *Heimskringla I*, ed. Bjarni Aðalbjarnarson, Íslensk fornrit, vol. 26 (Reykjavík: Hið íslenzka fornritafélag, 1941), pp. cxxix-cxxx.

17. Rebuttals of this kind through character ennoblement or denigration are common in saga literature.

18. See *Heimskringla I*, pp. cxxv-cxxvi.

19. See Jón Jóhannesson, *Gerðir Landnámabókar* (Reykjavík: Félagsprentsmiðjan, 1941), pp. 70-71.

20. See Ludvig Holm-Olsen, "Til diskusjonen om Sverris sagas tilblivelse," in *Opuscula*, vol. II, 2, ed. Jonna Louis-Jensen, Jón Helgason, and Peter Springborg, Bibliotheca Arnamagnæana, vol. 25 (Copenhagen: Munksgaard, 1977), pp. 55-67.

21. See G. M. Gathorne-Hardy, *A Royal Imposter: King Sverre of Norway* (London: Oxford University Press, 1956).

22. See Paul Schach, "Prophetic Dreams of Future

Renown in Old Icelandic Literature," Mosaic 4 (1971): 52-62.

23. See his "Notes on the Sverris Saga," Germanic Review 3 (1929):262-76.

24. See Carol Clover, The Medieval Saga (Ithaca, N.Y., 1982), p. 182.

25. Byskupa sögur, ed. Guðni Jónsson, 1:158.

26. The question of whether the concept of good fortune in saga literature is of Christian or of pagan origin has long been debated. For a recent contribution to the debate see Peter Hallberg, "The concept of gipta-gæfa-hamingja in Old Norse literature," in Proceedings of the First International Saga Conference, University of Edinburgh 1971, ed. Peter Foote, Hermann Pálsson, and Desmond Slay (The Viking Society for Northern Research, University College, London, 1973), pp. 143-83.

Chapter Four

1. Anthony Faulkes, ed., Two Icelandic Stories: Hreiðars þáttr, Orms þáttr (London: Viking Society for Northern Research, University College, London, 1951), p. 2.

2. This tale is found in Íslendinga sögur, ed. Guðni Jónsson, 12:107-18. Translations of four of the tales discussed in this chapter are included in Hrafnkel's Saga and Other Stories, trans. Hermann Pálsson (Penguin Books, 1971), pp. 94-129.

3. See Olsen, "Kongekrøniker og Kongesagaer," p. 51.

4. This tale is found in Íslendinga sögur, ed. Guðni Jónsson, 12:303-10.

5. See Faulkes, Two Icelandic Stories, pp. 20-22.

6. See Heimskringla, trans. Lee M. Hollander, pp. 732 and 734-35.

7. This tale is found in Íslendinga sögur, ed. Guðni Jónsson, 4:265-76.

8. For the Icelandic text of this story, see Íslendinga sögur, ed. Guðni Jónsson, 5:387-97.

9. Olsen, "Kongekrøniker," p. 70.

10. See Vera Lachmann, Das Alter der Harðarsaga, Palaestra 183 (Leipzig: Mayer & Müller, 1932), pp. 222-23; Sigurður Nordal, in Vestfirðinga sögur, Íslenzk fornrit, vol. 6 (Reykjavík: Hið íslenzka

fornritafélag, 1943), pp. lxx-lxxcii; Jacoba M. C. Kroesen, Over de Compositie der Fóstbrǽðra saga (Leyden: Universitaire Pers, 1962); Einar Ól. Sveinsson, Ritunartími Íslendingasagna (Reykjavík: Hið íslenzka bókmenntafélag, 1965), pp. 155-57; Jónas Kristjánsson, Um Fostbrǽðrasögu, pp. 292-310; Klaus von See, "Die Überlieferung der Fóstbrǽðra saga," skandinavistik 6 (1976):1-18.

11. Hallberg, The Icelandic Saga, p. 68.

12. For further examples in English translation, see Jónas Kristjánsson, Um Fóstbrǽðrasögu, pp. 322-24.

13. See Paul Schach, "Favoritord, Stylistic Variation, Absolute Prosa, and Suchlike in the Islendingasögur," in Studies for Einar Haugen, ed. E. S. Firchow et al. (The Hague-Paris: Mouton, 1972), pp. 498-510.

14. See Cecil Woods, "The Reluctant Christian and the King of Norway," Scandinavian Studies 31 (1959): 65-72 and Paul Schach, "The Theme of the Reluctant Christian in the Icelandic Sagas," Journal of English and Germanic Philology 81 (1982):186-203.

15. See Dag Strömbäck, The Conversion of Iceland (London, 1975), pp. 68-88.

16. Turville-Petre, Origins, p. 54.

17. See Bjarni Einarsson, Skáldasögur. Um uppruna og eðli ástaskáldasagnanna (Reykjavík: Bókaútgáfa Menningarsjóðs, 1961), pp. 228-29.

18. Hallberg, Old Icelandic Poetry, p. 145.

19. See Paul Schach, "The Influence of Tristrams saga on Old Icelandic Literature," in Old Norse Literature and Mythology: A Symposium, ed. Edgar G. Polomé (Austin and London: University of Texas Press, 1969), pp. 103-5.

20. See Hallberg, Old Icelandic Poetry, pp. 143-44. But see also Einar Ól. Sveinsson, "Kormakr the Poet and His Verses," Saga-Book 17 (1966):18-60, especially pp. 57-58.

21. See Íslenzk fornrit, vol. 8, p. lxxx.

22. See Bjarni Einarsson, Skáldasögur, pp. 50-51 and 290-91.

23. Andersson, The Old Icelandic Family Saga: An Analytic Reading (Cambridge, Mass., 1967), p. 149.

24. This motif has been preserved in the Faeroese ballad cycle Sjúrðarkvæði ("Romance of Sigurd") and

in Niflunga saga. See Þiðreks saga af Bern, ed.
Guðni Jónsson (Reykjavík: Íslendingasagnaútgáfan,
1954), 2:513.

25. The first fifteen chapters were destroyed in the
fire of 1728 in Copenhagen. They have been reconstruc-
ted from notes and from memory by Jón Ólafsson, who
had made transcripts of a vellum borrowed from the
Royal Library in Stockholm.

26. De Vries, Altnordische Literaturgeschichte, 2d
ed., vol. 2 (Berlin: Olsen, 1967), p. 388.

27. See Olsen, "Kongekrøniker og kongesagaer," p.
70; Jónas Kristjánsson, Um Fóstbræðrasögu, pp.
164-65.

Chapter Five

1. See Ciklamini, Snorri Sturluson, pp. 13-34 and
the literature cited there.

2. The evidence for Snorri's authorship is summarized by Sigurður Nordal in his edition of Egils
saga, Íslenzk fornrit, vol. 2 (Reykjavík: Hið
Íslenzka fornritafélag, 1933), pp. lxx-xcv; argumentation against it is provided by Jan de Vries, Altnordische Literaturgeschichte, 2d ed., vol. 2, pp.
348-50.

3. See Ralph West, "Snorri Sturluson and Egils
saga: Statistics of Style," Scandinavian Studies 52
(1980):163-93; Widding, "Islændingasagaer," in
Norrøn Fortællekunst, pp. 84-85.

4. See Paul Schach, "Antipagan Sentiment in the
Sagas of Icelanders," in Gripla I, ed. Jónas
Kristjánsson (Reykjavík: Stofnun Árnamagnússonar,
1975), pp. 105-34.

5. See Ciklamini, Snorri Sturluson, pp. 43-63.

6. See Heusler, Die altgermanische Dichtung, 2d
ed. (Potsdam, 1941), p. 235; Turville-Petre, Origins,
p. 224; and especially Clover, The Medieval Saga
(Ithaca, N.Y., 1982), chap. 2 and the literature cited
there.

7. See de Vries, Altnordische Literaturgeschichte, 2d ed., vol. 2, p. 292.

8. See Schach, "Symbolic Dreams of Future Renown,"
pp. 69-71.

9. See Sigurður Nordal, "Sagalitteraturen," p. 226.
See also Hallberg, Ólafr Þórðarson hvítaskáld,

Knýtlinga saga och Laxdæla saga. Ett försök till språklig författerbestämning, Studia Islandica 22 (Reykjavík, 1963).

10. Heimskringla, trans. Lee M. Hollander, p. xxv.

11. See Magnus Olsen, "Om troldruner," Edda 5 (1916):223-46.

12. For a verse translation, see Hollander, The Skalds, pp. 90-98. Only the first stanza is quoted in the saga.

13. See Andersson, The Icelandic Family Sagas. An Analytic Reading (Cambridge, Mass., 1967), p. 108.

14. The sources of Laxdæla are thoroughly discussed by Heller in his monograph Die Laxdæla saga. Die literarische Schöpfung eines Isländers des 13. Jahrhunderts (Berlin: Akademie-Verlag, 1976).

15. W. P. Ker, Epic and Romance. Essays on Medieval Literature, 2d rev. ed. (New York: Macmillan & Co., 1908), p. 209.

16. Einar Ól. Sveinsson, ed., Laxdæla saga, Íslenzk fornrit, vol. 5 (Reykjavík: Hið Íslenzka fornritafélag, 1934), p. lxvii.

17. See A. Margaret A. Madelung, The Laxdæla Saga: Its Structural Patterns (Chapel Hill: University of North Carolina Press, 1972), p. 13; Heinrich Beck, "Brynhilddichtung und Laxdæla Saga," in Festgabe für Otto Höfler, ed. Helmut Birkhan (Vienna: W. Braumüller, 1976), pp. 1-14; Rolf Heller, Die Laxdæla Saga (Berlin, 1976), pp. 150-52.

18. Hallberg, The Icelandic Saga, p. 137.

19. Turville-Petre, Origins, p. 246; Andersson, The Icelandic Saga, p. 171.

20. See Marina Mundt, Sturla Þórðarson und die Laxdæla saga (Bergen-Oslo-Tromsö: Universitetsforlaget, 1969); Hallberg, Ólafr Þórðarson hvítaskáld; A. Margaret A. Madelung, "Snorri Sturluson and Laxdœla: The Hero's Accoutrements," in Saga og språk: Studies in Language and Literature, ed. John M. Weinstock (Austin, Texas, 1972), pp. 45-92.

21. See Heller, Die Laxdœla Saga, pp. 151-52.

22. See Schach, "The Helgafell Episode in Eyrbyggja saga and Gísla saga," in Saga og Språk, pp. 113-46.

23. See Olsen, Hørg, Hov og Kirke, pp. 278-85.

24. See Clover, The Medieval Saga, chap. 4.

25. See Schach, "The Generation-Gap Theme in the Íslendinga sögur," pp. 367-69.

26. See Heller, "Das Alter der Eyrbyggja saga im Licht der Sprachstatistik," Acta Philologica Scandinavica 32 (1978):53-66.

27. See de Vries, Altnordische Literaturgeschichte, 2d ed., vol. 2, p. 371.

28. See Íslendingabók, chap. 1, and especially Heimskringla, trans. Lee M. Hollander, p. 5.

29. See A. U. Bååth, Studier öfver Kompositionen i Några Isländska Ättsagor (Lund, 1895), p. 159.

30. See Einar Ól. Sveinsson, Njáls Saga, pp. 80-180 and passim.

31. See Halldór Hermannsson, The Book of the Icelanders, p. 85 (note 2 to chap. 8).

32. See Íslendinga sögur, ed. Guðni Jónsson, 1:205 and 212.

33. See Schach, "Character Creation," pp. 263-67.

34. See Barði Guðmundsson, Höfundur Njálu (Reykjavík: Bókaútgáfa Menningarsjóðs, 1958), pp. xiv-xv and 225-34.

35. See Heusler, trans., Die Geschichte vom weisen Njál, Thule, vol. 4 (Düsseldorf-Köln: Eugen Diederichs Verlag, 1914), p. 17.

36. See Magnus Magnusson and Hermann Pálsson, trans., Njáls Saga (Baltimore: Penguin Books, 1960), p. 26. For a well-argued alternative interpretation, see Hallberg, "Njáls Saga--a Medieval Morality?" Alþjóðlegt Fornasagnaþing (Reykjavík, 1976).

37. See Einar Ól. Sveinsson, Njáls Saga, p. 169.

38. Ibid., pp. 174-80.

39. On the digression ad aliud extra materiam see Clover, The Medieval Saga, chap. 1.

40. For a perceptive interpretation of the purpose and function of this episode, see Richard F. Allen, Fire and Iron. Critical Approaches to "Njáls saga" (Pittsburgh: Pittsburgh University Press, 1971), pp. 157-62.

41. See Njáls Saga, p. 163 and n. 2.

42. Ibid., pp. 73-75.

43. See Sigurður Nordal, Sturla Þórðarson og Grettis saga, Studia Islandica 4 (Reykjavík: Ísafoldarprentsmiðjan, 1938). (English summary, pp. 29-32.)

44. See Sigurður Nordal, Sturla Þórðarson, pp. 18-19.

45. See Kathryn Hume, "Beginnings and Endings in the Icelandic Family Sagas," Modern Language Review 68 (1973):593-603 and "The Thematic Design of Grettis

saga," Journal of English and Germanic Philology 73 (1974):469-86.

46. See Guðni Jónsson, ed., Grettis saga, Íslenzk fornrit, vol. 7 (Reykjavík: Hið Íslenzka fornritafélag, 1936), pp. lv-lvii, and Schach, "The Influence of Tristrams saga," pp. 111-21.

47. See Schach, "Character Creation," pp. 263-67.

48. See Raymond W. Chambers, "Beowulf's Fight with Grendel and Its Scandinavian Parallels," English Studies 11 (1929):81-100.

49. See Robert J. Glendinning, "Grettis Saga and European Literature in the Late Middle Ages," Mosaic 4 (1970):49-62.

50. See Hume, "The Thematic Design of Grettis saga," p. 472.

51. See Andreas Heusler, trans., Die Geschichte vom weisen Njál, Sammlung Thule, vol. 4 (Düsseldorf-Köln: Eugen Diederichs Verlag, 1922; reprint ed., 1965), pp. 7-10, and Die altergermanische Dichtung, 2d ed. (Darmstadt, 1957), p. 212.

Chapter Six

1. See Kurt Schier, Sagaliteratur (Stuttgart: Metzler, 1970), pp. 43-44.

2. See Jón Jóhannesson, ed., Austfirðinga sögur, Íslenzk fornrit, vol.11 (Reykjavík: Hið Íslenzka fornritafélag, 1950), pp. lxvi-lxviii.

3. See Rolf Heller, "Studien zu Aufbau und Stil der Vápnfirðinga saga," Arkiv för nordisk filologi 78 (1963):170-88.

4. See Jan de Vries, Altnordische Literaturgeschichte (Berlin, 1967), 2d ed. vol. 2, p. 437.

5. See Jónas Kristjánsson, "Íslendingadrápa and Oral Tradition," in Gripla I, ed. Jónas Kristjánsson (Reykjavík: Stofnun Árna Magnússonar, 1975), p. 86, and Jón Jóhannesson, Austfirðinga sögur, pp. xx-xxii.

6. See Schach, "Some Observations on the Generation-Gap Theme in the Icelandic Sagas," pp. 361-67.

7. Thus Óskar Halldórsson, Uppruni og þema Hrafnkels sögu (Reykjavík: Hið Íslenska bókmentafélag, 1976), pp. 58-67 and 73-74. For an alternative interpretation, see Hermann Pálsson, Art and Ethics in Hrafnkel's Saga (Copenhagen: Munksgaard, 1971).

8. On this story, see Jón Jóhannesson, Austfirðinga sögur, pp. lxxxvi-xcii.

9. See Knut Liestøl, "Reykdœla Saga. Tradisjon
og Forfattar," in Festskrift til Finnur Jónsson
(Copenhagen, 1928), pp. 29-44.

10. See Carol Clover, "Scene in Saga Composition,"
Arkiv för nordisk filologi 89 (1974):57-83.

11. See Björn Sigfússon, ed., Ljósvetninga saga.
Reykdæla saga og Víga-Skútu, Íslenzk fornrit, vol.
10 (Reykjavík: Hið Íslenzka fornritafélag, 1965),
pp. lxi-lxii.

12. On this work, see Lee M. Hollander, trans.,
Víga-Glúm's Saga (New York, 1972), pp. 9-16 and
especially G. Turville-Petre, ed., Víga-Glúms Saga,
2d ed. (Oxford, 1960), pp. ix-lvi.

13. See Björn Sigfússon, "Ingólfs þáttur í
VígaGlúmssögu," Arkiv för nordisk filologi 52
(1937): 62-69.

14. See Andersson, The Icelandic Family Saga, pp.
252-61.

15. On this work, see Marlene Ciklamini, "The
Concept of Honor in Valla-Ljóts Saga," Journal of
English and Germanic Philology 65 (1966):303-17.

16. Andersson, The Icelandic Family Saga, p. 181.
On this work, see Peter G. Foote, "An Essay on the Saga
of Gísli and its Icelandic Background," in The Saga
of Gísli, trans. George Johnston (Toronto, 1963), pp.
93-134.

17. See G. Turville-Petre, "Gísli Súrsson and His
Poetry," Modern Language Review 39 (1944):374-91.

18. See Sturla Thórdarson, Íslendinga saga (chap.
55) and the anonymous Arons saga (chap. 12) in Sturlunga saga, ed. Guðni Jónsson, 2:130 and 3:451.

19. See Foote, "An Essay on the Saga of Gísli," pp.
131-33.

20. See Björn K. Þórólfsson and Guðni Jónsson,
eds., Vestfirðinga sögur, Íslenzk fornrit, vol. 6
(Reykjavík: Hið Íslenzka fornritafélag, 1943), pp.
v-xiii.

21. On this story, see Gwyn Jones, trans., The
Vatnsdalers' Saga (Princeton, 1944), pp. 1-18 and
129-58.

22. Ker, Epic and Romance, p. 229.   See also de
Vries, Altnordische Literaturgeschichte, 2d ed., pp.
403-6.

23. On this work, see Jónas Kristjánsson, "Landnáma and Hænsa-Þóris saga," in Opuscula, vol. II, 2, ed. Jonna Louis-Jensen (Copenhagen: C. A. Reitzels Boghandel A/S, 1977), pp. 134-48, and Walter Baetke, ed., Hænsa-Þóris saga (Halle [Saale]: VEB Max Niemeyer Verlag, 1953), pp. 1-31.

24. See Annálar og Nafnaskrá, ed. Guðni Jónsson, pp. 2 and 78.

25. On this work, see Erik Wahlgren, "Fact and Fancy in the Vinland Sagas," in Old Norse Literature and Mythology (Austin and London, 1969), pp. 19-80, and Magnus Magnusson and Hermann Pálsson, trans., The Vinland Sagas (New York, 1966), pp. 7-43.

26. On this story, see Gunnlaugs Saga Ormstungu, ed. P. G. Foote, trans. R. Quirk (London, 1957), pp. ix-xxvii, and Robert F. Cook, "The Character of Gunnlaug Serpent-Tongue," Scandinavian Studies 43 (1971):1-21.

27. See Sigurður Nordal, "Sagalitteraturen," p. 255.

28. See Schach, "Symbolic Dreams," pp. 71-73, and especially Clover, The Medieval Saga, chap. 4.

29. Cook, "The Character of Gunnlaug Serpent-Tongue," p. 21.

Chapter Seven

1. Twelve nineteenth-century sagas are included in Íslendinga sögur, ed. Guðni Jónsson.

2. See King Harald's Saga, trans. Magnus Magnusson and Hermann Pálsson (Baltimore, 1966), chaps. 6-10, for examples of his stratagems.

3. For the Icelandic text with English translation, see Schach, "Favoritord," pp. 509-10.

4. On the father-son conflict in this story, see Margaret Schlauch, Romance in Iceland (Princeton, 1934), pp. 113-18.

5. On this saga, see Jóhannes Halldórsson, ed., Kjalnesinga saga, Islenzk fornrit, vol. 14 (Reykjavík: Hið Íslenzka fornritafélag, 1954), pp. v-xx.

6. On this saga, see Richard Perkins, "The Dreams of Flóamanna Saga," Saga-Book 19 (1975-76):191-238 and the literature cited there.

7. On the interpretation of hjálmlaukar and laukar, see Perkins, "The Dreams," pp. 223-32.

8. See Jóhannes Halldórsson, Kjalnesinga saga, pp. lxx-lxxiv.

9. See Olsen, Hørg, pp. 34-49.
10. See Jónas Kristjánsson, Eyfirðinga sögur, pp. lxxvii-lxxxvii.
11. Ibid., pp. lxx-lxxxvii.
12. See Jenny M. Jochens, "The Church and Sexuality in Medieval Iceland," Journal of Medieval History 6 (1980):377-92.
13. For translations of the tree dreams in Heimskringla and the Íslendingasögur, see Schach, "Some Parallels," pp. 360-61.
14. See The Book of Settlements, p. 97.
15. See Heinz Dehmer, Primitives Erzählungsgut in den Íslendinga-Sögur (Leipzig: J. J. Weber, 1927), p. 111.
16. See Carl F. Bayerschmidt, "The Supernatural in the Sagas of Icelanders," in Scandinavian Studies, ed. Carl F. Bayerschmidt and Erik J. Friis, pp. 39-53.
17. See Jochens, "The Church and Sexuality," p. 380.

Chapter Eight

1. For a recent study, see Jónas Kristjánsson, "Learned Style or Saga Style?" Speculum Norroenum: Norse Studies in Honor of Gabriel Turville-Petre, ed. Ursula Dronke et al. (Odense: Odense University Press, 1981), pp. 260-99.
2. For a dissenting opinion, see Anne Heinrichs, "'Intertexture' and Its Functions in Early Written Sagas: A Stylistic Observation of Heiðarvíga saga, Reykdæla saga, and the Legendary Ólafssaga," Scandinavian Studies 48 (1976):127-45. But note the concession, pp. 143-44.
3. See Claiborne W. Thompson, "Moral Values in the Icelandic Sagas: Recent Re-Evaluations," in The Epic in Medieval Society: Aesthetic and Moral Values, ed. Harald Scholler (Tübingen: Max Niemeyer Verlag, 1977), pp. 347-60.
4. See Gerd Wolfgang Weber, "Irreligiosität und Heldenzeitalter: Zum Mythencharakter der altisländischen Literatur," Speculum Norroenum, ed. Ursula Dronke et al., pp. 474-505.
5. Sturla Þórðarson, Hákonar saga gamla, chap. 228 (Konunga sögur, ed. Guðni Jónsson, vol. 3, p. 335).
6. Kurt Schier, "Iceland and the Rise of Literature

in 'terra nova,'" in <u>Gripla I</u>, ed. Jónas Kristjánsson (Reykjavík: Stofnun Árna Magnússonar, 1975), pp. 168-87.

7. Thus Weber, <u>Irreligiosität</u>, pp. 504-5.

8. See Otto Springer, "The Style of the Old Icelandic Family Sagas," <u>Journal of English and Germanic Philology</u> 38 (1939):107-28.

Selected Bibliography

Bibliography of Old Norse-Icelandic Studies, 1963-.
Edited by Hans Bekker-Nielsen and Thorkil Damsgaard
Olsen. Copenhagen: Munksgaard, 1964-. Annual
bibliography.
FRY, DONALD F. Norse Sagas Translated into English:
A Bibliography. New York: AMS Press, 1980.
HANNESSON, JÓHANN S. The Sagas of Icelanders
(Íslendinga sögur). (Supplement to Islandica 1
and 24.) Islandica 38. Ithaca, N.Y.: Cornell
University Press, 1957.
HERMANNSSON, HALLDÓR. The Sagas of the Kings and the
Mythical Heroic Sagas. (Two bibliographical supple-
ments.) Islandica 26. Ithaca, N.Y.: Cornell
University Press, 1937.
SCHIER, KURT. Sagaliteratur. Sammlung Metzler 78.
Stuttgart: J. B. Melzlersche Verlagsbuchhandlung,
1970.

Current bibliographical references to Old Norse sagas
and related literary genres can be found in the quarter-
ly Germanistik (1960-) and in the annual bibliography
of the Publications of the Modern Language Association (1921-). The entries in the Kulturhistorisk
leksikon for nordisk middelalder fra vikingetid til
reformationstid (1957-77) and the Kindlers Literatur
Lexikon (1970-74) provide good bibliographies for
genres and for individual works.

BACKGROUND MATERIALS

The Book of Settlements: Landnámabók. Translated
by Hermann Pálsson and Paul Edwards. Winnipeg,
Canada: University of Manitoba Press, 1980.
FOOTE, PETER, and DAVID M. WILSON. The Viking Achieve-
ment: The Society and Culture of Early Medieval
Scandinavia. London: Sidgwick & Jackson, 1970.
JÓHANNESSON, JÓN. A History of the Old Icelandic
Commonwealth. Íslendinga saga. Translated by

Haraldur Bessason. University of Manitoba Icelandic Studies, vol. 2. Winnipeg: University of Manitoba Press, 1974.

Laws of Early Iceland: Grágás. Translated by Andrew Dennis, Peter Foote, Richard Perkins. Winnipeg, Canada: University of Manitoba Press, 1980. The codex regius of Grágás with materials from other manuscripts.

OLSEN, OLAF. Hørg, Hov og Kirke. Historiske og arkæologiske vikingetidsstudier. Copenhagen, 1966.

STRØMBÄCK, DAG. The Conversion of Iceland. A Survey. Translated and annotated by Peter Foote. University College London: Viking Society for Northern Research, 1975.

SVEINSSON, EINAR ÓL. The Age of the Sturlungs: Icelandic Civilization in the Thirteenth Century. Translated by Jóhann S. Hannesson. Islandica 36. Ithaca, N.Y.: Cornell University Press, 1953.

TURVILLE-PETRE, E. O. G. The Heroic Age of Scandinavia. London and New York: Hutchinson's University Library, 1951.

————. Myth and Religion of the North: The Religion of Ancient Scandinavia. New York: Holt, Rinehart & Winston, 1964.

LITERARY HISTORY AND CRITICISM

AÐALBJARNARSON, BJARNI. Om de norske kongers sagaer. (Oslo, 1937).

ANDERSSON, THEODORE M. The Icelandic Family Sagas: An Analytic Reading. Harvard Studies in Comparative Literture, 28. Cambridge, Mass.: Harvard University Press, 1967. Includes plot summaries and analyses of twenty-four Íslendinga sögur.

BAETKE, WALTER. Uber die Entstehung der Isländersagas. In Berichte über die Verhandlungen der Sächsischen Akademie der Wissenschaften zu Leipzig. Philosophisch-historische Klasse, 102, part 5. Berlin: Akademie-Verlag, 1956, pp. 1-108.

BEKKER-NIELSEN, HANS, THORKIL DAMSGAARD OLSEN, and OLE WIDDING. Norrøn Fortællekunst: Kapitler af den norsk-islandske middelalder-litteraturs historie. Copenhagen: Akademisk Forlag, 1965.

CLOVER, CAROL. The Medieval Saga. Ithaca, N.Y.: Cornell University Press, 1982.

EINARSSON, STEFÁN. A History of Icelandic Litera-
    ture. New York: Johns Hopkins Press for ASF,
    1957.
ELLEHØJ, SVEND. Studier over den ældste norrøne
    historieskrivning. Bibliotheca Arnamagnæana vol.
    26. Copenhagen: Munksgaard, 1965.
FRANK, ROBERTA. Old Norse Court Poetry. The
    Dróttkvætt Stanza. Islandica 42. Ithaca and
    London: Cornell University Press, 1978.
HALLBERG, PETER. The Icelandic Saga. Translated
    with an introduction and notes by Paul Schach.
    Lincoln: University of Nebraska Press, 1962.
_____. Old Icelandic Poetry: Eddic Lay and
    Skaldic Verse. Translated with a foreword by Paul
    Schach and Sonja Lindgrenson. Lincoln and London:
    University of Nebraska Press, 1975.
HELGASON, JON. Norrøn Litteraturhistorie. Copenha-
    gen: Levin & Munksgaard, 1934.
_____. "Norges og Islands digtning." In Littera-
    turhistorie B. Norge og Island. Edited by Sigurður
    Nordal. Nordisk kultur, 8B. Oslo: Aschehoug;
    Stockholm: Bonnier; Copenhagen: Schultz, 1953, pp.
    3-110.
HELLER, ROLF. Die Laxdœla saga. Die literarische
    Schöpfung eines Isländers des 13. Jahrhunderts.
    Berlin: Akademieverlag, 1976.
HEUSLER, ANDREAS. Die altgermanische Dichtung. 2d
    rev., augm. ed. Potsdam: Athenaion, 1941. Re-
    print. Darmstadt, 1957.
LEACH, HENRY GODDARD. Angevin Britain and Scandina-
    via. Harvard Studies in Comparative Literature,
    vol. 6. Cambridge, Mass.: Harvard University
    Press, 1921.
LONNROTH, LARS. European Sources of Icelandic Saga-
    Writing: An Essay Based on Previous Studies.
    Stockholm, 1965.
_____. Njáls Saga. A Critical Introduction.
    Berkeley: University of California Press, 1976.
NORDAL, SIGURÐUR. "Sagalitteraturen." In Litteratur-
    historie B. Norge og Island. Nordisk kultur, 8B.
    Oslo: Aschehoug; Stockholm: Bonnier; Copenhagen:
    Schultz, 1953, pp. 180-273.
PAASCHE, FREDERIK. Norges og Islands litteratur
    indtil utgangen af meddelalderen. 2d ed. (with
    supplements by Anne Holtsmark). Oslo: H. Asche-
    houg, 1957. Includes bibliographical notes on schol-

arly literature between 1924 and 1956.

SCHLAUCH, MARGARET. Romance in Iceland. Princeton:
Princeton University Press; New York: ASF, 1934.

SVEINSSON, EINAR ÓL. Dating the Icelandic Sagas. An
Essay in Method. University College London:
Viking Society for Northern Research, 1958.

TURVILLE-PETRE, E. O. G. Origins of Icelandic Literature. Oxford: Clarendon Press, 1953.

ANNOTATED AND BILINGUAL EDITIONS

First Grammatical Treatise. The earliest Germanic
phonology; an edition, translation (from the Old
Norse), and commentary (by) Einar Haugen. 2d rev.
ed. London: Longman, 1972.

The First Grammatical Treatise. Introduction, text,
notes, translation, vocabulary, facsimile, edited by
Hreinn Benediktsson. Rekjavik: Institute for Nordic
Linguistics, 1972.

Gunnlaugs saga Ormstungu. The Saga of Gunnlaug
Serpent-Tongue. Edited with introduction and notes
by Peter G. Foote. Translated from the Icelandic by
R. Quirk. London: Thomas Nelson & Sons, 1957.

Hrafnkels saga Freysgoða. Edited with introduction
and glossary by Frank Stanton Cawley. Cambridge,
Mass.: Harvard University Press, 1932.

The Poetic Edda. Volume I. Heroic Poems. Edited
with translation, introduction, and commentary by
Ursula Dronke. Oxford: Clarendon Press, 1969.
Atalkviða, Atlamál in Grœnlenzko,
Guðrúnarhvöt, Hamðismál.

Saga Heiðreks Konungs ins Vitra. The Saga of King
Heidrek the Wise. Translated from the Icelandic
with introduction, notes, and appendices by
Christopher Tolkien. London: Thomas Nelson & Sons,
1960. Hervarar saga ok Heiðreks konungs.

Jómsvíkinga Saga. The Saga of the Jomsvikings.
Translated from the Icelandic with introduction,
notes, and appendices by N. F. Blake. London:
Thomas Nelson & Sons, 1962.

Strengleikar. An Old Norse Translation of Twenty-one
Old French Lais. Edited by Robert Cook and Mattias
Tveitane. Norrøne tekster nr. 3. Oslo: Norsk
historisk kjeldeskriftinstitutt, 1979.

The Vinland Sagas. Edited with an introduction,
variants, and notes by Halldór Hermannsson.

Ithaca, N.Y.:   Cornell University Press, 1944.
Völsunga saga. The Saga of the Volsungs. Edited
    and translated with an introduction, notes, and
    appendices by R. G. Finch. London: Thomas Nelson &
    Sons, 1965.
Völuspá: The Song of the Sybil. Translated by
    Paul B. Taylor and W. H. Auden with the Icelandic
    text edited by Peter H. Salus and Paul B. Taylor.
    Iowa City, Iowa: Windhover Press, 1968.
Þorgils Saga ok Hafliða. Edited by Ursula Brown.
    London: Oxford University Press, 1952.
Víga-Glúms Saga. Edited by G. Turville-Petre. 2d
    ed. Oxford: Clarendon Press, 1960.

COLLECTIONS AND SERIES

Altnordische Saga-Bibliothek. Halle a.S.:   Max
    Niemeyer, 1892-1929. 18 vols. Annotated texts with
    introductions.
Altnordische Textbibliothek. New series. Halle
    (Saale): M. Niemeyer, 1952-. (In progress.) Texts
    edited with introductions, notes, and glossaries.
    Includes Bandamanna saga, Gunnlaugs saga,
    Hrafnkels saga.
Bibliotheca Arnamagnæana. Copenhagen: Munksgaard,
    1941-. (In progress.) Monographs in the field of
    Old Norse and Icelandic studies.
Byskupa sögur. 3 vols. Sturlunga saga. 3 vols.
    Annálar og Nafnaskrá. Edited by Guðni Jónsson.
    2d ed. Akureyri: Íslendingasagnaútgáfan, 1953.
    The seventh volume contains the annals and a common
    index of names to the other six volumes.
Editiones Arnamagnæanæ. Copenhagen: Munksgaard,
    1958-. (In progress.) Editions of Old Norse and
    Icelandic texts.
Fornaldar sögur Norðurlanda. Edited by Guðni
    Jónsson. 4 vols. Akureyri: Íslendingasagna-
    útgáfan, 1954.
Íslendinga sögur. Edited by Guðni Jónsson. 13
    vols. 2d ed. Akureyri: Íslendingasagnaútgáfan,
    1953. The last volume contains the names of all
    persons, places, peoples, families, literary works,
    animals, and objects (ships, swords, etc.) that
    occur in volumes 1-12.
Íslenzk fornrit. Reykjavík: Hið Íslenzka fornrit-
    afélag, 1933-. (In progress.) The standard edi-

tions of Íslendingabók, Landnámabók, Heimskringla, Orkneyinga saga, and most Íslendinga
sögur and þættir.
Konunga sögur. Edited by Guðni Jónsson. 3 vols.
Akureyri: Íslendingasagnaútgáfan, 1957. Contains Óláfs saga Tryggvasonar by the monk Odd,
the legendary Óláfs saga ins helga, the Elzta
saga, Sverris saga, and Hákonar saga Hákonarsonar.
Nordisk filologi. Copenhagen: Munksgaard; Oslo:
Dreyers forlag; Stockholm: Svenska bokförlaget,
1950-. (In progress.) Texts with introductions and
variant manuscript readings of Eddic and skaldic
poetry, the Prose Edda, sagas, etc.
Riddara sögur. Edited by Bjarni Vilhjálmsson. 6
vols. Akureyri: Íslendingasagnaútgáfan, Hauka-
dalsútgáfan, 1954.
Sturlunga saga. Edited by Jón Jóhannesson, Magnús
Finnbogason, and Kristján Eldjárn. 2 vols.
Reykjavík: Sturlunguútgáfan, 1946.
Thule. Altnordische Dichtung und Prosa. 24 vols.
Jena: E. Diederichs, 1922-34. Reprint. Düssel-
dorf, 1963-67. Vol. 1 revised. The most comprehensive collection of translations of Old Norse prose
and poetry. The reprinted volumes contain valuable
bibliographical information.

TRANSLATIONS

Arrow-Odd: A Medieval Novel. Translated with an
introduction by Paul Edwards and Hermann Pálsson.
New York: New York University Press; London:
University of London Press, 1970. Orvar-Odds
saga.
The Confederates and Hen-Thorir. Two Icelandic Sagas.
Translated by Hermann Pálsson. Edinburgh: South-
side, 1975. Bandamanna saga and Hænsa-Þóris
saga.
Egil's Saga. Translated by Gwyn Jones. With intro-
duction and notes. Syracuse: Syracuse University
Press for ASF, 1960.
Egil's Saga. Translated by Christine Fell and John
Lucas. Toronto: University of Toronto Press;
London: Dent, 1975.
Egil's Saga. Translated with an introduction by
Hermann Pálsson and Paul Edwards. Harmondsworth,

England: Penguin Books, 1976.
Eirik the Red and Other Icelandic Sagas.   Selected
    and translated with an introduction by Gwyn Jones.
    London and New York: Oxford University Press, 1961.
    Eiríks saga rauða, Hænsa-Þóris saga,
    Vápnfirðinga saga, Þorsteins þáttr
    stangarhöggs, Hrafnkels saga, Gunnlaugs saga,
    and Hrólfs saga kraka.
Eyrbyggja Saga.   Translated from the Old Icelandic by
    Paul Schach.   Introduction and verse translations by
    Lee M. Hollander.   Lincoln and London: University
    of Nebraska Press and ASF, 1959.   Reprint. 1977.
Eyrbyggja Saga.   Translated by Hermann Pálsson and
    Paul Edwards.   Edinburgh: Southside, 1973.
The Elder Edda.   A Selection.   Translated from the
    Icelandic by Paul B. Taylor and W. H. Auden.   Intro-
    duction by Peter H. Salus and Paul B. Taylor.   Notes
    by Peter H. Salus.   New York: Random House, 1970.
Erex Saga and Ívens Saga.   The Old Norse Versions of
    Chrétien de Troyes's Erec and Yvain.   Translated,
    with an introduction, by Foster W. Blaisdell, Jr.,
    and Marianne E. Kalinke.   Lincoln and London:
    University of Nebraska Press, 1977.
The Faroe Islanders' Saga.   Translated with an intro-
    duction by George Johnston.   Ottawa: Oberon, 1975.
    Færeyinga saga.
Four Icelandic Sagas.   Translated with an introduc-
    tion and notes by Gwyn Jones.   Princeton: Princeton
    University Press; New York: ASF, 1935.   Hrafnkels
    saga, Þorsteins saga hvíta, Vápnfirðinga
    saga, and Kjálnesinga saga.
Grettir's Saga.   Translated by Denton Fox and Hermann
    Pálsson.   Toronto: University of Toronto Press,
    1974.
Heimskringla.   History of the Kings of Norway.   By
    Snorri Sturluson.   Translated with introduction and
    notes by Lee M. Hollander.   Published for the ASF.
    Austin: University of Texas Press, 1964.
Hrafnkels Saga.   Translated by John C. McGalliard.
    In World Masterpieces.   Edited by Maynard Mack.
    New York: Norton, 1956.   3rd ed. 1973, vol. 1, pp.
    745-65.
Hrafnkel's Saga and Other Icelandic Stories.   Trans-
    lated with an introduction by Hermann Pálsson.
    Baltimore: Penguin Books, 1971.   Includes
    Þorsteins þáttr stangarhöggs, Ölkofra þáttr,

Hreiðars þáttr heimska, Halldórs þáttr
stangarhöggs, Auðunar þáttr vestfirzka, and
Ívars þáttr Ingimundarsonar.

Gautrek's Saga and Other Medieval Tales. Translated
by Hermann Pálsson and Paul Edwards. With introduction. New York: New York University Press, 1968.
Contains Gautreks saga, Bósa saga ok Herrauðs,
Egils saga ok Ásmundar, Þorsteins saga bæjar-
magns, and Helga þáttr Þórissonar.

Hrolf Gautreksson: A Viking Romance. Translated by
Hermann Pálsson and Paul Edwards. Toronto: University of Toronto Press, 1972.

*Karlamagnús Saga. The Saga of Charlemagne and His
Heroes.* 3 vols. Translated by Constance B.
Hieatt. Mediaeval Sources in Translation, 13, 17,
and 25. Toronto: Pontifical Institute of Medieval
Studies, 1975-1980.

King Harald's Saga: Harald Hardradi of Norway. From
Snorri Sturluson's *Heimskringla.* Translated with
an introduction by Magnus Magnusson and Hermann
Pálsson. Baltimore: Penguin Books, 1966.

The Laxdoela Saga. Translated from the Old Icelandic
with introduction and notes by A. Margaret Arent.
Seattle: University of Washington Press for ASF,
1964.

Laxdæla Saga. Translated with an introduction by
Magnus Magnusson and Hermann Pálsson. Harmondsworth, England: Penguin Books, 1969.

Njáls Saga. Translated from the Old Icelandic with
introduction and notes by Carl F. Bayerschmidt and
Lee M. Hollander. New York: New York University
Press for ASF, 1955.

Njal's Saga. Translated with an introduction by
Magnus Magnusson and Hermann Pálsson. Baltimore:
Penguin Books, 1960.

Orkneyinga Saga. Translated with introduction and
notes by A. B. Taylor. London and Edinburgh:
Oliver & Boyd, 1938.

Orkneyinga Saga. The History of the Earls of Orkney.
Translated from the Icelandic and introduced by
Hermann Pálsson and Paul Edwards. London: Hogarth
Press, 1978.

A Pageant of Old Scandinavia. Edited by Henry
Goddard Leach. Princeton: Princeton University
Press, 1946. Reprint. Freeport, N.Y.: Books for
Libraries Press, 1968.

Poems of the Vikings. The Elder Edda. Translated by
    Patricia Terry with an introduction by Charles W.
    Dunn. Indianapolis and New York: Bobbs-Merrill
    Co., 1969.
The Poetic Edda. Translated from the Icelandic with
    an introduction and notes by Henry Adam Bellows.
    New York: ASF, 1923. Reprint. 1968.
The Poetic Edda. Translated with an introduction and
    explanatory notes by Lee M. Hollander. 2d rev. ed.
    Austin: University of Texas Press, 1962.
The Prose Edda by Snorri Sturluson. Translated by
    Arthur G. Brodeur. New York: ASF, 1916.
The Prose Edda of Snorri Sturluson. Tales from Norse
    Mythology. Selected and translated by Jean I.
    Young. Berkeley and Los Angeles: University of
    California Press, 1964.
The Saga of Gisli. Translated from the Icelandic by
    George Johnston with notes and an essay on the Saga
    of Gisli by Peter Foote. Toronto: University of
    Toronto Press, 1963.
The Saga of Grettir the Strong. Translated by G. A.
    Hight. Edited with introduction, notes, and indexes
    by Peter Foote. London: Dent; New York: Dutton,
    1965. Everyman's Library.
The Saga of Hrafn Sveinbjarnarson: The Life of an Ice-
    landic Physician of the Thirteenth Century. Trans-
    lated with an introduction and notes by Anne
    Tjomsland, M.D. Islandica 35. Ithaca, N.Y.:
    Cornell University Press, 1951.
The Saga of Hrolf Kraki. Translated by Stella M.
    Miles. Oxford: Blackwell, 1933.
The Saga of Tristram and Ísönd. Translated with an
    introduction by Paul Schach. Lincoln: University
    of Nebraska Press, 1973.
The Saga of the Volsungs. Translated by Margaret
    Schlauch. New York: Norton, 1930. Reprint. New
    York: ASF, 1949, 1964. Reprint. New York: AMS
    Press, 1976.
The Skalds. A Selection of Their Poems with Introduc-
    tions and Notes. By Lee M. Hollander. Princeton:
    University of Princeton Press for ASF, 1945.
    Reprint. Ann Arbor Paperbacks: University of Michi-
    gan Press, 1968.
The Story of Kormak the Son of Ogmund Edited by
    Grace J. Calder. The hitherto unpublished transla-
    tion of Kormáks Saga by William Morris and

Eiríkr Magnússon. With an introduction by Grace
J. Calder and a note on the manuscript work of
William Morris by Alfred Fairbank. London: William
Morris Society, 1970.

Sturlunga Saga. Volume 1. The Saga of Hvamm-Sturla
and The Saga of the Icelanders. Translated from
the Old Icelandic by Julia H. McGrew. Introduction
by R. George Thomas. New York: Twayne Publishers,
for ASF, 1970.

Sturlunga Saga. Volume II. Shorter Sagas of the Ice-
landers. Translated from the Old Icelandic by
Julia H. McGrew and R. George Thomas. New York:
Twayne Publishers, for ASF, 1974.

Survivals in Old Norwegian of Medieval English,
French, and German Literature. Edited and trans-
lated by H. M. Smyser and F. P. Magoun. Baltimore:
Waverly Press, 1941.

Sverissaga. The Saga of King Sverri of Norway.
Translated by J. Sephton. London: David Nut, 1899.

Three Icelandic Sagas: Gunnlaugs Saga Ormstungu;
Bandamanna Saga; Droplaugarsona Saga. Translated
by H. M. Scargill and Margaret Schlauch. Princeton:
Princeton University Press, 1950.

Víga-Glúm's Saga and the Story of Ögmund Dytt.
Translated from the Old Icelandic with introductions
by Lee M. Hollander. New York: Twayne Publishers,
for ASF, 1972.

The Vatnsdalers' Saga. Translated with an introduction and notes by Gwyn Jones. Princeton: Princeton
University Press for ASF, 1944.

The Vinland Sagas: The Norse Discovery of America.
Grænlendinga Saga and Eirík's Saga. Translated
with an introduction by Magnus Magnusson and Hermann
Pálsson. New York: New York University Press,
1966.

Index

Adalbert, archbishop of Bremen, 9, 26
Adam, 39
Ægir (god of the sea, Rán's husband), 107
Age of the Sturlungs. See Sturlung Age
Ágrip af Nóregs konunga sögum (Compendium of sagas about kings of Norway), 15, 31, 35–36, 46, 53
Alfífa, queen of Denmark, 55
alliteration, 7, 35, 44, 54, 63, 99, 130, 145
Andersson, Theodore M., v, 91, 108, 112, 140
Ari Thorgilsson the Learned, 2, 8, 10, 23, 24–35, 46, 48, 50, 56, 101, 116, 118, 128, 148, 175
Arinbjörn (in Egils saga), 104–7
Arnald, bishop of Greenland, 26
Arna-Magnæan Foundation of Iceland, 99
Arngrímur Jónsson, scholar, 39, 41
Árni Magnússon, scholar, 124
Arnkel Thórólfsson (in Eyrbyggja saga), 115
Ásdís Bárðardóttir (in Grettis saga), 128

Ásgard ("abode of the Æsir"), 98
Asia, 39
Ástríd, queen mother of Denmark, 66
Athelstan, king of England, 60, 104–6, 108
Atlakviða (Lay of Atli), 6
Atli (Attila), king of the Huns, 5–6, 143
Atli (in Grettis saga), 126
Aud the Deepminded, 36
Audun the Red, 38
Augustus, Roman emperor, 40
Auðunar þáttr, 75
avarice, 22, 72, 105, 147, 165–66

Bååth, A. U., 117
Babylonian cherubim, 17
Baetke, Walter, v
Baldur, 98, 120
Baltic, 104
Bandamanna saga, 147–48, 154
baptism, 27, 54, 134, 147, 151, 162, 166–67, 174
Bardi Gudmundarson (in Heiðarvíga saga), 93–95, 125
Bárðar saga Snæfellsáss, 157, 167–68, 170
Beck, Heinrich, 109

Bede, 32
Benedict, Saint, 53
Benediktsson, Jakob, 29
Beowulf, 6, 40, 127
Bergthóra Skarpheðins-
    dóttir (in Njáls
    saga), 121
Bergthórshvol, 119, 121
Berserker, 91, 104, 106,
    113, 125, 146, 173
Bersi (in Kormáks
    saga), 85
Bible, 32, 51, 66, 172
"Birchlegs," 59, 61
Bjarg, 125
Bjarkamál, 55
Bjarnar saga Hítdæla-
    kappa (Saga of Björn,
    the Hítadal champion),
    86-90, 110, 133, 151,
    175
Bjarni Herjólfsson (in
    Grænlendinga saga),
    45, 151
Björn (in Bjarnar
    saga), 87-90, 96, 126,
    152, 175
Björn Breidvíkinga-
    kappi, 115-16
Blund-Ketil (in Hænsa-
    Þóris saga), 149-50
Boccaccio, 127
Bolli Bollason (in Lax-
    dæla saga), 112-14
Bolli Thorleiksson (in
    Laxdæla saga), 108,
    110-12
Book of Joshua, 28
Book of Settlements.
    See Landnámabók
Borg, estate, 103, 106,
    106, 152
Borgarfjord, 90, 93
Brand Sæmundarson, bish-
    op of Hólar, 68
Breidfjord, 26
Bremen, 9

Brennu-Njáls saga.
    See Njáls saga
British Isles, 3, 8,
    69
Brján, Christian king
    of the Irish (in
    Njáls saga), 122
Brodd-Helgi (in Vápn-
    firðinga saga), 133
Brown, Ursula, 18-19
Brynhild (German Brün-
    hild), 6, 111
Byskupasögur, iv, 164

Catalogus regum Norwagi-
    ensium, 34-35
Charlemagne, 56
Christ, 121
Christianity, iv, 3, 7-
    10, 18, 26-27, 42, 53,
    56-57, 66, 83, 85, 89,
    92, 96, 110, 120-23,
    132, 134, 138, 140,
    144, 146-47, 150-51,
    154, 159, 174-77
Ciklamini, Marlene, iv,
    101
Clontarf (1014), battle
    of, 135
Clover, Carol, 62
Code of church law, 11
Code of civil law, 11
Constantinople, 92, 95,
    112, 127, 135, 155
conversion (999), 4, 8
Cook, Robert F., 154

David, king of Israel, 67
De excidio Trojae
    (Dares Phrygius), 32
Denmark, 26, 39, 41-43,
    58, 75, 87
Dialogues (Gregory the
    Great), 53
digression, 47, 62, 76,
    85, 103, 120, 122, 138,
    173

Disciplina clericalis,
  124, 140
dragons, 87, 165-66
Drangey, 127-28
Drápa, 7, 49, 76, 83,
  107, 152
dreams, 41, 64, 67, 79,
  89, 100, 110, 117, 132,
  135, 139, 141, 144,
  151, 159-61, 165, 167-
  69
Droplaug, 131-32, 168
Droplaugarsona saga,
  131-32, 136, 143, 168
Dróttkvætt ("court
  meter"), 7, 49, 86
Dublin, 37
Dýrafjord, 143

Eastfjords, 1
Edda, Elder (Poetic),
  5-6, 59, 99, 108, 143,
  166
Edda, Prose (Snorri's),
  39, 57, 85, 97-99, 120,
  132
Edna Kjarvalsdóttir, 37
Egil Skallagrímsson, 54,
  102-8, 114
Egils saga Skallagríms-
  sonar, 15, 96-97, 102-
  8, 129, 172, 175-76
Egils þáttr, 71
Einar Skúlason, poet, 49
Einar Thveræinbg, 17
Einars páttr Sokka-
  sonar (Tale of Einar,
  son of Sokki), 26
Einarsson, Bjarni, 84
Eirík, Earl of Hladir,
  57-58, 108, 152
Eirík Bloodaxe, king of
  Norway, 35-36, 103-6
Eirík Oddsson, histori-
  an, 30-31

Eirík the Red, 26, 150-
  51, 159
Eiríks saga rauða, 40,
  150-51
Eiríksfjord, 26
Ellehøj, Svend, 24, 34-
  35, 49
Elzta saga Óláfs hel-
  ga, 48-50, 55-56, 63,
  71
England, 76, 104
Erfidrápa (Memorial
  lay), 49
Erling, Norwegian earl
  (in Sverris saga), 60-
  61, 63, 65
Erling Skjálgsson, 53,
  55
Esdras, 144
Ethelred, king of En-
  gland, 152
Europe, 147
excursus. See digres-
  sion
Exodus, 170
Eyjafjord, 17
Eyjólf Sæmundarson, 35
Eyrbyggja saga, 5, 36,
  62, 91, 113-16, 129,
  131, 142, 157, 159, 173-
  74
Eystein, archbishop of
  Nidarós, 13, 33, 35,
  60-65
Ezekiel, 17

Færeyinga saga, 42,
  140
Faeroe Islands, 1, 42-44,
  60
Fáfnir, a dragon, 6, 59,
  166
Fáfnismál, 59
Fagrskinna, 46
fate, 86, 120-21, 153

father-son conflict.
See generation gap
Faulkes, Anthony, 71
Fifth Court, 8
Finnboga saga ramma,
155-56, 161
Finnbogi, 146, 155-56,
170
Finnur Jónsson, 34-35,
56, 152, 159
First Grammatical Treat-
ise, The, 23-24, 33
Flateyjarbók, Iceland-
ic codex, 79
Fljótsdæla saga, 155,
168-69
Flóamanna saga, 159-60
Flokkr, 7, 76, 152
Flos pregrinationis, 33
Flosi, 117, 121-23
Foote, Peter, 143-44, 152
foreshadowing, 37, 41, 51-
52, 57, 70, 88, 110,
117, 124, 129, 132,
138, 140, 165, 168, 172
Fornaldarsögur, iv,
155, 157, 159, 162,
165, 167, 170
Fóstbrœðra saga, 76-
79, 81
France, 156
"free-prose" doctrine, v
Frey, 8, 27, 135-36, 139-
40
Freydís, 151
Freyfaxi, 135
Fridrek, Norwegian mis-
sionary bishop, 72
Frigg, 98
Friðþjófs saga, 157
Fróda, 115-16
Fylgja, 139

Geisli, a drápa com-
posed by Einar Skúla-

son in honor of St.
Ólaf, 49
General Assembly (al-
þingi), 3-5, 8, 11,
14, 16-18, 26-27, 56,
64, 66, 68, 93-94, 108,
110, 119, 122, 132,
135, 152, 174
generation gap theme, 52,
115, 124, 134, 157,
170, 173
generic farce, 166-68
Genesis, 41, 169
Germanic mythology, 8
Gerpla, novel by
Laxness based on Fóst-
brœðra saga, 81
Gísla saga Súrssonar,
142-45, 154, 172
Gísli Súrsson, 142-45,
173
Gizur Hallsson, scholar,
32-33, 58, 65
Gizur Ísleifsson, second
bishop of Iceland, 10-
11, 18, 69
Gizur Thorvaldsson, 21-22
Gizur the White, 9, 33
Glám (in Grettis
saga), 125
Glendinning, Robert, 127
God, 54, 58, 60, 62, 66-
68, 84, 121
Godi (goði), 3-5, 14,
146
Godord, (goðorð), 4,
135, 146-47
good fortune, 58, 66, 68,
174
Gorm the Old, king of Den-
mark, 39, 41
Grælendinga saga, 44-
45, 150-51
Grágás, law code, 61,
170

Grásíða, name of two
  famous weapons, 143
Greenland, 26, 45-46, 75,
  77-78, 151, 156, 159-60
Gregory the Great, 18
Grettir Ásmundarson, 36,
  123-28, 165, 170
Grettis saga Ásmundar-
  sonar, 52, 123-30, 165
Grettla. See Gret-
  tis saga
Grím Droplaugarson,
  132
Grímkel, bishop of Nor-
  way during reign of
  Saint Ólaf, 49
Grímsey, 17, 22
Grís (in Hallfreðar
  saga), 82-83
Gryla (first part of
  Sverris saga), 59
Gudbrand (Dala-Gudbrand),
  Norwegian chieftain,
  52, 54
Gudmund Arason the Good,
  bishop of Hólar, 14, 66
Gudmund the Mighty, 15,
  119, 126, 140-42
Gudríd (wife of Thor-
  finn karlsefni), 45-46,
  151
Gudrún Gjúkadóttir, 6, 143
Gudrún Ósvifrsdóttir,
  108, 110-13, 136
Gulathing, 3, 105
Gull-Þóris saga, 105,
  165
Gunnar (German Gunther),
  5, 6
Gunnar of Hlídarendi,
  117-20, 123, 173
Gunnars saga Kel-
  dugnúpsfífls, 160-61
Gunnars saga Þiðrandaba-
  na, 136-37, 168
Gunnhild, queen of Nor-
  way, 104-6, 109

Gunnlaug Leifsson, monk
  of Thingeyrar, 12, 14,
  58, 66-67
Gunnlaug Serpent-tongue,
  poet, 151-53
Gunnlaugs saga Orms-
  tungu (Saga of Gunn-
  laug Serpent-tongue),
  8, 151-55
Guðnason, Bjarni, 39
Gylfaginning (part of
  Prose Edda), 98-99

Hænsa-Þóris saga,
  148-50, 154
Haflidi Másson, 11, 18-
  19, 27
Haflidaskrá (Haflidi's
  scroll), 11
Hákon, earl of Hladir,
  41, 44, 57, 83, 163
Hákon Adalsteinsfóstri
  the Good, king of Nor-
  way, 21, 36, 106, 113
Hákon Eiríksson, Norwe-
  gian earl, 53, 57
Hákon Hákonarson, king
  of Norway, 46, 97
Hákonar saga góða, 113
Hákonar saga Hákonar-
  sonar, 101
Hálfdan the Black, king
  of Norway, 24, 35
Hálfdan Longlegs, son of
  Harald Fairhair and
  Snjófríd, 38
Hálfdanar saga svarta,
  100
Hall of Sída, 71-72,
  122, 175
Hall Teitsson, 10, 33
Hallberg, Peter, v, 4,
  47, 80, 84, 112
Halldórs þáttr, 74
Hallfred vandræoaskáld,
  72, 82-84, 88, 98, 102,
  110, 146, 151

Hallfreðar saga vandræð-
askálds, 82-85, 102,
146
Hallgerd (in Njáls
saga), 117-18
Hamlet motif, 60, 163,
169
Happy Warriors, The
(novel by Laxness), 82
Harald, earl in the Ork-
neys, 68
Harald Fairhair, king of
Norway, 2-3, 15, 24-25,
35, 39, 100, 102-3,
108, 114, 146, 158,
165, 167, 176
Harald gilli, king of Nor-
way, 30
Harald Gormsson, king of
Denmark, 16
Harald gráfeld, king of
Norway, 106, 109
Harald the Harsh, king of
Norway, 16, 73-76, 80,
86, 124, 135, 156
Haralds saga hárfagra,
35
Haralds saga hins
harðráða, 100
Haraldssona saga, 30
Harðar saga ok Hólmver-
ja, 164-65
Hastings, battle of, 53
Háttatal (part of
Snorri's Edda), 21,
97
Hauk Erlendsson, Sir,
scholar and lawman, 29,
80, 124
Hauk Valdísarson, poet,
132, 135
Haukadal, 10
Haukdæla þáttr, 32
Hauksbók, 28, 80, 150
Hávarðar saga Ísfirð-
ings, 166

Hebrides, 28, 114
Heimskringla, 16, 22,
30, 43, 46, 59, 86, 97,
100-102, 129, 159, 173,
175
Heiðarvíga saga, 90-
95, 123, 164, 175
Hel (goddess of the under-
world), 107
Helga the Fair, 152
Helgafell, 113-14, 116,
137
Helgason, Jón, 33
Helgi Ásbjarnarson, 131-
32, 136
Helgi Droplaugarson, 132,
168-69
Helgisaga Óláfs konungs
Haraldssonar, 15, 50-
51, 56-57, 59, 71-72,
77, 79, 82, 99, 124
Heller, Rolf, 109, 112,
133
Helluland, 167
Hen-Thórir, 148-50
Herford, convent in West-
phalia, 9-10
Heusler, Andreas, v, 110,
119, 158
Hildebrandslied, 6
Hildigunn (in Njáls
saga), 121, 123
Hildiríd (in Egils
saga), 102-3
Historia de antiquitate
regum Norwagiensium,
33, 49, 53
Historia Norvegiae,
33-35
Historia regum Britanni-
ae, 28
History of the Archbish-
ops of Hamburg-Bremen.
See Adam of Bremen
Hítardal, 90, 149
Hjalti Skeggjason, 15, 72

Hjardarholt, 75
Hjörungavág, battle of,
  41-43
Hlídarendi, 117, 119
hóf (cardinal virtue
  in Íslendingasögur),
  22, 95, 116, 129, 142,
  173-74, 176
Höfuðlausn, 106
Hólar, 10-11, 19, 23, 66-
  67
Hollander, Lee M., 42,
  62, 101
Holy Land, 12, 38
Hörd (in Harðar saga),
  164-65
Höskuld (Njál's foster
  son), 120-23, 175
Höskuld Njálsson, 117
Hrærek (deposed king of
  Norway), 15
Hrafnkatla. See
  Hrafnkels saga
Hrafnkel, priest of Frey,
  135-36
Hrafnkels saga Freys-
  goða, 135-36, 154,
  164, 168
Hrefna (in Laxdæla
  saga), 111
Hreiðars þáttr, 72-73
Hrút (in Njáls saga),
  117
Hryggjarstykki, 30-31
Hume, Kathryn, 128
Húnavatn, 90
Hungrvaka, 18, 31-33

Iceland, 1-2, 16, 18, 23,
  25-26, 34, 45, 53, 67,
  70, 75, 77, 87-88, 90-
  92, 95, 101, 103, 108-
  11, 118, 125-26, 136-
  37, 146, 155-56, 158-
  61, 165, 167, 169-70,
  175-76

Icelandic Annals, 1, 26,
  45
Icelandic Commonwealth,
  19
Icelandic nationalism, 29
Ingi, king of Norway, 35
Ingibjörg (in Hallfreðs
  saga), 83
Ingolf Arnarson, 2, 159
Ireland, 109, 122
Isidor of Seville, 32,
  150
Ísleif Gizursson, first
  bishop of Iceland, 2,
  9-11, 26
Íslendinga saga (Histo-
  ry of the Icelanders),
  101, 143, 148
Íslendinga sögur iv-v,
  12, 22, 51, 61-62, 76,
  90, 94, 99, 101-2, 112,
  117, 131, 142, 150, 154-
  57, 159, 164, 169-73,
  175, 177
Íslendinga þáttr, 57
Íslendingabók, 2, 8,
  10, 24-28, 31-32, 34,
  56, 128, 148, 175-76
Íslendingadrápa, 132,
  135
Ívars þáttr, 74, 87

Johannes Scotus, 32
Jóhannesson, Jón, 28-
  29, 137
John the Evangelist,
  Saint, 17
Jómsvíkinga saga, 41-
  42, 57
Jómsvikings, 41-42, 115
Jón Haraldsson, earl of
  Orkney, 36
Jón Loptsson of Oddi,
  13, 20, 24, 39, 65-66,
  68
Jón Ögmundarson, bishop

of Hólar, Saint, 10-12, 66-67, 98
Jón Olafsson, 91
Jóns saga helga, 11, 66-68, 71, 98
Joseph, 169

Kálf Árnason, 53
Kári (in Njáls saga), 117, 120-23
Karl Jónsson, abbot of Thingeyrar, 14, 35, 59-63, 136, 173
kennings, 6, 35, 76, 83-86, 98-99, 157
Ker, W. P., 108, 147
Ketil flatnef, 108, 114
Ketil Thorsteinsson, bishop of Hólar, 19, 25, 32, 46
Kirkjubæ, monastery, 64
Kjalnesinga saga, 158-59, 161, 164
Kjartan Ólafsson, 57, 108-11, 133
Klæng Thorsteinsson, bishop of Skálholt, 11, 23, 31-32, 67
Knút (Canute the Great), king of Denmark and England, 50, 52, 54, 72, 87
Knýtlinga saga, 101
Kolbítr ("coal-biter"), 162
Kolfinna (in Hallfreðar saga), 82-83, 85
Kolskegg (in Njáls saga), 118
Konungasögur, iv, 96, 99, 108, 112, 159, 164, 167, 171
Konungsbók (Codex regius), 99
Kormák, 84-86

Kormáks saga, 84-86, 96, 151
Kriemhilde, 151
Kristjánsson, Jónas, 48, 77, 80, 96, 148
Kristni saga, 10, 18, 58
Kroesen, Jacoba M. C., 77
Króka-Ref, 156, 164
Króka-Refs saga, 156
Kveld-Úlf, 102-4, 108

Lachmann, Vera, 76
Landnáma. See Landnámabók
Landnámabók, 1, 4, 15, 23, 28-29, 118-19, 124, 129, 148, 151, 159, 161-63, 166-67, 175
Laugar, 110
Laxdæla saga, 36-37, 57, 108-13, 116, 129, 133, 136, 143, 172
Laxness, Halldór, 81
Leif Eiríksson, 45, 151
Leiðarvísir ok borgaskipan, 12
Liestøl, Knut, 138
Lilja, a poem, 99
Livy, 62
Ljósvetninga saga, 140-41, 146
London, 52
Long Serpent, 56, 162
Lönnroth, Lars, 56, 176
Lund, 12

Maccabees, 170
Madelung, A. Margaret A., 109
Magnús, earl of Orkney, Saint, 38
Magnús Barelegs, king of Norway, grandfather of

Jón Loptsson, 24, 68
Magnús Einarsson, bishop
   of Skálholt, 31-32
Magnús Erlingsson, king
   of Norway, 13, 59-63,
   65
Magnús the Good, king of
   Norway, 24, 43, 46, 73
Magnús Ólafsson, king of
   Norway, 55
Magnusson, Magnus, 4, 120
Markland ("Woodland")
   (Labrador), 45
Markús Skeggjason, law-
   speaker, 11, 27, 40
Matthew, 159
Mediterranean sea, 38
Melabók, 28
Melbrikta Tooth, earl of
   the Scots, 38
Melkorka, 109
Michael, Saint, 142
Michaelmas, 142
Miklagard (Constantino-
   ple), 112
miracles and portents, 55
Mörd, 120
Morkinskinna (Rotten
   skin), 16, 46, 74, 124
Möðruvallabók, 131,
   139, 168
Munkathverá (founded
   1155), 12, 140

National Assembly. See
   General Assembly
Nesjar, battle of, 53
Nibelungenlied, 6, 151
Niblung. See Niflung
Nidarhólm, 33
Nidarós (Trondheim), 12-
   15, 35, 49-50, 65
Niflung, 58, 108-9, 111
Nikulás, bishop of Nor-
   way, 61

Nikulás Bergthórsson,
   abbot, 12
Njál Thorgeirsson, 116-
   23
Njála. See Njáls
   saga
Njáls saga, vi, 36,
   62, 116-23, 129, 131,
   142, 172-73, 175-76
Nordal, Sigurður, 31, 76-
   77, 101, 124, 151
Nóregs konungatal, 24,
   39
Norway, 2-3, 16-17, 23,
   26, 28, 30, 33, 35-36,
   45-46, 49, 53, 55-56,
   59-61, 65, 67, 72-73,
   75, 86, 92, 100-102,
   104, 106, 108-11, 125-
   26, 132-33, 136, 142,
   144, 146-47, 152, 155-
   56, 158, 160-62, 165,
   167, 175-76

Odd Snorrason, monk, 24,
   34, 56-59, 67, 72
Oddaverjar, 39
Oddi, 10, 21, 36, 39
Oddný (in Bjarnar
   saga), 87-90
Oddný (in Ivars
   þáttr), 74
Odin, 39, 57, 102, 107,
   120, 139-40, 167
Ólaf, king of Sweden, 15,
   71
Ólaf Haraldsson the Saint,
   king of Norway, 15-17,
   33, 37, 42-44, 48-57,
   60-63, 66, 71-72, 77-
   79, 87-88, 95-96, 99-
   101, 126, 141, 167, 173
Ólaf pái, 109-10
Ólaf Thórdarson, 99,
   101, 113

Ólaf Tryggvason, king of
Norway, 8, 12, 24, 27,
33-34, 44, 52, 54, 56-
59, 72, 82-83, 88, 96,
98, 100, 102, 108, 110,
151, 162, 166-67
Ólafs saga hins helga,
17, 36, 43, 99-100
Ólafs saga Tryggvaso-
nar, 56-59, 62-63,
100, 111
Ulkofra þáttr, 147
Ölsen, Björn Magnússon,
152
Olsen, Magnus, 105-6
Olsen, Olaf, 5
Olsen, Thorkil Damsgaard,
76, 96
Orkney, 36, 39, 84
Orkneyinga saga, 36-39,
120
Urlygsstadir, battle of,
21, 143
Urvar-Odds saga, 159
Oswald, king of England,
38
Ovid, Ars amatoria, 67

Paasche, Fredrik, 32
Pál Jónsson, bishop of
Skálholt, 39, 64-65,
68-69, 133
Páls saga byskups, 68-
69
Pálsson, Hermann, 120
Passio et miracula beati
Olavi. See Eystein,
archbishop of Nidarós
Paul, Apostle, 64, 176
plot interlace, v, 62,
117, 142
polycentric composition,
62
prophetic dreams, 60, 153

Ragnarök, 98

Ragnheid Thórhalls-
dóttir, 68
Rán (goddess of the
sea), 107
Reginsmál, 166
Reykdæla saga ok Víga-
Skútu, 137-40, 154,
175
Reykjavík, 2
riddarasögur, iv, 112,
152, 155, 157, 170
Rímur, 99, 159
Ring des Nibelungen
(Richard Wagner), 6
Rögnvald kali, earl of
Orkney, Saint, 36-38,
120
Rome, 9, 12, 18, 32-33,
45, 72, 75, 123, 128,
156
Rouen, 52
Russia, 87

Sæmund Jónsson, 20, 39
Sæmund Sigfússon the
Learned (1056-1133), 1,
10-11, 13, 24-25, 34-
35, 39, 46, 56-57, 67-
68
Sagas of Icelanders, iv-
v, 9, 15, 28, 175
Samuel, the prophet, 60,
120
Scandinavia, 2, 6-7, 11,
21, 69, 177
Schier, Kurt, 131, 137,
176
Scotland, 2, 36, 39, 149
See, Klaus von, 77
Shakespeare, 6
Sigfússon, Björn, 138,
140
Sighvat Sturluson, 21,
140
Sighvat Thórdarson, 48-
49, 52

Sigmund Brestisson, 43-44
Sigríd the Haughty,
  queen of Sweden, 51-52,
  57-58
Sigurd (German Sieg-
  fried), 5, 6
Sigurd, earl of Orkney,
  37
Sigurd Eysteinsson, 36
Sigurd Haraldsson, king
  of Norway, 32, 60
Sigurd the Jerusalem-
  farer, king of Norway,
  35-36, 46
Sigurd the Mighty, 38
Sigurd Munn, 36
Sigurd slembidjákn, 30-
  31, 73
Sigurd Sow, king of Nor-
  way, 52-53, 63, 73-74
Sigvaldi, earl of Den-
  mark, 72
skáldasögur ("stories
  about poets"), 78
skaldic poetry, 5-8, 96,
  98-100, 108, 116, 139-
  40, 143, 152-53
Skáldskaparmál, 98-99
Skálholt, 9-11, 13, 26,
  31-32, 69
Skalla-Grím, 102-4, 106,
  108, 170
Skapti Thóroddsson, law-
  speaker, 8-11, 27, 72,
  119, 126
Skarðsárbók, 28
Skjöld (OE Scyld), 39
Skjöldunga saga, 39-
  41, 100
Skúli, earl (later duke)
  of Norway, 20-21
Snæfellsnes, 113, 158,
  167
Snjófríd, 35
Snorri, son of Karlsefni,
  46

Snorri the Chieftain
  (goði), 2, 74, 91-95,
  113-16, 126
Snorri Sturluson, 5, 7,
  16-17, 20-22, 30-31, 36-
  37, 43, 46, 54, 59, 62,
  70, 97-103, 105-6, 122
Sonatorrek, 107, 110
Spes, 127-28
Springer, Otto, 177
Starkad the Old, 40-41
Stefnir Thorgilsson, 72
Steingerd, 84-86
Steins þáttr, 72
Stevenson, Robert Louis,
  113
Stiklastadir, battle of,
  37, 49, 55
Strömback, Dag, 84
Sturla Sighvatsson, 143
Sturla Thórdarson, chief-
  tain (1115-83), 20
Sturla Thórdarson, histo-
  rian, 1, 29, 34, 58,
  99, 101, 113, 124, 143,
  148, 165
Sturlubók, 28-29, 148,
  165
Sturlung Age (1200-1280),
  19-22, 91-92, 97, 116,
  122, 136, 147, 154, 173-
  74
Sturlunga saga, 21,
  101, 119, 147, 164, 175
Sturlungs, 39, 113
Styrmir the Learned, 29-
  30, 59, 124, 165
Styrmisbók, 28-29
Svarfdæla saga, 162-
  64, 170
Svein Alfífuson, king of
  Norway, 55
Svein Ásleifarson, 37
Svein Forkbeard, king of
  Denmark, 58, 75, 156
Svein Knútsson, king of

Denmark, 49
Svein Úlfsson, king of
   Denmark, 45, 66-67
Sveinsson, Einar Ólafur,
   36, 77, 86, 109, 118,
   123
Sverrir Sigurdarson, king
   of Norway, 35-36, 59-
   63, 65, 68, 100, 120
Sverris saga, 59-63,
   70, 101, 173
Svöld, battle of, 58
Sweden, 40-41, 52, 58, 83-
   84, 152

Tegnér, Esaias, 157
Teit Ísleifsson, 10, 33
Thangbrand the Priest,
   132
Theodoricus monachus, 33-
   35, 49, 53, 72, 105
Thingeyrar, 11-12, 14,
   48, 56, 59, 66, 147-48,
   175
Thingvellir, 4, 16
Thomas, Apostle, 90
Thór, 8, 57-58, 79, 85,
   98, 151, 159, 167, 169
Thóra Magnúsdóttir, 68
Thórd Kolbeinsson, poet,
   87-90
Thórd Sturluson, 21
Thorfin karlsefni, 2, 45,
   151
Thorfinn, earl of Orkney,
   37
Thorgeir (in Fóst-
   bræðra saga), 77-78,
   80
Thorgeir, lawspeaker, 26-
   27, 140
Thorgerd Egilsdóttir,
   110
Thorgils Oddason, 18-19,
   27

Thórir of Gardar, 126,
   128
Thorkel Gellisson, 26
Thorkel krafla, 146-47,
   174
Thorlák Runólfsson, bish-
   op of Skálholt (d. 1133),
   18-19, 25, 31, 32
Thorlák Thórhallsson,
   bishop of Skálholt,
   Saint, 13-14, 35, 63-
   66, 68-69, 133, 160
Thorleif the Christian,
   133
Thormód Bersason, poet,
   15, 48, 50, 55, 77-79
Thórólf (in Eyrbyggja
   saga), 115, 173
Thórólf Skallagríms-
   son, 103-5
Thorstein (in Grettis
   saga), 126-28, 155
Thorstein Egilsson, 108
Thorvald, (in Kormáks
   saga), 85-86
Thráin Sigfússon, 117
Thránd of Gata, 43-44
Thuríd Snorradóttir,
   115-16
Translatio sancti
   Olavi, 49
Tristrams saga, 84, 124
Trójumanna saga, 151
Trondheim, 56
Turf-Einar, adversary of
   Harald Fairhair, 38
Turville-Petre, E. O. G.,
   24, 30, 32, 112

Ulfljót's Law, 3, 161

Vagn (in Jómsvíkinga
   saga), 42
Valla-Ljót, chieftain,
   141

Valla-Ljóts saga, 141,
    154, 163
Vápnfirðinga saga, 132–
    34, 164
Varangian guard, 127
Vatnsdæla saga, 15,
    145–47, 154–55, 173–75
Veraldar saga, 31–32
Víga-Glúm, 138–40, 143
Víga-Glúms saga, 138–40
Víga-Styr, 91–92, 113, 173
Víglund, 157–58
Viglundar saga, 157–58
Viking Age (ca. 780–
    1070), 2
Víkinga vísur, 53
Vínland, 1–2, 26, 40,
    44–46, 151
Völsunga saga, 6
Vries, Jan de, 92, 100,
    116, 133

Wales, 122
Weber, Gerd Wolfgang, 176
Westfjords, 135–36
William the Conqueror, 53

Ynglinga saga, 100
Ynglinga tal, 100
Yngvi, king of the Turks,
    25
York, 106

þættir (sg. þáttr),
    iv, 48, 67, 71–76,
    87, 131, 134, 138, 140,
    175
Þorláks saga byskups,
    63–66, 68
Þormóðar þáttr, 50,
    55, 71
Þórólfsson, Björn K.,
    144
Þorsteins saga hvíta,
    133–34
Þorsteins saga Síðu-
    Hallssonar, 37, 135
Þorsteins saga stangar-
    höggs, 134–35, 157
Þorsteins saga uxa-
    fóts, 161–62
Þórðar saga hreðu, 156–
    57, 161

DATE DUE

DEMCO 38-297